Animal, Vegetable, DIGITAL

Experiments in New Media Aesthetics and Environmental Poetics

ELIZABETH SWANSTROM

The University of Alabama Press
Tuscaloosa

The University of Alabama Press
Tuscaloosa, Alabama 35487–0380
uapress.ua.edu

Typeface: Minion, Eurostile and Miller

Manufactured in the United States of America
Cover illustration: *Double Helix* by Rafael Araujo (2012), acrylic and Indian ink on canvas; courtesy of the artist (www.rafael-araujo.com)
Cover design: Michele Myatt Quinn

∞

The paper on which this book is printed meets the minimum requirements of American National Standard for Information Sciences—Permanence of Paper for Printed Library Materials, ANSI Z39.48–1984.

Cataloging-in-Publication data is available from the Library of Congress.
ISBN: 978-0-8173-1895-6
E-ISBN: 978-0-8173-8929-1

For Ben Masselink (1919–2000)

The force that through the green fuse drives the flower
Drives my green age; that blasts the roots of trees
Is my destroyer.
And I am dumb to tell the crooked rose
My youth is bent by the same wintry fever . . .

—Dylan Thomas,
Collected Poems, 1934–1953

Contents

Acknowledgments

Animal, Vegetable, Digital had its genesis at Umeå University in northern Sweden, and I remain inspired by the many people who assisted me in its early stages there, both in HUMlab, a creative space for digital humanities work, and in Institutionen för språkstudier (Department of Language Studies). James Barrett, Ele Carpenter, Coppélie Cocq, Carl-Erik Enqvist, Emma Ewadotter, Van Leavenworth, Maria Lindgren Leavenworth, Cecilia Lindhé, Jenna Ng, Marita Nilsson, Johan Van Boer, and Berit Åström commented on early versions of the manuscript, and this book benefitted from their generous attention. I am also grateful to Patrik Svensson, who invited me to be a member of the HUMlab community in the first place, to the Kempe Foundation, which provided the financial support that made my fellowship at HUMlab possible, and to Finn Arne Jørgensen, who was kind enough to invite me back.

My position as a Kay Fellow in the English Department at Brandeis University was also invaluable for providing the time and financial support necessary to do prelimary research, and I am thankful for the mentorship I received there from Caren Irr, John Plotz, and Ramie Targoff; for the countless kindnesses bestowed by Shannon Hunt and Lisa Pannella; for the excellent company of my fellow Kay Fellow, the classicist Eirene Visvardi, and for the friendship, hospitality, and good counsel of the incomparable Paul Morrison.

Moving from New England to northern Sweden to Southern Florida within a three-year time span was an adventure of a lifetime, and I count myself lucky to have ended up at the English Department at Florida Atlantic University (FAU). I could not have hoped for a more supportive and collegial environment. I am especially thankful for Carol McGuirk, whose careful and perceptive reading made this manuscript stronger, for Ayşe Papatya Bucak, Adam Bradford, John Golden, and Wendy Hinshaw, whose generous comments were invaluable to me as I wrote and revised, for Kate Schmitt, Taylor Hagood, Andy Furman, and Eric Berlatsky for their kind words and encouragement, for my graduate student Travis Finch for his efforts in hunting down the whereabouts of Midori-san (the Blogging Plant) in Japan, and for Babette Cieskowski and Bridget Sweet, the talented undergraduate students at FAU who gave their time in order to collaborate with me on this book's website.

I am additionally indebted to the following people outside of FAU: Wolf Kittler, for sharing his insights about ancient oracles and introducing me to H. W. Parke's fascinating study about stochastic prediction in antiquity; Alan Liu, for inviting me to participate in the *Agrippa Files*, and, indeed, for offering me so many opportunities to partake of digital culture when I was a graduate student at the University of California at Santa Barbara; Joseph Tabbi, whose editorial incisiveness helped make the project stronger; and Rita Raley, whose critical acumen is matched only by her generosity. This book would not have been possible without her careful attention and expert guidance, at every conceivable stage of its development. My gratitude to her is beyond measure.

My friends Karen Bishop, EM Lewis, Inga Kiderra, Kim Knight, Linda Mastrangelo, Matthew Amati, and Martin Rosenstock gave me their constant encouragement, and my family—Patrick and Janice Swanstrom, my sister Erika, and my brother Joss, as well as Lynne Rae Olson and the entire Svatos clan—their love and support.

Finally, I thank Scott Anton Svatos, my husband, collaborator, and partner-in-crime, for his love, camaraderie, and, as always, his sense of humor. When I began this project he offered the following cautionary note: "I once was an animal who spent so much time on the digital that I became a vegetable." I have tried, not always successfully, to heed his warning.

Animal, Vegetable, DIGITAL

Experiments in New Media Aesthetics and Environmental Poetics

Introduction

Animal, Vegetable, Digital

Thou hast a voice, great Mountain . . .

—Percy Shelley, "Mont Blanc: Lines Written in the Vale of Chamouni" (1817)

Call me!
+ 43 5254 30089

—The Vernagtferner Glacier (2007–present)

Dial-a-Glacier

The Vernagtferner Glacier lies on the southwest edge of the Austrian Alps, approximately nine thousand feet above sea level. In a Google Earth satellite image taken in 2014, the glacier appears stately and serene, frozen literally in space and figuratively in time, a majestic monument to nature's constancy. Nothing could be further from the truth. Like all glaciers, the Vernagtferner is on the move. It surges and recedes annually, crushing noisily everything in its path and carving out new pathways in the process. Its very name—roughly translated as the "distantly be-gnawed one"—speaks to these rugged cycles.[1] These are normal, natural processes. All alpine glaciers surge in the springtime, and, historically, the Vernagtferner has been a precocious jumper.[2] But the Vernagtferner is no longer leaping. It is leaking. Its annual melt-and-surge occurs, but it does not reconstitute itself the way it used to. It is losing mass. Every spring it loses more. Eventually, the Vernagtferner will leap no more.[3] But the Vernagtferner is an unusual sort of glacier. It lacks multiple outlets for downstream travel. When it melts, its waters shoot swiftly and powerfully in one direction. Because of this singular flow, its water surges are easy to measure, making the Vernagtferner one of five glaciers in the entire world—alpine, arctic, or otherwise—whose annual mass balance, that is, its difference in mass in winter and summer, can be tracked by all viable means ("Vernagtferner," Bavarian Academy). This data allows scientists to extrapolate about the general health of all glaciers. The Vernagtferner, to use a pun, is the tip of the iceberg, metonymic of the high-stakes ecological problems that have emerged in the waning age of the Anthropocene.

Its swift decline is a clarion call. It requires a response. But what kind? And how? In 2006, Kalle Laar, a contemporary German sound artist who focuses on all manners of acoustic expression, formed a novel response to the problem of disconnect by launching the *Call me!* project. How can we connect with the glacier in a way that affects us emotionally, he asked, so that the statistics about it might begin to feel more real? How can we confront it in a manner that is experiential and participatory rather than merely spectatorial or voyeuristic? Given our age of ubiquitous computing and social networking, his answer might seem obvious. He invited people to call it. Laar's *Call me!* initiative is "a series of interactive projects in acoustical emotional field research . . . on the global impacts of climate change" (Laar). Beginning with the Vernagtferner, he and a small team of technicians hiked to the glacier's gauging station, bringing with them a computer, a radio transmitter, a steel-framed tripod, a solar panel, a microphone, many cables, duct tape, and a telephone. Drawing from and supplementing the station's solar-powered electricity, they hooked up the microphone to a very long extension cord and dropped it into one of the glacier's watery crevasses. There, it could pick up all the interesting sounds that the glacier made as it melted and flowed. They then hooked up the microphone to the computer. By using custom-coded software, they translated its strange acoustic medleys into machine-readable sound files, binary packets of information ready for sending across the Internet. They hooked up the computer to a transmitter and bounced the signal to the Vodafone mobile network, who assigned the glacier a numeric address: + 43 5254 30089. The glacier had its own phone line and was ready to take calls. As Laar relates in his description of the project, "Calling the Glacier invites the caller to get in touch . . . when a caller makes the decision to dial this number, he will find himself there, in real time, any time, from anywhere." Laar maintains that he does not seek to provide "sensational reporting from strange, far-away worlds, but . . . a personal experience of a process that concerns us all." For Laar, it is the sound of the glacier's decline, melting and groaning in real time, which calls attention to its turmoil. It is the voice of the glacier that matters, rather than its visual features.

In this respect the *Call me!* project has an impressive literary precedent. Percy Shelley's famous paean to "Mount Blanc" celebrates the awesome power of that mountain, using the waters of the Arve to structure the poem's ascent, until "Mont Blanc appears—still, snowy, and serene" (61). But Shelley doesn't linger long on its visual serenity; he pays more attention to the geographic turmoil of the region, "where the old Earthquake-daemon taught her young" (72), and describes its destructive potential in breathtaking terms: " . . . not a city, but a flood of ruin / Is there, that from the boundaries of the sky / Rolls its perpetual stream; vast pines are strewing / Its destin'd path, or in the mangled soil . . . / The dwelling-place / Of insects, beasts, and birds, becomes its spoil" (107–115). Although he is writing about the ice of Mount Blanc, the description applies as well to the Vernagtferner, which is in the same southwest region of the Alps, just further south and further west, on the French side of things. Shelley calls attention to how its power reverberates through all creation: "Thou hast a voice, great Mountain, to repeal / Large codes of fraud and woe; not understood / By all, but which the wise, and great, and good / Interpret, or make felt, or deeply feel" (80–83). This is an amazing statement—a call to action, one that argues that the glacier's voice is also the voice of justice, with a power to "repeal large codes of fraud and woe." Furthermore, it suggests that the best of us have some kind of obligation to make this voice understood—to "interpret" it, to "make it felt," or at the very least to feel it "deeply." But as powerful and important as Shelley's poem is for legislating (poetically speaking) the mountain's authority, it is in some ways as lofty as the peaks it describes. It conjures a feeling, to be sure, but it does not quite create what one might call a personal connection to the glacial peaks. Shelley's description of the glaciers as sinister, predatory forces does not help in this respect. "The glaciers creep," he writes, "Like snakes that watch their prey, from their far fountains" (100–101).

Even so, Shelley expresses the glacier in a way that is experiential and engaging rather than merely spectatorial. The glacier is present, not just as an immobile hunk of ice but as an active entity with a powerful *voice*. But Shelley was writing in a very different climate, culturally and meteorologically, during the so-called Little Ice Age, the time between the 1500s and the 1800s, which was marked by prolonged dips in temperature (Mann). The Alps were hit by the volatile freezing and melting patterns, and the Vernagtferner was a particularly volatile force, one that leaped dramatically in one-hundred-year cycles. We are living in different times. Shelley's glaciers are not our glaciers. Or, rather, our glaciers are the melting remnants of these once-powerful forces.

Call me! draws attention to their decline. Since *Call me!* debuted, callers have been able to call the glacier with a cell phone or a landline and listen to a live feed of its glacial sounds.[4] Callers can marvel at the glacier's hisses, trickles, and pops, its rushes and groans.[5] By making the sounds of the glacier accessible, Laar hopes to call attention to its plight, as well as the larger consequences of anthropogenic global warming, by bringing it to human scale. It is difficult to internalize its reality when the glacier seems so vast, formidable, and physically remote. Because of its massive size—the Vernagtferner is over eight thousand kilometers square—it defies human perspective. The complex causes of its decline are similarly hard to grasp. Glacial melting is a result of global warming, but this term, "global warming," is itself shorthand for a cluster of processes, objects, entities, and networks. We know that the consequences of climate change are reshaping not just our shorelines but the very surface of the planet, but we know this like we know any number of facts, which is not the same as "knowing" them in an emotional and experiential way. These facts are hard to put in human terms, even harder to get an individual handle on. Getting to the bottom of them is not as simple as identifying a single culprit and eliminating it. But recognizing the problem of disconnect can help us reframe the conversation. The challenge becomes one of engagement as much as education, less about gathering data to convince people of already established facts and more about *presenting* these facts so that the information hits home.[6]

As Laar writes of the project, "active calling provides the possibility of individually experiencing locations normally unreachable and mostly neglected by headline news." Instead, it is "the individual emotional contact created by listening live to the sounds . . . that is much more important. Activating this perspective in connection with social, political and scientific aspects is the aim of *Call me*!" (Laar). The phone call highlights the glacier's peculiar agency by giving the glacier a voice, or, more precisely, amplifying and transmitting that voice to the human ear. By recording it and broadcasting it, the phone call illuminates the glacier's vulnerable material features. It also calls attention to *this* glacier, not as a remote, vast abstraction, severed from human contact, but as a real-world site of fragility, worthy of protection and conservation. Instead of cutting humans out of the picture, a frequent tendency in conservation practice and aesthetics, the glacier invites connection. So far, the project seems to have struck a cord. In its first year alone, over twenty thousand people called the glacier, and the phone line remains active.

The project is weird, wonderful, and terribly important. Through its use of digital technology, it helps us appreciate and experience connections to nature in ways that abstract statistics cannot. It reminds us that it is the special power of aesthetics, of art, to explore different ways of knowing and experiencing the world, and that it is through art that we can articulate connections between ourselves and natural spaces, as precarious as these might be, not merely by contemplating mimetic representations of these spaces but by full-frontal aesthetic encounters that demand our active and conscious participation.[7]

I open with a summary of the *Call me!* project because this work clearly encapsulates many of the central concerns that *Animal, Vegetable, Digital* articulates. By making use of computational technology as a primary aesthetic component, explicitly foregrounded and out in the open, digital artists like Laar are opening up promising avenues for exploring connections between human beings and the natural world. Such works foster a diversity of connections to the natural world, not in spite of their digital status but because of it. *Call me!* is indicative of a new, exciting class of art that takes advantage of the unique features of the digital medium to offer productive engagements with the natural world and to reintegrate humanity into natural circuitry.

Throughout this book I explore how such works provide opportunities for experiencing human-environmental contingency, for demonstrating the human body's coextension with the environment, for aiding in conservation practices, and for expressing the agency of natural spaces. It is my argument that digital art, largely excluded from environmental criticism since its inception, has the potential—if not yet perfectly realized—to reconnect us to nature, remind us of our own embodied materiality, and reaffirm our kinship with other living and nonliving things.

Deserts of the Real

Laar's work is not anomalous.[8] Artists are increasingly forging connections between digital aesthetics and ecological poetics that are viable and vibrant, but their efforts have not, as yet, been widely acknowledged. The reasons for this are complex, but at their base lurk deep-rooted cultural beliefs that tell us that nature is opposed to digital technology. From the height of the Cold War to the turn of the twenty-first century, particularly, our cultural narratives tend to treat nature and computers as mutually exclusive entities. In this schema, nature is pure and innocent, whereas digital technology is malevolently self-determining; nature is present and active, whereas digital technology enables dangerous notions of disembodiment and immateriality; nature allows us to experience the physical world fully, whereas digital technology wants to destroy it, or at the very least enable our escape from it. In such works, digital technology distances us from the real world, distracts us from our physical bodies, and erodes the already precarious connection we hold to natural spaces. Indeed, if the many popular narratives about technology-run-amok that emerged during this time period can be considered "indicator species," then films such as *The Matrix*, *Blade Runner*, and *The Terminator* signaled a world on the brink of environmental devastation and human enslavement to the machine.[9] By the time Morpheus changed the channel of his old-fashioned television set in order to tune Neo in to the blasted and polluted earth in the first *Matrix* film in 1999, Baudrillard's concept of the "desert of the real" had been well rehearsed in a variety of cinematic dystopias.

In such narratives it is the artificially intelligent computing machine that causes such environmental destruction in the first place and then creates an alternate, simulated reality to distract us from it.[10] To add insult to injury, representations of simulated spaces in both literature and cinema have not offered much in terms of an appealing alternative to real-world ruin. Rather than presenting any kind of ecological harmony between an individual self and a larger ecosystem, they have tended to express flat, geometric nightmares with no place for organicism, physicality, or humanity. Instead, within such narratives, "the real world is the devastated remnant of our planet" (Bolter and Gromala 125).[11]

Blaming these technological agents, however, obscures a much larger network of culpability, both in our fictions and in our reality. Follow the causal chain in each of these films, and one goes from Agent Smith to the Matrix, Nexus 6 to the Tyrell Corporation, and Skynet to Cyberdyne. Do the same with *Alien, 2001*, and *Moon*, and one follows Ash to "The Company," the HAL-9000 to NASA, and GERTY to Lunar Industries. A commercial interest in the mining of natural resources drives the treachery in *Alien*, *Moon,* and *Blade Runner*. The AI's decision to enslave humanity in *The Matrix* is a direct result of an energy shortage. Their exploitative actions result from a shortage of resources, in the form of solar power, diminishing fossil fuel, manual labor, or, in the blunt parlance of *Avatar*, "Unobtanium."[12]

Such anxieties might have made some sense during the Cold War, when the computer was so tied to the fear of nuclear destruction and, indeed, devastation of all kind, but they make less sense now, when the reality of our material world seems so volatile and *present*. Computational technology, in fact, has helped put our environmental problems into excruciatingly detailed relief. And yet the notion that such technology contains within it, per se and in situ, the potential to create environmental devastation continues to appear in our cultural narratives. The Cold War has ended, so why do we still suffer from this distrust and unease? The personal computer might be a recent phenomenon, but our suspicion of technology is a longer-term problem, with an extensive history. The same suspicious stance toward technology in general has been growing, hardy as a vine, wholly entwined with the epistemological scaffolding of scientific inquiry, which has been thriving since the Enlightenment.

The Enlightenment zeitgeist, in its celebration of the intellect, rational thought, and reason, served to partition nature from human culture.[13] And it is to this time period that we can trace the particular fear of the sinister potential of *computational* technology, albeit in a predigital form: to Gottfried Wilhelm von Leibniz, who in the *Monadology* (1714) uses the metaphor of the machine-like mill to suggest something of the mind's eerie relation to the body; to Thomas Hobbes, who in *De Corpore* (1655) reduces the process of rational thought to computation; and to René Descartes, who in *Meditations on First Philosophy* (1641) offers mathematics as proof positive of the existence of an eternal soul. We bear the scars of this epistemological framework. A distrust of computation emerges from a rigid system of categorization, an epistemological misstep that we inherited from the scientific revolution.[14] In this system, subjects are not just distinct from objects but are their masters. Nature is not a site of its own autonomous agency. It is a scientific laboratory. Art and technology are separated, no longer combined with the poetic potential of *techne*. Instead of a realm of shared experience and participatory engagement, nature becomes cordoned off from us. A hierarchical system of knowledge organization emerges in its place that prevents us from making the very connections to nature we now so desperately need to make.[15] But more flexible taxonomies are available to us. These include ancient and contemporary frameworks that can allow us to see continuities between "natural" and "technological" objects more readily, by pointing to their intersections and overlaps rather than to any categorical purity they might possess.[16] One of the most accessible of these takes the form of a children's word game, and it is from this game that this book takes its title.

Animal, Vegetable, Mineral

"Animal, Vegetable, Mineral" is a word game that emerges as a popular form in the Victorian period.[17] Its objective is to deduce the identity of an unknown object after asking a series of questions about it. Questions may vary, but the query that launches every game comprises three words: "animal, vegetable, mineral?" Armed with the answer to this first question, the player then begins her crossexamination in order to hone in on the mysterious object, in effect creating an idiosyncratic taxonomy for it. It is a superb game for sharpening deductive reasoning, but it is also an instructive game to play when trying to hone in on the peculiar status of the digital object in our current moment of computational frenzy. Why? Because it doesn't work. A player might start with "mineral," but this won't take her very far, since any digital object has the potential to leak out, leach from, and leech onto the other categories. Digital objects have a Protean quality. Like the ancient Greek god the adjective takes its name from, the more you try to pin them down, the more shifty and recalcitrant they become. Aligning computation with this simple game reminds us that digital technology—its cords, its chips, its microcircuits and screens; the animals who make it, make use of it, and in certain cases are made by it; as well as the countless ecological features with which it cocirculates and upon which its distribution depends—shares the same elemental components as everything else in the material world and that the status of digital objects is far from settled. This is no more evident than when one looks to contemporary artifacts and art objects that make use of digital technology to offer engagements with "natural" spaces.

Our natural spaces are, conventionally, composed of the same animal, vegetable, and mineral domains that start off the children's game, but the status of nature is no more settled than it was at the dawn of the environmental movement. Determining the dominant feature that a particular slice of earth has to offer remains an important and politically charged pastime (this space is reserved for mineral mining; that space is an animal sanctuary; this other one a site where corn crops are grown and harvested, etc.). To make matters more interesting, this new category of the digital has been rubbing against these three with increasing friction. The past thirty years have seen an astonishing increase in digital technology worldwide. This increase in computational technology has been matched only by what has become both a scholarly and a mainstream pastime: assessing it. In spite of this attention, there has not been much careful reflection about the ways this technology might have something to contribute to our understanding of natural spaces and to environmental practice in general, nor has there been any serious or sustained discussion of how environmental poetics and new media aesthetics might engage with each other in positive ways.

All real-world instances of animal, vegetable, and mineral entities are, of course, always already continuous and interwoven, porous and connected rather than perfectly distinct categorical specimens. It is my suggestion simply that this new category of the digital can bring these connections into relief, not merely in an abstract manner but through a variety of experiential engagements. *Call me!* is an excellent example of a work that accomplishes this. It creates an experience that is participatory, engaging, and measurable in time. The computational features of the project enable connections in a variety of animal-vegetable-digital circuits. In such an arrangement the human being does not stand apart from the object. Instead the work highlights a collision of human and nonhuman entities and processes, and encourages interactive engagement. Thinking of such works in terms of this simple children's game permits us to reenvision ways that our artworks can function not as still sites of contemplation in which categories of subject and object are maintained but as lively networks that invite our participation.

Such works—and the study of them—constitute an emerging field. This field is composed of a variety of artists and practitioners who have received diverse levels of scholarly attention. As such, there is not yet a coherent theoretical apparatus for assessing them. But while there is no firm framework in place, there are several individual pieces of scholarship that address aspects of animal-vegetable-digital intersections, from practical,[18] historic,[19] and aesthetic perspectives.[20] More broadly, scholarship within the fields of digital aesthetics and ecocriticism offer crucial insights. Although the relation between these two areas has yet to be theorized carefully,[21] both share an interest in interrogating modernist conceptions of identity, challenging the concept of an autonomous subjective unity, and exploring connections between individual identity and a larger technological matrix (digital aesthetics) or ecology of relations (ecocriticism). Ecocriticism as a whole challenges human exceptionalism in a variety of ways: by rejecting the notion of a divinely "given" natural world over which man holds dominion (see Lynn White's classic (and contested) essay, "The Historic Roots of Our Ecological Crisis"); by calling attention to the ways that the body of a bird is as intricate a piece of engineering as anything created in a lab or a factory (see Joseph Meeker's essay "The Comic Mode"); by demonstrating a continuity between living matter and the inorganic matter it returns to when it dies (see Selden Whitcomb's reading of William Cullen Bryant's "Thanatopsis"); and by recognizing how nature communicates not in human language but in patterns and signs of every kind (see Fred Turner's "Cultivating the American Garden"). Digital objects and ecological ones are not intrinsically oppositional, nor are the networks they form mutually exclusive. But even given their overlapping interests, the two fields of research that such objects represent have different objectives and preoccupations.

Digital aesthetics is preoccupied with the advancement of technology, ecocriticism with the importance of natural ecology; digital culture is concerned with coding, computation, and simulation, ecocriticism with questions of sustainability, finite resources, and environmental holism. But both also have competing and problematic notions of transcendence. Early criticism in digital culture was largely fascinated with the computer's potential to transcend the material, natural world—a tendency that the digital artist

Talan Memmott refers as the "Narcisystem," a neologism that signifies "our fetishistic attachment to the enclosed circuits linking the human subject and the apparatus" (Raley, "Living Letterforms" 889). Conversely, although ecocritical research often eschews the technological, it has tended to consider nature itself in transcendent terms that are not always, to quote Donna Haraway, "faithful to . . . materialism" (1).[22]

Rather than attempt to force these two fields to snap in place, one upon the other, I have chosen to zoom out from both to bridge the eco-digital divide. To focus on ways that contemporary art can confound modern epistemological thinking without falling prey to problematic notions of transcendence, this project joins the dialog initiated by the fields of Science and Technology Studies (STS) and object-oriented ontology (OOO), although my emphasis is upon aesthetic interventions rather than scientific, philosophical, or political ones.[23]

Object-oriented ontology is a philosophical framework that includes, in the arena of being, objects of every kind, flattening categorical distinctions between animal, vegetable, mineral (and digital) entities. It is, as Levi R. Bryant writes in *The Democracy of Objects*, a philosophy that takes issue with "a *monarchy* of the human in relation to all other beings where some instance of the human is treated as that which overdetermines all other beings and where the primary order of the day is always to determine how individual minds relate to other objects" (39). Object-oriented ontology instead "strives to think a *subjectless* object, or an object that is for-itself rather than an object that is an opposing pole before or in front of a subject" (19). It does so without resorting to notions of transcendence and idealism. Object-oriented ontology views digital objects as continuous with natural objects and sees nature as an intricate ecology composed of diverse agents, including human ones, but without letting these human ones hold center stage.[24] This is a notion of a material and participatory nature, one that complicates categorical distinctions between animal, vegetable, and mineral realms—as well their vexing attendant subcategories: human being, technological being, being alive, nonliving being. It instead foregrounds and celebrates their collusions and collisions. In such a model of nature, objects of all ranks and kinds conjoin, interact, and separate with promiscuous zeal. Every object is a transmitter, every object is a receiver, and every object is a messenger that carries within it the smeared and internalized residue of the other objects. Nothing stands apart from it. It is a physical and inclusive concept of nature whose antecedents we can trace back to Empedocles.[25]

Within the larger purview of OOO, I am particularly drawn to Bruno Latour's scholarship, which simultaneously undermines human exceptionalism and provides an alternative model for thinking about what it means to be human that has nothing to do with Descartes' deadly dualisms. In fact, the word "subjectivity" in the Cartesian sense makes zero sense in Latour's formulation. Instead, "agency" occurs as a process of translation across multiple agents, only one of which might be human. Fittingly, Latour calls his approach Actor-Network-Theory, also known as ANT.[26] Latour's ANT provides a model of agency that is dependent not upon a suspect notion of self-assured human sovereignty but upon the relations one has with the objects and entities in one's world.[27] Latour never excludes the human from consideration in such a schema. Rather, he shows just how mercurial human agency becomes when one sees the human as a single component within a network of actors. In an essay for *Common Knowledge*, Latour provides a powerful example of this, describing a scenario in which a person picks up a gun and, as a result, becomes changed from how he was before, without it: "You are another subject because you hold the gun; the gun is another object because it has entered into a relationship with you" (33). Far from demonstrating a simplistic notion of one-way causality (such as the NRA's facile slogan, "guns don't kill people, people kill people"), his essay calls attention to the indisputable way that objects participate in any performance of agency.[28] These objects are not limited to guns or weapons but include all features of the material world, digital, natural, and otherwise.[29] Such an approach is not unique to Latour. Affinities with this sensibility inhere in a variety of related areas (including posthumanism, cybernetics, and bio-art). What is unusual about Latour's approach is the way he historicizes this stance. Nowhere does he claim to argue for (yet another) "new," "post," "peri," "epi," or "meta" ontology. On the contrary, he demonstrates continuity between a contemporary, object-oriented notion of ontology on the one hand and the way that "being" is configured and conceived of in the premodern world on the other. But while Latour looks to the past for alternative worldviews, his approach to the past is not nostalgic. Instead, his impulse to reconsider a premodern sense of being has profound, positive implications for our own time.[30] Throughout *We Have Never Been Modern*, Latour highlights moments in the history of scientific inquiry that point toward an understanding of nature as complex, social, material, and continuous with human nature. By paying attention to such moments, Latour shows OOO in action, demonstrating that nature has a complex and viable alternate history, worthy of recovery.[31]

Yet Latour's concept of nature, as such, is problematic. In *The Politics of Nature*, Latour questions "nature" as a viable concept, making the provocative claim that nature no longer serves as a useful category,[32] that "natural" agents hold no special importance over any other agents, and that resorting to the concept of nature hampers political and ecological progress: "we shall have to imagine . . . what a politics finally freed from the sword of Damocles we call nature might be like" (1). I share Latour's sentiment, but only provisionally. It would, indeed, be wonderful if we no longer needed this term because we had, as a species, accepted that our status within a vast, thickly threaded web of interdependence is partial, provisional, and always wrapped up with the well-being of the networks of objects around us on every conceivable scale of largeness and smallness. Until this vision comes into fruition, we are left with the cultural baggage *and* cachet of the term "nature."[33] And even if this term is, as Latour suggests, an amalgam of "Greek politics, French Cartesianism, and American parks"[34] (*Politics 1*) with questionable value, we should not cash out what little value it might possess for nothing. "Nature" is a loaded term, to be sure, and if we pick and poke at it enough we risk razing it to total insignificance.[35]

In *Vibrant Matter*, a book that shares an OOO perspective, Jane Bennett voices a similar concern about Latour's flattening of categories, not "nature" in this case but "human." Bennett offers a complementary framework for viewing the objects of the world as both material and animate. Her ambition is to "turn the figures of 'life' and 'matter' around and around, worrying them until they start to seem strange" so that "in the space created by this estrangement, a *vital materiality* can start to take shape" (vii). This objective is wholly achieved and gracefully executed. Like Latour, she calls for a "leveling" or "horizontalizing" and makes the bold claim that "to begin to experience the relationship between persons and other materialities more horizontally, is to take a step toward a more ecological sensibility" (10).[36] At the same time that Bennett champions Latour's model of leveling, however, she also articulates her concerns about the flattening of agency that he advocates, writing that she "cannot envision any polity so egalitarian that important human needs, such as health or survival, would not take priority. . . . To put it bluntly, my conatus will not let me 'horizontalize' the world completely. I also identify with members of my species, insofar as they are bodies most similar to mine" (104). This beautifully written book generates an enormous amount of respect and inspiration, but one can put the matter a bit more bluntly: such a statement suggests that the conatus in question wants to have its cake and eat it too. This is understandable. The identification with one's species is a natural tendency, one that makes sense in terms of our evolutionary history, which is so dependent upon cooperation. But if one were to think more about how one's conatus, that is, the "innate inclination of a thing to continue to exist and enhance itself," is dependent upon the conatus of others, it might be possible to reframe this proclivity ("conatus"). Additionally, Bennett's assertion that "important human needs" should take priority over those of the other entities with which we share the world does not depart from the status quo, since human needs quite clearly already do.

In *The Democracy of Objects*, Levi R. Bryant offers a slightly different vision of flattening that speaks to these concerns. His vision of OOO is one that marks a "profound decentering of the human and the subject" on the one hand, yet "nonetheless makes room for the human, representation, and content" and provides "an accompanying attentiveness to all sorts of nonhuman objects or actors coupled with a refusal to reduce these agencies to vehicles of content and signs" (27).[37] Through his notion of "onticology," in particular, Bryant offers a way out of this impasse.[38]

I draw inspiration from all of the above works, and I share with their authors an interest in cultivating a worldview that challenges traditional, human-centric hierarchies. Taking a cue from Latour, in particular, I am interested in looking back to a rich and complicated past in which technology and environment are intermeshed, and in which art is a key component in weaving them together. In *We Have Never Been Modern*, Latour writes: "Let us keep what is best about them, above all: the premoderns' inability to differentiate durably between the networks and the pure poles of Nature and Society, their obsessive interest in thinking about the production of hybrids of Nature and Society, of things and signs, their certainty that transcendences abound, their capacity for conceiving of past and future in many ways other than progress and decadence, the multiplication of types of nonhuman different from those of the moderns" (133). In the pages that follow, I seek continuities between the past and the present, just as Latour advocates above. It is a challenge, of course, to argue that the computer—that modern technology par excellence—has an ancient history, let alone a natural one, but the challenge is welcome. The use of computational technology is as old, at least, as written history and as such has many surprising affinities with antiquity, even in its current, digital form.

Animal, Vegetable, Digital

Digitization is the wholly material process by which information is encoded and translated into binary language that a computer can process. The result of this encoding is that such information becomes programmable information and, because of this, malleable in ways that analog information is not. The two terms, analog and digital, have come to be understood only as points of contrast to each other, but it is worth thinking of them in partnership. Analog is continuous data. It is "of the world." It flows, unfolds, and reforms like a certain stream described by Heraclitus. And yet, like that stream, each moment of its apprehension is a distinct and unique snapshot in time. Discrete. Analog artifacts, such as paintings, sound recordings, photographs, and film, are differentiated according to their respective mediums. Put crudely, a painting is the result of putting paint into contact with a surface that can hold or absorb it. A photograph is the result of exposing light-sensitive surfaces to light through various processes of development. One cannot be changed easily into the other. In contrast to this, information that is converted to a digital format is *de*differentiated. Digital artifacts, whether they take the appearance of photographs, films, sound recordings, or written words, are all made of the same material, which is to say machine-readable binary code. Digital data is discrete, made up of a finite amount of zeros and ones.[39] A digital photograph is no signature of light. A digital song is no recording of sound. Instead, each is a translation of a continuous medium into strings of binary code, of bits and bytes in multiples of eight, each bit an absence or presence of a certain voltage of electricity, which a computer "reads" and translates into light, sound, color, type. This makes the translation of image to sound to word to motion a fluid, Protean process, one that complicates questions about ekphrasis, synesthesia, and performance, questions that were seen as puzzling even in the ancient world. Seen this way, the "natural" and the "digital" are both part of a greater connective force, not a discontinuous one. Instead of adversaries, the two faces of the head of Janus emerge, one looking forward, the other looking back, distinct but conjoined.[40] Dylan Thomas implies something of this continuity when he aligns the natural with the technological by referring to the stem of a flower as a "fuse" in an early poem, "The force that through the green fuse drives the flower," the first stanza of which forms the epigraph to this book. I suggest that this goes both ways: the same "force . . . that drives the flower" is the force that powers us, our technology, and, as grandiose as it may sound, our cosmos.

Throughout *Animal, Vegetable, Digital*, I identify and explore four *aesthetic techniques* that show potential for forging connections between digital aesthetics and ecological poetics that promote a networked, object-oriented sensibility. These include *coding*, *collapsing*, *corresponding*, and *conserving*. Coding refers to the way artists make use of expressive and operational computer code to complicate distinctions between the text and its reader and, hence, the reader and her world. Collapsing names the ways that digital artworks encourage confusion between biological and technological boundaries and challenge assumptions about the human body's "natural" perimeters. Corresponding refers to the process of translation between natural and human-readable signs that enables communication. And conserving is the way that digital art and artists aim to democratize conservation efforts on large and small scales of intervention.

Laar's *Call me!* employs all of these techniques. Like many works of art that focus on climate change, global warming, and imperiled ecosystems, it delivers its message forcefully. It is an important message, to be sure, and the project as a whole clearly highlights the environmental stakes. The works that I consider in my chapters, however, are not exclusively activist-driven, although they have important implications for re-framing activist practice. Instead of focusing on sites of ecological fragility, I consider works of art that encourage making connections between human beings and natural systems by promoting an object-oriented sensibility.

Coding

Chapter 1 refutes the narrative history that tells us that code is transcendent, immaterial, and evil.[41] Code has not always been perceived as antithetical to materialism, organic or otherwise.[42] While contemporary computer code develops as a highly abstract language as a result, in large part, of military cryptography and technologies of taxation, it also emerges from a much wider cultural and aesthetic milieu. Nearly ten years before Alan Turing was grappling with the Enigma Machine's many encrypted mysteries, authors of science fiction were imagining similarly complex systems of communication and encryption whose syntax depended upon natural objects, such as flowers and leaves, to imagine what path the evolution of encryption might take.[43] An illustration from a 1930 issue of *Astounding Stories of Super Science*, for example, which accompanies the short story "A Problem in Communication," depicts a fictional coding system wholly inspired by botanical and insect morphology and suggests that the languages of symbolic abstraction and natural signs are related pursuits (Breuer). The histories of both computer technology and natural history are filled with moments such as these. By looking at them, a compelling and *alternative* story emerges about code's relation to natural spaces, one that emphasizes organicism, holism, and the interconnected agency of all things.

Throughout this chapter, I demonstrate how computer code evokes and illuminates natural sign systems. In key pieces of digital art, the use of both operational and expressive code reveals the work's mode of production, such that it is hard to distinguish between the built world of the simulation and the coded processes that have made them possible. One of the most successful and striking examples of this is the appearance of code on the level of the interface, which functions to weave the reader within the text, as in Char Davies' immersive environment *Osmose*. Codework in this case destabilizes the illusion of a coherent subjectivity, undermines Cartesian space, and challenges human exceptionalism by enveloping the human within its spaces. Next, I turn to William Gibson's *Agrippa (A Book of the Dead)*to analyze the way that codes of various kinds, most especially in the form of natural signs, inhere within the work's material and poetic "mechanisms" and endure over time to challenge any simple eschatology.

Collapsing

Zeus and Leda, Hyacinth and Apollo, Phaeton and his sisters—ancient myth is filled with moments in which anthropomorphic forms shift into natural objects: animal (swan), vegetable (hyacinth), mineral (amber).[44] Ovid's is the most famous compendium, although Lucian's lunar infantry, composed of mushroom- and asparagus-wielding moon-men (who are also, reproductively speaking, moon-maidens) is more fantastic still.[45] There is a robust literary tradition of shape-shifting, traceable from the myth of Lycoan to the werewolves in the *Twilight* series.[46] In my second chapter I examine key works of digital art that collapse and expand the boundaries of the human body in ways that are consistent with ancient expressions of metamorphosis and significantly distinct. I examine the Xbox game *Kinectimals*, in which children play with animal avatars on their television screens, and "Tornado," an online arcade-style game that allows users to become a cyclone. Such works collapse boundaries between the self and the ecosystem that surrounds it and allow their players to explore the resulting confusion and comingling of human and nonhuman forms. Additionally, I look at a simulation entitled *Empress & Hierophant* in Second Life, which encourages its users to alter the physical boundaries of the body through the construction of avatars. One way in which visitors to *Empress & Hierophant* play with the concept of the sublime power of nature is by reconfiguring Caspar David Friedrich's "Wanderer above the Sea of Fog" so that the Wanderer becomes female, digital, and malleable. This type of collapse results in a multiplicity of "human" bodies and a proliferation—and celebration—of *literary* forms.

Corresponding

Chapter 3 addresses the aesthetic strategy of correspondence, that is, the artwork's ability to express its own material conditions in human terms, aided by digital technology. Drawing upon Stephanie Strickland's *slipping-*

glimpse, and S.W.A.M.P.'s *Spore 1.1*, I examine how natural objects such as plants and ocean currents generate their own mode of signification. Such works elicit empathy and, as such, provide the means to consider "natural agency" in a way that has not, since Novalis, been carefully explored. Again, such instances emerge from a robust mythological tradition. An example that highlights the expressive potential of natural agents is the story of King Midas' servant. This servant, who cannot keep the secret that his master has the ears of an ass, needs to unburden himself of this information and whispers the scandalous details into a hole in the ground. He thinks his privacy is assured, but he is wrong: "a thick bed of quivering reeds began to shoot up there, and . . . stirred gently, then, by the wind they repeated the buried words, and testified against his master" (Ovid 11.172–193). The reeds in this story are illustrative of a larger tendency that permeates literature. In virtually every world religion and literary tradition, features of the natural landscape—the soil, the stones, the rivers, the trees, and the various creatures that reside within them—are imbued with powerful, often divine, agency. In the ancient world, Homeric epic teems with natural objects with powerful import. Flowers, trees, eagles, and swans are always both themselves and signs of divine activity and transformation. As John Berger puts it in *Why Look at Animals?*, "animals entered the imagination as messengers and promises . . . [with] magical functions, sometimes oracular, sometimes sacrificial" (4). At some point the voices of these vital agents lost their authority. Typically, we call this moment "modernity," an oversimplification but at least an economic one, in that so much about technology, progress, rationality, and liberty is packed in those four syllables. Through instances of correspondence, I suggest that digitally enabled works of art help recover something of this loss.

Conserving

The fourth and final chapter considers digital artworks and projects in relation to conservation efforts. However, it moves away from the somber and alienating aesthetics that have traditionally characterized conservation efforts in order to reimagine conservation as something democratic and social, by focusing on digital works that aim to foster conservation—of natural spaces and energy—through game play. Games and game-like features undergird various digital applications that target domestic conservation efforts. In particular, I consider how popular applications such as Playdom's *(Lil) Green Patch* and the German-based search engine *Ecosia* have had real-world consequences for conservation efforts. Such works also emerge from literary traditions that date back to antiquity. Some of these traditions are useful for helping recover a sense of a holistic ecology. The notion of the genius loci (the "spirit of a place," a concept central to both the ancient Romans and the romantic poets), for example, appears in many games in the form of avatars, sprites, and nonplayer characters. Such "spirits" can help us think of a place—both as itself and the agents within it—as worthy of respect and empathy. Other traditions are less useful. The equally ancient notion of the wilderness as a space of temptation and primitivism continues to inform conservation aesthetics, but its long-enduring status does little to recommend it. Many such games, unfortunately, hearken back to this ancient concept, as well as to a more modern variant, that is, *cultural* primitivism. Several games that purport to "save" natural spaces in Central and South America do so in ways that uncomfortably invoke tropes of colonialism and conquest. Even as such works offer positive engagements with natural spaces, they raise issues about conservation efforts in general, the economics of online activism, and the sense of virtue we might feel in playing such games and participating in such efforts. Nevertheless, because they force us to think through the complicated politics of global, cooperative conservation efforts, they are well worth exploring, and this chapter points to their potential to democratize conservation.

The pages that follow provide a preliminary framework for thinking about partnerships between digital aesthetics and environmental poetics. They identify four ways that digital art engages with both: coding, collapsing, corresponding, and conserving. While this list is far from exhaustive, it is my hope that it will provide a starting point for identifying other strategies and tactics for imagining how digital art might do good work in our natural world. The ambition of this book is to consider ways that digital technology and digital art can access a dynamic and participatory version of nature. The works it explores offer opportunities for human and nonhuman agents to inflect and shape their shared environments, as well as each other. They grant a special access to objects, to nature, and to ways of configuring consciousness. We are already engaged with nature, but it is not often that we reflect or think about how the world shapes us and how, in turn, we shape the world, not only by our actions but also by the simple fact of our being organic bodies made up of the same stuff that makes up the world. Digital art demonstrates and celebrates this simple and beautiful fact: the human organism in its entirety permeates and is permeated by what surrounds it.

1
Coding
Creating and Erasing Worlds of Signs

> Philosophy is written in this grand book, the universe, which stands continually open to our gaze. But the book cannot be understood unless one first learns to comprehend the language and read the letters in which it is composed.
>
> —Galileo, *The Assayer* (1623)

> Bits have arrived, they're not going away, and we must learn how to live with them.
>
> —Mark Hurst, *Bit Literacy* (2007)

What Is Code?

All things that can be read, watched, and listened to online are readable, watchable, and audible because of computer code. Code manages the fuel efficiency of the cars we drive and the energy consumption of our home appliances; it animates and controls the dendrites of network communication as we know it. Yet as crucial as computer code is, we seldom see it. Unlike Neo in the *Matrix*, code remains hidden to most of us, obscured by its output or masked by its interface. In spite of this invisibility (which is not an inevitable precondition of its existence but is still something more than mere convention), code is a real and material language with the purpose of communicating commands to microprocessors in a computer. A machine-readable program, when compiled or interpreted by a computer processor, executes a series of commands and is called "operational" because it tasks the computer with performing some kind of operation (filing, counting, sorting, calculating, creating, deleting, mapping, etc.). Recently, however, instances of code have emerged from the obscurity of their source files and made their appearance on screens both large and small. When this happens, code becomes "expressive" and functions as an aesthetic trope: visible, readable, sensible.[1] In certain special cases, it serves to emphasize our relationship with the natural world. This expressive type of code has a human audience and allows us to consider how computer code is *experienced*, that is, the manner in which it functions cognitively, affectively, and phenomenologically.

In this chapter I look at examples of digital art that use computer code in this peculiar way: William Gibson's *Agrippa (A Book of the Dead)* and Char Davies' immersive art installation *Osmose*. In each, code instructs a computer, yet it also asserts its presence to the reader. It engages the user by manifesting as a part of the artwork on the screen (as in *Osmose*) or through its very act of self-erasure (as in *Agrippa*). The works offer complex ecologies composed of animal, vegetable, and computational agents. In both works, computer code is not merely an invisible set of instructions that control the computation. It is foregrounded and sensible; it both organizes and contributes to the thickly layered topographies of each work and world. Because code in such instances helps foster an ecological model that is rooted in materialism, it will be useful to have a basic understanding of what computer code is, how it operates, and how I am using the term in this context. The following, then, is an attempt to demystify code.

Blockhead and Bole

This should be easier to do than it is. The dictionary definition of "code" isn't all that elusive. A code is "a system of words, letters, figures, or other symbols used to represent others" ("code"). This broad definition works for computer code, a system of symbols that represents other symbols and even whole systems of symbols. But computer code is also something else, something physical. Even its etymology speaks to its materiality: the term "code" emerges from the old French word *code*, or "system of laws, law-book," which itself emerged from the Latin term *codex* or *caudex*, which signified a "tree trunk, wooden tablet or book" as well as "a wooden stump to which petty criminals were tied in ancient Rome" ("codex"). It was also the suggestive word for a "dolt" or a "blockhead." Hence the contemporary term "code" marks an intersection between mineral (the book, the bollard), vegetable (the tree), animal (the blockhead), and digital (the code) realms.[2] The etymologies of the related terms "calculus" and "digital" are similarly suggestive: a *calculus* in Latin is a pebble used for accounting and, by extension, the name of the counting table at the time of financial reckoning; *digitus* is the Latin term for the human fingers used for counting; and a certain type of *tabella* (tablet) is one of the Latin names of the surface upon which very specific, very procedural curses were inscribed.[3]

Several extant critical investigations have grappled with code's puzzling status in ways that simultaneously clarify and frustrate. In his investigation of information aesthetics and creative labor in the *Laws of Cool*, Alan Liu discusses "transcendental data"; in "There Is No Software," Friedrich Kittler laments the "de-differentiated" nature of code; in *How We Became Posthuman*, N. Katherine Hayles describes the transmission of data as a process of "flickering signifiers." These frameworks discuss information technology's material nature in great detail; they also demonstrate how high the stakes have been raised for humanist and aesthetic inquiry in the age of information. At the same time, however, the vocabulary that each enlists has paradoxically highlighted code's inaccessibility (transcendence), erasure (de-differentiation), and instability (flickering) instead of its material properties.

William Gibson, the cyberpunk pioneer who made personal computing, hacking, and coding such popular subjects in the 1980s, once related an anecdote that speaks to this problem. In an author's note to his first trilogy, set in the "sprawl" of the Eastern Seaboard of the United States, he describes his initial conception of how a computer stores information in the following terms: "I'd assumed the data was just sort of, well, held. In a glittering mesh of silicon. Or something" (qtd. in Bukatman 87).[4] Gibson's misconception gives voice to, echoes, and is at least partially responsible for spawning our own initial misconceptions about the material nature of code, a misconception he promotes in his early fiction. Code in *Neuromancer* is configured as lattices of "intrusion countermeasure electronics," shortened to "I.C.E," abstract, beautiful, and divorced from materiality. But if computer code is not something suspended in a silent, crystalline lattice of silicon—a miniaturized ice cave of Krypton—then what is it? We don't have a common understanding of what it is, how it works, or how to locate it.[5]

According to IIEEE Software, "Whereas hardware is physical, software is intangible. . . . It cannot be touched" ("software"). Given that intangible forces are often equated with supernatural ones, it is not too surprising that code in this sense (i.e., immaterial and ethereal) has evolved as an antihumanist—and antienvironmental—force. Dystopian science fiction has made a villain out of code since the dawn of personal computing. In Gibson's *Neuromancer* (1984), hieroglyphic computer code imprisons the main character on a remote strand of beach, whose silver-hued sands stand in contrast to the way the novel depicts the polluted beaches of the real world's Eastern Seaboard; and "black I.C.E." is the name for code that kills. Code is the means of corporate control and provides a nearly insurmountable blockade against social mobility. Fifteen years later, in the phenomenally popular *Matrix* film franchise of the late 1990s, green and rain-like code underwrites the structure the matrix, an oppressive computer simulation that hides an environmentally devastated earth from its enslaved human population. Code is what conquers humanity, and every instance of its visibility is a reminder of this subjugation. Code also devalues individuality by objectifying all living subjects. (We might recall the character Cipher pointing to lines of code and saying, "All I see is blonde, brunette, redhead," without referring to any specific person.) In a dystopian science fiction film from 2011, the main character is a hapless airplane pilot who, in spite of his vehement protests, must live the last eight minutes of his life over and over until he can uncover the solution to a terrorist plot on a city-bound train. The name of the film, *Source Code*, is also the name of the computer program within the film that makes possible this endless loop of dying and suffering. Such works have prepared a negative poetics, have primed us to think of code as abstract, lethal, and controlled by the elite.[6]

But even as it is guilty of some of the dystopian aspects that are expressed in contemporary works such as *Neuromancer* and the *Matrix*—particularly in terms of its difficulty and abstraction—code is both local and locatable. But where? We might have a hunch that computer code is "out there" somewhere, remotely, in the cloud, perhaps, or "in there," on or in one's computer, locally, but neither assumption is quite right. Cloud computing is the name of a popular informational product model, but it also provides a suggestive metaphor that fits too easily within notions of transcendence; and although one saves and stores data locally on one's own computer (in a file in a folder in a platter on a hard drive) the notion of it as a self-contained kernel of information is not accurate either. Computer code, at its base, controls electric voltage to store, retrieve, calculate, and manipulate information. This part of its syntax—electric voltage and its absence—gets things done. But in spite of dystopian narratives about the sinister agency of code, the act and execution of coding is thoroughly tied up with human actions. Accordingly, it will be useful to demonstrate how different codes might come to be involved in the execution of a simple command. The best way to do this is not to "see" it—to do so would be difficult, since running code is, at its heart, a series of electrical events—but to see "coding" in practice.

As a way to foreshadow their interplay within *Agrippa* and *Osmose*, consider the different valances of code in the following scenarios:

1) A computer programmer is in charge of writing a program to control and monitor CO2 emissions of a new line of hybrid vehicles. The coding language she uses is "Misra C," a powerful, low-level language customized for the auto industry.[7] Her final product must resolve the following questions: How will the car's computer receive information from its fueling system? How will it display that information so the driver can make sense of it? How will the system troubleshoot when parts are defective, and how will it communicate its efforts to

do so to the driver? Between the program she authors and its execution in the car, several other systems of code are at work. She will use the language of Misra C to write the software; Misra C will compile into machine language; machine language will translate into binary code; binary, in turn, will translate into the presence or absence of voltage, which *then* instantiates a command (acceleration, use of fuel, etc.). All of this happens sequentially in lines of code but instantly in time; my narration highlights how one system of symbols represents another system of symbols every step of the way. *Code* refers at once to a highly abstract language (Misra C), to the software that the programmer eventually composes in it, the intermediary machine language, and binary. *Coding* refers to the work of writing these commands into a set of machine-readable instructions. One is a language, the other a practice.

2) A lepidopterist puzzles over the distinction between the giant-skipper (*Megathymini*) and other members of the skipper (*hesperiidae*) family.[8] Although the giant-skipper has enough phenotypical (visibly expressed) traits to suggest that it constitutes an entire skipper subfamily rather than a species, our entomologist isn't so sure. How will he test his theory? Variously and thoroughly: 1. He consults his list of known states and behaviors of butterflies (there are eighty), and checks each off for each butterfly in the form of + (present), – (absent), or ? (unknown); 2. He combines and collates that information into binary code, which condenses the information and allows him to eliminate improbable branches more swiftly than the +–? grid allows; 3. He takes images of each butterfly type, measures the color values of each, and conducts a "pixel-by-pixel image color subtraction" from the images to identify how distant the patterns and colors are from type to type (Grishin). 4. Finally, he consults the GenBank section of the Nucleotide database at the National Center for Biotechnology Information research hub and uses a program called MUSCLE (*MU*ltiple *S*equence *C*omparison by *L*og-*E*xpectation) to collate and contrast the skippers' genotypes. By comparing the DNA sequences of four genes of the giant-skipper to those of the closely related grass-skipper, leonard-skipper, and awl, he determines that the giant-skipper is not, in fact, sufficiently low on the tree of butterfly branching (the nadir of the butterfly genealogy is that point on its family tree where it parts ways with the moth) to count as a subfamily. Instead, it is the striped policeman (*Coeliades forestan*), who forms the base branch from which all skip-

pers stem. As in our first scenario, code occurs every step of the way in a variety of forms—as letters, symbols, numbers, and colors. As binary, code stands for the absence or presence of a genetic trait. The letters C, A, T, and G denote the occurrence of nucleotides within a genetic sequence. And the color-coding of butterflies allows our scientist to measure variations in hue across his samples. *Code* here might be difficult and abstract, but it is always in the service of clarifying the properties of natural signs. It provides a way to simplify an overabundance of data.

3) A student of aesthetics (or linguistics, anthropology, sociology, political science, or history—all are applicable) reads Roland Barthes' *S/Z*, which famously parses Balzac's *Sarrasine* according to a "volley" of related, interlocking codes (154). Code here does not refer exclusively to an individual language, such as French or English—or Misra C, binary, or DNA, for that matter. Nor does code suggest a single encryption with a single key. Instead, codes for Barthes are *patterns* that emerge within a text. Although the text itself is composed from a larger language set (French), these patterns nevertheless manage to exceed that text and ricochet through the multiple sign systems that constitute culture at large—and vice versa. Instead of viewing the text as a closed system, Barthes illustrates throughout *S/Z* one of his most crucial insights about reading in general: " . . . a text is not a line of words releasing a single 'theological' meaning . . . but a multi-dimensional space . . . a tissue of quotations drawn from the innumerable centres of culture" (*Image, Music, Text* 146). Interpretation is always subjective and interpretative, but it is never conducted within a vacuum of any individual system of signs. Instead, literary codes are porous and refractive; they don't merely "contain multitudes," they generate them.

What insights do these scenarios provide? Each worker in the examples just given would most likely have no interest in the other, at least not on a practical level. Our mythical programmer would probably have little patience for thinking through code's historical implications or its relation to moths; I imagine that her thinking would be pragmatic and oriented toward solving a problem. Our entomologist's approach to code is bound by his interest in the butterfly and its world; it has nothing to do with either hybrid cars or Roland Barthes (something by Vladimir Nabokov might have been a better choice). The student of aesthetics, who unbraids different plaits of codes within a text only to reweave them into an interpretation of his own, has little interest in how to translate his insights into machine-readable commands or how it is that the curvature of a butterfly's antenna might help identify a species.

Nevertheless, these examples from widely divergent domains share points of connection: each illuminates the ways that code, in all of its forms—as process, product, pattern, mark of culture, linguistic signifier, and genetic shorthand—is continuous with the material world. Thinking about code's historical development in this way helps bring the computer back to earth. This should be a fundamental enterprise for something that holds so much power over the way we produce and consume information, not to mention over how it mediates the natural world. As media scholar Roberto Simonowski writes in his essay in *Beyond the Screen*, "code is an indispensable aspect in every discussion of digital arts. Since it is code [t]hat makes everything happen on the screen or on the scene, everything happening is subject to the grammar and politics of code" (137). Put simply, there is no escaping the fact that all computer technology is dependent upon computer code. It is the most potent sign system of our time.[9]

This truth, however indisputable, presents two sizable challenges in terms of analysis. In the first place, to the uninitiated, computer code may appear as an impenetrable wall, composed of unfamiliar symbolic abstractions arranged according to inscrutable rules. Second, acknowledging that machine language underpins all acts of digital expressions is akin to acknowledging that natural language is what determines all forms of literary expression. Both statements are true, but the scale of their implications is vast. Where can one even hope to begin if every line of code has the potential for cultural valence? In literary studies, at least, we have the benefit of thousands of years of aesthetic philosophy to guide us, to show us how to parse natural language effectively, to deploy it to create literary experiences, and to aid us in our reading and analysis of it. We do not yet, however, have a system in place that allows us to do the same for machine language. This is not to say we are helpless. Several writers have grappled with the aesthetics of code, especially within the context of literary-textural analysis. John Cayley's essay, "The Code Is Not the Text (Unless It Is the Text)," provides a useful cautionary note in terms of this type of inquiry. Cayley defines codework as "a term for literature which uses, addresses, and incorporates code: as underlying language-animating or language-generating programming, as a special type of language in itself, or as an intrinsic part of the new surface language." He describes a tendency for people to set up a simple equivalence between the operational code and its expression, and cautions against, as his title suggests, the interpretation of code in this manner, since such a "reading simplifies the intrinsically complex address of writing in programmable media" and runs the risk of leveling all of code's material valences so it becomes subsumed under a textual model, transforming the code into a "simple text-to-be-read, whereas there are real questions of how such work is to be grasped as an object" (Cayley). Cayley is not opposed to the analysis of code per se, nor to considering its aesthetic potential, yet he explicitly urges a move away from an approach that sees code as identical to natural language, or as a way to use one language to decipher the other: "My aim is to disallow a willful critical confusion of code and text, to make it harder for critics to avoid addressing one or the other by pretending that they are somehow equivalent."

In an essay written a year earlier on how code functions within hypertext fictions, Rita Raley makes a similarly strong case for analyzing code. Instead, however, of focusing on the problem of transparency, Raley emphasizes the circuit of communication that occurs between reader, code, and processor in order to point to code's complicated status as an aesthetic object. As she puts it, "both operator and machinic processor are crucial components of the performance of the system. The performance that encompasses user and the machinic system is an interactive one and to some degree collaborative" ("Reveal Codes" 10). In other words, while *running* code might be inaccessible to textual analysis, as Cayley argues it is, the human and machine audience are still actively engaged in that operation. In addition to these important resources, Critical Code Studies, led by Mark Marino, is tackling the aesthetics of code head-on.[10] These efforts are important but have not had much to say about how code functions as an explicitly material agent within a natural ecology.

Code is not only not immaterial; it is *diversely* material, at once a sign system, a series of electrical pulses, a catalyst for physical state changes within a computer and what a computer controls (a car, the display of color of a butterfly's wing, a .pdf of *Sarrasine*), a purchasable product in the form of software, and a mediator between human intention and machinic action. Code is an object, takes an object, is responsible for manipulating objects. It is, in fact, inseparable from the machinic apparatus that it commands. The practice of coding also signifies an uncomfortable zone of artistry that is always balancing individual methods of creative problem-solving and artistic expression against corporate, automated systems. In terms of aesthetic practice, code is both operational and expressive. A machine-readable program, when compiled or interpreted by a computer processer, executes a series of commands and is called "operational" because it tasks the computer with performing some kind of operation (filing, counting, sorting, calculating, creating, deleting, mapping, etc). Expressive code, on the other hand, has a human audience. In the pages that follow, I highlight two pieces of digital art that employ code—computer and otherwise—novelly, in ways that reveal connections between code and natural ecologies across every conceivable model of inscription.[11]

Osmose

Leaf, Tree, Forest, Cloud: The Nature of Expressive Code

In the deepest section of the immersive art installation *Osmose*, the user "swims" through reefs and shoals of bright green code. To arrive at this section, she has donned a virtual reality rig outfitted to respond to her bodily motions. She has learned to control her breathing and lean her body slightly to change direction and explore the strange, organic contours of this highly simulated world. After navigating through interactive natural spaces, such as "Leaf," "Tree," "Forest," and "Cloud," she has emerged here, in "Code," the layer of the installation that makes all the others possible. The code here is visible, tangible, and as such pushes beyond the purely operational. At the same time that it points to the computational processes that have gone into the creation of the art installation, it signals organicism and conveys a sense of ecological holism. Code is the same generative script that creates natural and artificial realms. In this, the "natural" spaces of *Osmose* are more like the emanations of a divine source than they are copies of transcendent forms, more Plotinus than Plato.[12]

Created in 1995, *Osmose* is the work of Char Davies, a Canadian artist who specializes in using digital technology to create immersive environments. In common usage, the term "osmosis" refers to "a gradual, often unconscious process of assimilation or absorption" ("osmosis"). In scientific usage, it means the way different substances become diffused and integrated into one another: "diffusion of a fluid through a semi-permeable membrane from a solution with a low solute concentration to a solution with a higher solute concentration until there is an equal concentration of fluid on both sides of the membrane" ("osmosis"). It is instructive to keep both definitions in mind when thinking about *Osmose*. Within the piece the two substances that exchange and interchange with each other are the human and the environment. Instead of maintaining a distinction between them, the human and the natural are repositioned so that they are one and the same. The human breathes and the earth moves, *not* because the human acts as the "prime mover" but because the human and the earth are coconstituted, composed of the same substance. In *Osmose*, this substance is code.

In the words of Davies, *Osmose* is "is an immersive interactive virtual-reality environment installation with 3D computer graphics and interactive 3D sound, a head-mounted display and real-time motion tracking based on breathing and balance." This is a standard set-up in virtual environments. To experience the piece fully, however, additional hardware is required, specific to Davies' work. The user dons a "body sensor vest" programmed to respond to the user's bodily movements and breathing patterns: "In to rise, out to fall, while leaning gently to change direction" (Davies, *Osmose*). By emulating the movement of scuba divers, each breath and tilt of the body aids in navigation and helps to naturalize the user to the space. By the time the user gets to the deepest layer, naturalized to "Code," she has entered into a fully immersive experience. In fact, "immersant" is the name Davies gives to the user: "I wanted to integrate 'code' as a visible element into *Osmose* in order to draw attention to the technological means by which the work was made. I wanted to emphasize that, even while the contents of the work consist of representations of 'nature,' the immersive experience takes place within a highly technologized construction" (Davies, *Osmose*). This highly technologized abstraction becomes coextensive with the human body experiencing it. In her planning and design, Davies notes the physiological marks of the encounter: "Rather than incorporate visual references to coding throughout the work, we specifically located the code so that it would be experienced as the 'substratum' of the *Osmose* environment. Accordingly, it can only be encountered by going *down* through the surface of the ground and through the subterranean earth, an act achieved by exhaling deeply so that one effectively sinks" (Davies, *Osmose*). Layering code beneath natural features—"ground," "subterranean earth," and so on—suggests that the code layer is continuous with these same natural features. Code forms and frames the immersant's experience; it cannot be divorced from the content it generates, cannot be divorced from the hardware it operates, because it is coextensive with these mechanisms. And because breathing is what propels the immersant, code becomes linked to the functioning of the human body, as well.

Breathing Code

Once the immersant moves through "earth" and reaches "code," she appears to meet an impenetrable wall of abstraction, one that anticipates the dehumanizing code of the *Matrix* film franchise by five years. But the code here is traceable, real; it ties to individual operations and controls the hardware that makes them manifest. Davies' description of such technological specs is significant: "*Osmose* runs on a silicon graphics ONYX, with connections to a crystal river acoustatron, miniguear, and a Macintosh quadra for sound control" (*Osmose*). Terms such as "silicon," "onyx," "crystal," "river," and even "Macintosh," signal brand names, of course, not literal natural features, but by emphasizing these names in the project description, Davies cannily reminds us of the organic nature of computer technology itself, which is made of the most basic elements around—sand, glass, water—and grounded in natural objects.

Davies provides a screen shot of "Code" on her project's website ("Code"). This screen shot is a mere sliver of the coding that has gone into creating the simulation, but it gives a sense of the whole, both in terms of its expressive output and the computational operations it performs. *Osmose* is not a lightweight piece of coding: "More than 20,000 lines of additional code were written to render the images in real time, read the motion sensor data, control the sound equipment, etc." (Davies, *Osmose*). The syntax of this expressive code is operational, meaning that it conforms to the grammatical structure required by a computer for processing. As such, it seems impossible for a human reader to comprehend. Indeed, the clearest word in this snapshot is the word "LOST," which may well indicate how an immersant might initially feel as she breathes her way through this perplexing space. Yet the code here is also expressive and aesthetic, in that it is meant to be encountered and experienced.

So let us attempt to parse the code more carefully, in terms of its expressive *and* operational values. At least three lines of code refer to an array, which in programming language indicates a series of variables contained in one grouping. In this case the array is named "LEAF," presumably linking to the "leaf" landscape in the simulation, although we have no way of verifying this without looking at the rest of the actual code. We see also that there is a "FOR" operation, which indicates that there is a conditional statement that needs to be present for the operation to be executed. We see that there is a line that indicates a relationship between the word "GEAR" and the action of a "FADE" equated to a value of zero. If we flip the snapshot horizontally, we additionally see a command that says "SEND MATERIAL" in the foreground and, in the background, a line that pairs the words "REMOVE" and "COMMENTS" with another conditional statement (this time an "IF" instead of a "FOR"). As enticing as decoding this code might be, we reach the limit quickly. Even if we had fluency in the programming language used to create the work, we only have a snapshot and cannot hope to decode its operational secrets. Yet we have not come close to exhausting its significance. Equally suggestive are its *expressive* elements, that is, those elements that would be meaningless to a computer processor but are suggestive to us.

In the first place, the code is green, signaling both the color of the environmental movement and the computational aesthetics of the 1980s—a time period marked by the popularization of the personal computer, whose default format setting was a black background screen and colorful sans-serif font.[13] By invoking simultaneously these two things that have all too often been seen as opposed to each other, Davies collapses them into one mutually informing aesthetic trope. Second, because the code branches from a core, trunk-like structure, it has much in common visually with other images of trees within the work. And because the array it lists is named "LEAF," a word that appears multiply within this snapshot, the code suggests actual leaves adorning this exceedingly abstract tree.

While this layer of code might form the work's substrate, as Davies suggests it does, it is both expressive *and* operational—operational in the sense that it is this same code that the artist has used to create the rest of the work, expressive in the sense that the code has been aestheticized, turned green and made visible to the human eye. Davies' overt use of code as a tool of production and active aesthetic element ties it both to natural artifacts ("leaf," etc.) and embodied action (breathing). Its presence demonstrates code's multivalence. It is a sign system, a work composed within that system, an environment, and a mimetic entity. Like Leibniz' monad, the code here is a microcosm of the whole, the whole, in turn, a manifestation of the micro.[14] Moreover, and just as suggestively, the code here recalls the other spaces of *Osmose*, particularly in the way that it hangs upon the x, y, and z axes of a three dimensional grid. This grid-like "tree" of code echoes the "orientation grid" that opens the work.

Greening the Grid

The grid is an example of codework both in its operational sense, as a physical instance of graph theory used to structure the environment, and in its expressive and cultural valences, as I am using the term here. It signals and is coextensive with the structural underpinnings of *Osmose*. In this respect the grid does the same work that expressive code does. It calls attention to the tools of its production by making these tools visible on the level of the interface, by having the immersant *experience* them. As such, it sets up a dramatic contrast between the grid as a tool, consistent with the conventional way that computer graphics are configured, and the more organic spaces the immersant will encounter. The orientation grid provides an effective opening not only because it hints at computer graphics but also because it invokes and challenges the way the grid has functioned as an aesthetic trope in the literary and visual arts since at least the seventeenth century. Ever since Descartes described the coordinate system as a way to measure space precisely and to situate one's (extended) self in relation to it, the grid has held a troubling relation to nature. As a tool of mapping and orientation, the grid imposes a conceptual and abstract scaffolding upon the world, one that has enabled many human achievements (architecture, cartography, navigation—no small things!). But a tool is never just a tool; it is also always a cultural object. In her influential work on the cultural and artistic history of grids, for example, Rosalind Krauss argues that the grid represents the rationality of modern thought at the expense of the material world. She puts the matter succinctly: "[The grid] is what art looks like when it turns its back to nature . . . a way of abrogating the claims of natural objects to have an order particular to themselves" (50). This is a strong argument, illuminated through Krauss' examples of the evolution of images of windows-as-grids, which grow in stature until they eclipse the world. As the grid gains confidence, the world it measures recedes into the background, ultimately effaced.

The grid in this sense seems an apt grandparent of the grids in *Osmose*. As Boyce Byerly writes in "Spatial Cognition," the grid within human-computer interaction (HCI) is a "space . . . measured exactly by a series of Cartesian coordinates, making stimuli easy to quantify." And as Jodey Castricano, a Canadian-based researcher who focuses on HCI, writes in her analysis of *Osmose*, reliance on the Cartesian coordinate system "allows for quantification of subjective experience . . . [and] *produces* this experience perceptually in the form of dualisms such as the subject-object distinction, which has made its way into HCI theories of perception and cognition." As in Krauss' analysis, grids in Castricano's view concern themselves with measuring and quantifying and, as such, maintain a clear distinction between subjects and objects and, hence, human and environment. Yet grids are not just cultural objects but also natural ones. Grids as material structures exist throughout nature. They do not always inhere in right angles and rigid xy intersects, nor in human windows (or human-computer interfaces) as manifestations of human intellect. The grid also acts as an organizing principle for all animals who must make their homes, build their nests, design their honeycombs, dams, dens, reefs, and lairs. The grid need not even be tied to a living thing: it appears in crystals, rocks formations, mountain ranges, snow banks, waves of water, cloud formations, and plateaus. A recent artwork called "Rules of Six" acknowledges and takes advantage of this fact: an "experiment in self-assembly . . . [it] applies algorithms mimicking natural patterns to six-sided forms of varying sizes, the hexagon being an incredibly efficient and durable structure found in honeycombs and geological formations." The artists envision using these patterns as a template for urban spaces, and "the result suggests an urban-scale landscape that is grown more than planned" (Hosey 143). Such a project gives us an inverse understanding of the grid. Instead of "turning its back" on nature, the grid *emerges* from nature and our own living spaces adapt to its model.[15] *Osmose*'s grids do the same.

Even as a human tool, the grid as a mode of organization need not be antinatural. Thoreau—a land surveyor who walked the land and measured it—analyzed and documented the features of his world in tabular form, nature as database.[16] Nearly three hundred years before Thoreau, Blaise de Vigenère, in his *Traicté des chiffres* (1586), created a charming puzzle, a cluster of star-filled clouds called "The Book of Nature in the Sky." As Peter Pesic writes in his analysis of the work, "the positions of the stars encrypt a French versification of Psalms 19:1. . . . The cipher is made by dividing the picture into a 'trelli' of 320 squares in which stars can appear at a corner or at the center, indicating the letters by their position" (686). This puzzle-image consists of natural signs, human language, and scripture; together they suggest a harmony, and the grid is the organizing structure upon which this harmony hangs.

Even so, the grids in Davies' *Osmose* do invoke Cartesian rationality. In that the user is surrounded by—and lost within—the very abstraction that makes the simulation possible (the xyz space of computational graphics, upon which all subsequent images are mapped), this space provides an example of the computer's "flesh-eating" potential (Kroker and Kroker). One might recall the presentation of virtual reality in films such as *The Lawnmower Man* (1992) and *Johnny Mnemonic* (1995) for a reminder of this expression of virtual engagement, or the description of cyberspace as a "tight grid of pale blue neon" in William Gibson's *Neuromancer* (63). In such spaces the hapless human body appears wildly out of place, pressed flat upon a grid that unfolds to infinitely wide fields of abstraction and shares no contingency with the real world.

This cold, geometric space seems to be nothing but a void. No other bodies inhabit it; it is consistent with the criticism that emerged during the late 1980s and early 1990s, which claimed that virtual environments and digital technology divide human experience from the real world. The immersant might seem to typify the troubling image of a disembodied presence who floats, ghost-like, through abstract space. After all, one dons a vest and a head display, which could be seen as cutting one's self off from the "real" world, in order to view a space made possible by the abstraction of computational technology. This is true only to a certain extent. As mentioned previously, the belief in an unmediated encounter with a "real" world is hard to justify. The sensory perceptions, as well as the feelings of empathy and emotion and reciprocity of the immersant in relation to the world-spaces that make up the installation, all provide an antithesis to how we understood virtual worlds initially, that is, as incompatible with our flesh. Instead, the simulation offers the immersant insight into a built world and extends an invitation to participate in its creation.

For the immersant the physical body—with all of its functioning—is paramount, for it is only by the most basic human bodily function of breathing that she is able to move beyond the three-dimensional grid and enter into the work's more overtly organic spaces. Additionally, the orienting title of the grid is ironic. A "grid," in common usage, provides a way to get one's bearings, usually functioning as that part of a map that allows one to locate one's self via the abstraction. On a map of my university's campus, I can locate myself by following the third vertical grid line to where it connects to the second horizontal grid line; the point of intersection marks the building where I work. Similarly, the first moment of *Osmose* seems to promise to help the immersant find her bearings. Yet at the same time, it signals the failure of the grid to do so. The human, in *this* grid, does not stand apart from the abstraction. She swims within it, just as she does in real life. She cannot objectively read her position within a system of coordinates that enfolds her. Instead, she becomes part of the abstraction, part of the coded organizing structure. This does not negate her agency. Instead, it offers her an opportunity to explore her contingency with the world she inhabits.

As the immersant breathes, the grid recedes, allowing her to enter the central environment of *Osmose*, a space teeming with subtle movement: "the clearing." A river filled with glowing creatures flows across it, and soft points of lights come into view. At its center, a translucent yet highly textured tree spreads its bare, reddish branches toward a dark sky. This space is filled with signs of organicism. Not only do the features of tree, river, earth, and light figure prominently but there is also constant movement within the translucent shapes and layers that make up the clearing.

Code and Grids

In total, there are twelve such spaces in *Osmose*, all of which the immersant explores by breathing, leaning, tilting, and even "hovering" between worlds in what Davies refers to as "non-Cartesian space" (Davies, *Osmose*). The artist's reference to Descartes' coordinate system is significant; it criticizes the grid as a system of measurement more interested in objective quantification than in subjective experiences or qualia. Although the use of a coordinate system still underpins these environments—it would be impossible to create a simulation like *Osmose* without a three-dimensional conceptual grid because a coordinate system is still essential to the structure and design of any immersive HCI—Davies plays with this framework by making this abstraction yield to the more "organic" world it attempts to measure. *Osmose*'s immersant dispenses with the grid, but not in pursuit of a rational cogito. Instead, she is continuous with the whole system, just as the operational code is continuous with the expressive spaces it creates. Code is the key aesthetic trope that makes this continuity possible.

Code blurs the boundary between individual perceiving subject and the objects that make up the natural landscape; when users "breathe" and "sink" into code they see that the code that makes up the ecology of the art installation is tied to their own bodily processes, which are responsible for the connection between breath, motion, and navigation. Through code, the relationship between reader, spectator, and text becomes very fluid. This peculiar, code-enabled mode of engagement suggests a harmonious interdependence between the immersant and the space she explores; as such, it is extremely promising for thinking about ways to raise environmental awareness. By this I don't mean awareness specific to one political ideology or another, but rather to an awareness of the *stakes* of these confusing, competing, and often contradictory ideologies. One of the most important objectives that ecocritical discourse shares with object-oriented ontology is its desire to question (if not extirpate) the notion of human exceptionalism, the pernicious yet persistent belief that humans have dominion over nature. Here, in *Osmose*, the immersant does not stand apart from or above the world. Instead, she is fully imbricated within its fabric. The sense of immersion that *Osmose* engenders is not just a function of a cinematic, stereoscopic panorama. It also comes from how the images within the installation are layered on top of each other, moving in and out of focus. By layering natural imagery across all three dimensions of the (now invisible) grid, this collage-like mixing of foreground and background, within which images from both bleed through and intermingle, displaces the human user as the center and enframer of the world. Instead, the immersant is entangled with the landscape, and the code literalizes this connection.

Within *Osmose* and other such landscapes—as strange as they might seem—the presence of code has intriguing and salubrious effects on the structure of subjectivity in terms of the relation of the subject to its environment. In particular, code allows the subject to be able to see how she is connected to a world that is not limited to human components but includes, in addition to human components, biological components and data points. This can have positive consequences for our own perceptions of natural spaces in the real world, in that it allows us to see our actions unfolding in relation to other beings and entities, which has the potential to foster a greater sense of personal responsibility for the environs. The presence of code suggests that nature and self are not only constituted by the same generative language but also so commingled as to be indistinguishable. In the next piece of art I examine, code functions quite differently, takes multiple forms, and expresses different things, including memory, erasure, and, as I shall argue, the "mechanisms" of nature.

Agrippa

If an ecosystem is "a system formed by the interaction of a community of organisms with their environment," then *Agrippa* is an ecosystem in book form ("ecosystem"). It functions wholly differently from *Osmose*, however. Instead of an environment that invites the user to explore and partake of its many intriguing spaces, *Agrippa* functions as an archive of memories and artistic techniques. At its center lurks a highly subjective presence whose desires and insights shape the text and inform its readings. In this sense, *Agrippa* is traditional in its presentation of a specific, human identity and would seem to do very little to inform an object-oriented approach. And yet it does so very well. As an object and as a text, *Agrippa* names an aesthetic collision (and collaboration) that occurred in 1992 between several disparate natural and expressive (and commercial) domains: publishing, poetry, etching, bookbinding, typesetting, genetic coding, advertising, image making, performance, reading, and computer programming. The product of this collaboration took the final form of a "book."[17] The scare quotes are purposeful; *Agrippa* is not a book in any conventional sense of the term; or, to be more precise, the book-as-object is only one aspect of its puzzling existence. Instead, *Agrippa* names a queerly evocative series of textual objects—book, poem, floppy disk, aquatints, adverts, and pages of genetic code—all nested within a bulletproof Kevlar case.[18] Each of these objects has an author; together they form the work's dramatis personae.

Kevin Begos, Jr., was the publisher who commissioned, coordinated, and managed the project. *Dennis Ashbaugh* was the artist responsible for the book's "genetic portraits," striking columns of pale green "DNA-gel motifs," which resulted from his innovative process of aquatinting, a technique similar to copperplate etching (*Agrippafiles*). *William Gibson*, the famous science fiction author, composed the work's centerpiece, a meditation on the mechanism of memory (among other mechanisms, as we shall see), which took the form of a 293-line (305, counting spaces) poem entitled "Agrippa: (A Book of the Dead)."[19] The poem begins with a description of a family photo album, the Agrippa brand album that Kodak released in the 1920s, from which the poem takes its name. *An anonymous programmer* who went by the handle "Brash" created the computer code contained on the disk. When run on an early Macintosh, the program on the disk instructed the computer to scroll the poem once, and only once, and then erase itself. *The unsung members of the fruit fly family, genus* Drosophila, (a "very popular research creature," as the publisher has noted [Begos, "Printer's Copy"]) provided the DNA in the form of their "bicoid maternal morphogen," a partial sequence of which appears in the book's pages as a long series of Gs, Ts, Cs, and As, but which, apart from spatial and thematic proximity, bares no relation to the DNA expressed in Ashbaugh's "genetic portraits." And, finally, the typesetting and binding were achievements of the *Golgonooza printing press in New Hampshire*, which burned and branded each cover; set the type—here, arguably, the fruit fly had its revenge (the Gs, Ts, Cs, and As must have been a typesetter's bane)—and cut a floppy disk–size hole from the last few pages of each copy; then Smyth stitched the binding, that is, sewed through each signature with an industrial-strength sewing machine. The name of the press, Golgonooza, was a neologism lifted from Blake's "Jerusalem," whose etymological meaning, as Nelson Hilton has demonstrated in his explication of the word, suggests "a tissue of living words or word-creatures"—a weird name, in other words, made weirder on account of its aptness to this similarly weird project.[20]

In sum, the project made use of at least six different semiotic codes:

1. English-poetic (the poem)
2. Cultural-historic (the newspapers)
3. Genetic (the DNA code)
4. Visual (the green cells)
5. Book making (binding, setting, cutting, and selling)
6. Computer code (self-effacing)

Once the textual objects of poem, disk, "genetic portraits," and genetic code were bound into this tortured codex, the entire book was wrapped in gauze, like a burial shroud, and enclosed, like a corpse, within the case. The work is puzzling—impossible. It cannot possibly cohere. Yet it does. In its very collision of digital, poetic, and genetic codes, *Agrippa* offers an exemplary instance of the messy, violent, technologically rich, and naturally vibrant ecological model that *Animal, Vegetable, Digital* advocates. It is my argument that the "natural" features of the work cohere with other elements to suggest not a harmonious model of nature but what Steven Mentz, in his "post-sustainable" vision of nature, refers to as "the structure-breaking structure of all systems" (591), that is, the often violent and disruptive changes that occur regularly and systematically, although not always predictably, within nature.

The Critical Ecology

Before I delve into the particulars of my argument, it will be useful to provide a snapshot of *Agrippa*'s critical landscape. My reading is indebted to and builds upon work by Peter Schwenger, Alan Liu, and Matthew Kirschenbaum. It is also informed by the *Agrippa Files*, an online archive of artifacts related to and inspired by *Agrippa*, as well as the work I conducted as a member of the *Agrippa Files* team. All the scholarship that *Agrippa* has generated shares a central premise: the work is a self-reflexive expression of, flirtation with, and commentary upon destruction, or at least demonstrates a proclivity toward erasure and death. Yet this shared point of departure has yielded distinct, although not mutually exclusive, conclusions. Peter Schwenger's "*Agrippa*, or the Apocalyptic Book" views the work as a manifestation of an eschatological impulse. His reading identifies *Agrippa*'s theoretical and poetic antecedent as the concept of disappearance as it is outlined by Blanchot and Mallarmé, respectively. Alan Liu argues that the work expresses a special type of transcendence. His reading aligns the related technological mechanisms of erasure that appear in the work—photography, digital technology, and guns—and suggests that they cohere as the work's central "mechanism," usurping Nature's role as the prime organizer of existence and hence Nature's objects as the catalysts of sublime experience.

Matthew Kirschenbaum has provided a "forensic" reading, which traces the poem's manifestation within and across a variety of authorized and unauthorized medial forms—the computer code that contained, displayed, and erased it; the degraded visual copy in the form of a bootleg film that circulated after the poem's public transmission (that is, the "hack" referred to earlier); the text on William Gibson's own website, which contains discrepancies and typos; and finally an encryption emulator that translates the text into the code used to hide it. Kirschenbaum's reading highlights code's peculiar and resilient materiality as electric event and textual trace, and uses *Agrippa* to demonstrate that in spite of anxieties about the fragile and ephemeral nature of digitally encrypted information, such information has longevity.

These critics have read *Agrippa* carefully and thoroughly. I share with them an interest in the way moments of revelation—in the poem, in particular—speak to a larger system of (dis)organization at work in the entire piece. My focus, however, is on how natural signs and agents might be said to act and operate within it. These help to foster an ecological unity of disparate expressive systems—codes both literal and metaphoric. This is a messy, unraveling, and at times ugly ecology, perhaps, but an ecology nevertheless, of distinct signs that are aesthetically yoked.

The systems of code at work in *Agrippa* at large—computer, poetic, genetic, book—affirm this ecology. The gene sequence of the fruit fly is a shorthand of familial genetic expression: the repetition—with difference—that offers a set of conditions that may or may not be expressed. The body of the book looks like a coffin and hence suggests life, death, and mourning. Each instance appears battered and distressed, as if it were exhumed well into its process of decomposition. And the poem, as we shall see in just a moment, is itself a testament to memory, death, and creation. This leaves the computer code. How to analyze a text that is absent? Although it is the driving force behind the gimmick, one that erases the very product it displays, it at the same time speaks to a larger ecological unity—ecology in the etymologically accurate sense of the word from which it stems, *oikos*: a dwelling place. The code itself holds and evokes the world around it. As Matthew Kirschenbaum argues in *Mechanisms*, *Agrippa* in its entirety is an archive of technological inscriptions.

Designed to erase, *Agrippa*'s code might seem mystical, transcendental. And we might even see Gibson's early understanding of computation lurking somewhere throughout its pages.[21] Even so, the code that erases *Agrippa* also contains it. And, in fact, the poem remains, retrievable on the computer disk designed to negate it. The code on the disk has been hidden, anonymously authored, appropriately enough for a program tasked with erasure. Yet, in fact, the poem is still there. This is code as legerdemain: look at this while this other code does that. It was fitting that Penn Jillette was there to read the poem at the work's vernissage. Magician that he is, he staged its illusionary execution. In 2010, the "Cracking the Agrippa Code" team completed the second act of the show by bringing it back to life, by hosting a competition to see who might be able to hack *Agrippa*'s code and hence "recover" its contents. Even before the precise manner of encryption was cracked, some of the mystery of the erasure was negated. As in all good magic tricks involving resurrection, the trick lay in never having had an execution in the first place. A programmer from the Netherlands—a one "Freek Wiedijk"[22]—used mini vMac, a program that emulates an early Macintosh, to demonstrate this. He inserted the disk and "interrupted the program when it was scrolling its text, and used the Find function of the User Area to locate the string "'I h', or rather its hex equivalent 22492068, this being the start of the poem" (Wiedijk). Then, in Linux, he copied all of the data on the disk to a file and "cut the poem from that file" (Wiedijk).

In Mr. Wiedijk's output, an extraction from the whole kit and caboodle of data on the *Agrippa* floppy, Gibson's poem appears beneath and between the computer code. It was never displayed this way, never meant to be seen—in fact was explicitly meant *not* to be seen—but it inhered all the same. How? It will be useful to demonstrate how various computer codes might come to be involved in this trick. But first, a caveat: like Cayley, Kirschenbaum describes a certain risk involved in reading code; his concern is that people who approach code as a text to be read will be "lulled into assuming they must be witnessing electronic writing in something close to its natural state" (235). This note of caution is especially important with *Agrippa*, which involves so many codes that it is impossible to point to which one might count as "natural" in the first place. The "Cracking the Agrippa Code" website itemizes these for us: "There are four main aspects of the program that were revealed by the submissions: the compiled binary, the main cryptographic algorithm, the encryption effect that runs after the poem finishes scrolling, and the 'self-destruct' mechanism that prohibits running the program more than once" (DuPont). A walk-through of a few of the different levels of encoding that are possible, in any text, will show just how distant computer language in its "natural" state(s) is from our own.

It's Not Easy Being #00AF33

As we have seen, a machine-readable program is called "operational" because it is capable of executing a command or performing various operations. Before this happens, however, it exists as a text file. In order for it to operate, it needs to be translated from a high-level programming language (so named because it involves a high level of abstraction from the computer's hardware schematics) to a low-level one (so named because it departs very little from this): binary. We can—sort of—"see" this in action by looking at a simple program. One of the first commands that one learns in any programming language is the print or echo command, which prints text on the screen.[23] In a line of code written in PHP, for example, which tells the computer to display the sentence "it's not easy being green," the syntax is very familiar. It looks like this:

```
print ("it's not easy being green");
```

The structure of this command is very close to that of an English imperative. Yet before the processor can execute this command, it needs to be told how to do so, how to retrieve information, where it is "stored," and how and where to display it. The above code will get this done, but not before it is interpreted into machine-readable binary. In digital technology binary's two symbols consist of a one (1), which signifies the presence of electricity, and a zero (0), its absence. The same statement—"it's not easy being green"—in binary looks like this:

01101001 01110100 01011100 00100111 01110011 00100000 01101110 01101111 01110100 00100000 01100101 01100001 01110011 01111001 00100000 01100010 01100101 01101001 01101110 01100111 00100000 01100111 01110010 01100101 01100101 01101110 00101110 ("binary")

It is not as accessible, and there is a reason for that. Binary is not meant to be "read" by you or me. It is not like Morse telegraph, strung in one long line, sent across a wire, and decoded by a human—perhaps an electrified one—at the other end.[24] It *can* be rendered this way, and we can translate it so that we can read it, as we've just done above, but its expression is an electrical action that opens or closes an infinitesimally small circuit housed on a piece of silicon. Instead of a 1:1 correspondence between one letter and another, as in Morse (e.g., S-O-S corresponds to . . . --- . . .), it signifies multiple and often recursive events. These are just two examples of how we might encode this sentence, but there are many other possible ways that other types of code might come into play. If there were a concern in terms of file size, for example, the binary code might first be stored in hexadecimal form, a "short-hand for binary numbers . . . [with] 75% [fewer] characters" ("hexadecimal"). The same sentence above, in hex, would look like this:

49 74 73 20 6E 6F 74 20 65 61 73 79 20 62 65 69 6E 67 20 67 72 65 65 6E 2E

But most users aren't terribly worried about this level of management. Most of us are concerned with what we—not the computer—can read and see, on a web page, browser, and so on. In these cases, we "see" hex all the time, in the form of color values. Hexadecimal values take the basic building blocks—red, green, and blue—that a computer processor needs to mix up thousands of different colors. In a sequence of six digits, two each for red, green, and blue, the hex apportions color into quantifiable sections, on a spectrum of color density that ranges from zero (the lowest value) to F, the highest value, which looks like this:

0 1 2 3 4 5 6 7 8 9 A B C D E F

To display that same sentence against a green background, one would type the hexadecimal sequence #00AF33 into a text editor, surround it with the tags to set the background color of the HTML document, and view it in a web browser, creating on one's screen a field of green—the color of jealousy, fresh-cut grass, and the metonymic shade of both money and the environmental movement. In hexadecimal form, however, green is unrecognizable to most users. In the case of green (00AF33), we get zero portions of red, full portions of green, and zero portions of blue. If we wanted a more minty green, we might add some splashes of blue (00FF66). If we wanted more of a yellow-green we could mix in some red (AAFF00).[25] The same hex values show up differently on different computers, to the eternal frustration of graphic designers everywhere. As instructive as this is in terms of demonstrating McLuhan's truism that medial variations are also content variations, it is also an exercise in abstraction, in simple mathematics, that seems more cognitive than experiential. In this way, it seems immaterial and intangible and, consequently, opposed to the organic, hand-hewn aesthetics of environmentalism.

Yet this small sampling—even such tiny slivers of it—demonstrates the fact that while operational computer code in general is rational, formula-driven, and rule-based, it is nevertheless translatable and transformable. If we do the same thing with the code from *Agrippa* listed above, limiting ourselves to the last lines of the poem, we see the same translation occur in reverse. The binary sequence of "00011100 10100101 11010000 01100111 01101000 01101001 01101110 01100111 00101100 00001101 01101001 01101110 00100000 01110100 01101000 01100101 00100000 01101101 01100101 00011100 10100101 11100000 01100011 01101000 01100001 01101110 01101001 01110011 01101101 00101110 00100000 00100000 01101101 10110110 00000000," translates to the hexadecimal sequence "1ca5d0 67 68 69 6e 67 2c 0d 69 6e 20 74 68 65 20 6d 65 1ca5e0 63 68 61 6e 69 73 6d 2e 20 20 6d b6 00," which itself translates into English as "laughing, in the mechanism," the last three lines of Gibson's poem. In all its instances, the computer code, like all matter, inheres. And Brash, the programmer behind it, took pains to communicate that his code was context-specific: "As far as the code goes things are going well. The encryption portion, which actually has two different sections, is together and working fine. It has one very interesting feature in that it is context sensitive. The value, both character and numerical, of any particular character is determined by the characters next to it, which from a cryptoanalysis or code-breaking point of view is an utter nightmare" (*Agrippa Files*, "Brash"). In his explication of Brash's algorithm, Quinn DuPont takes down the complexity of the code a few notches, writing that Brash's claims of intricacy were overstated and that "the anonymous programmer of *Agrippa* chose a simple mechanism" (DuPont). Even so, the choice of the mechanism, simple or not, is relevant. Brash chose to "write a large string of data over a portion of the binary that contains necessary run routines. In the archived source code printout this self-destruct mechanism wrote 40,000 ASCII characters (ASCII code 255) to a specified offset, leaving a string of 320,000 binary 1's to corrupt the program" (DuPont). In addition to a context-specific, character-level encryption, Brash hid his code *in code*, hid not just needles in haystacks, but hay needles in stacks of hay.[26] And, "once the binary is run in emulation it changes itself, writing a string of genetic code back into the binary (diff)" (DuPont). At this point in the code's execution, the "320,000 binary 1's" become a six-thousand character sequence of Cs, Ts, Gs, and As, aesthetically linking genetic code to the code of the computer, as well as to Ashbaugh's images and the pages of the fruit fly's excerpted morphogen. What I want to emphasize from this summary of *Agrippa*'s use of computer code is how it works as a material ecology. Even when it "disappears" it inheres and, as Kirschenbaum shows us, endures: "Despite its being a uniquely volatile electronic object—its own internal mechanisms radically ephemeral by both intent *and* design—'Agrippa' has proven remarkably persistent and durable over the years" (Kirschenbaum, "Hacking Agrippa"). In this sense it is, like all matter, obedient to the laws of nature.

Revelations

It is the poem itself, however, that offers the most sustained expression of a natural ecology. In structure, the poem is simple, composed of six short parts: The poet opens an old family photo album and describes the photographs it contains. These trigger several personal memories, including a childhood memory of accidentally firing a gun, his adolescence in the South, his firing of a different gun, his move to Canada as a young adult, and a "present" moment of walking through a storm in Japan. The poem, like the book-objects that contain it, braids together several large-scale topics: time, death, history, memory (both public and private), and artistic expression. It presents a series of revelatory moments, each associated with the word "mechanism." This word appears eight times throughout the poem and refers variously, in order, to the following: the photo album, a camera, a gun, a gun again, the memory of the gun, the timers of traffic lights, grace, and rain. In each instance, these items are both the objects and instigators of the revelation.

Revelation is one way of poking through the fabric of time, of glimpsing its organizing structure.[27] But revelation is also often tied to natural signs that reveal, hint, or frustrate meaning. The revelatory moments in "Agrippa" are no exception. Throughout the poem, natural signs contribute to revelation, cohere as "mechanism" and, in doing so, exhibit transhistoric agency. By this I mean agency in the sense that Tobias Menely employs it in "The Present Obfuscation," an essay that considers the way that weather patterns worked to produce eschatological anxiety in the eighteenth century, specifically in William Cowper's *The Task*. This work, Menely argues, "is marked by the uncertainties and anxieties of a modern climate" (478). He analyzes the last three books of the work in terms of their apocalyptic import. Confounded by the unusual weather—a thick, sulfurous haze that drifts in to England from the north—Cowper puzzles over whether he can distinguish between such natural occurrences and the divine signs that will mark the end of days. In *The Task*, he eschews this problem by appointing himself as the medium of prophecy, anticipating "that blest moment [when] Nature throwing wide / Her veil opaque, discloses with a smile / The author of her beauties" (qtd. in Menely 488). Cowper's vision of nature here is one that lacks any power of its own. Rather, nature's veil is what obscures the order of provenance. In spite of this, Menely makes it exquisitely clear how much historical agency nature "herself" did in fact possess: "Unbeknownst to Cowper, a sixteen-mile volcanic fissure in southern Iceland opened on 8 June 1783. Laki was the most powerful and devastating volcanic eruption between Huaynaputina in 1600 and Tambora in 1815. . . . [Its eruption led] to the hottest summer recorded in England until 1995" (481). Throughout the essay, through his analysis of Cowper's poem, Menely makes a persuasive argument, summarized neatly in his essay's abstract: "Climate change poses a crisis, in the dual etymological senses of a decision and a turning point, because it unsettles the duration of the present, what returns and endures and so measures alteration" (Menely n.p.). Climate change is not a preoccupation of either *Agrippa* or "Agrippa." However, natural phenomena structure the poem's revelatory moments—as they structure, to an extent, all expressive works, political acts, and historical events. Menely points to Walter Benjamin to help conceive of nature as a powerful witness to unfolding time. In "On the Concept of History," Benjamin suggests that "the past carries with it a secret index by which it is referred to redemption. Doesn't a breath of the air that pervaded earlier days caress us as well?" ("On the Concept," 390). As Menely writes, "Benjamin's atmospheric tropes . . . the clouds, the air, and the sun . . . are witnesses to history's tumult, palpable figures for the 'tiny fissures in the continuous catastrophe'" (489). Although Benjamin's insights are couched in the language of catastrophe and apocalypse, in Menely's analysis his "atmospheric tropes" eschew eschatology; he "holds out hope, sustained in a metaphoric of meteorological legibility, that buffeted by arctic winds the clouds will still part, unveiling other destinies" (490). Similarly, in "Agrippa," the air of the past is here, now, an "atmospheric index" that offers continuity and defies a definitive eschatological impulse. The past bleeds through to the future but also speaks to the "urgency of the moment." These fissures are revealed concretely in natural signs in "Agrippa"; moments of revelation crystallize in natural forms. These forms do not negate how they appear in other guises, but they reinforce and share equal standing with them. There are several moments that support this reading:

1. *The Bullet in the Banister*: In the poem's second section, Gibson's act of opening the old photo album, retrieved from the "bottom drawers of veneered bureaus," recalls a childhood memory of a similar disclosure: finding a gun in "an attic trunk." The gun discharges and the bullet strikes the hardwood banister, which brings "a strange bright smell of ancient sap to life" (132). What "life" is being revived here? His own, since this moment marks a brush with death; and his father's, of course, and his grandfather's, as well as the other members in the "book of the dead" he's just been perusing. But the banister's scent pierces through all of these memories, recalling the hardwood, before that a beam, before that a tree, felled and cut, perhaps by the family mill. The first and last photographs in this section are of the family sawmill and point to this very place and process; the first describes the scent of pitch and "the sweet hot reek of the electric saw, biting into decades" (32). The last describes the "wrack of cut lumber" his grandfather surveys, the "cone of sawdust some thirty feet in height" (92) that stands behind him, and Gibson's own sensuous curiosity about it: "(How that feels to tumble down, or smells when it is wet)" (94). This moment then, while narratively about the blast of the gun and the danger it suggests through misfire, also speaks in an associative way about the continuity of life and objects over time, in this case, a tree's. I mean this in a way that is opposite of sentimental. Neither the act of cutting down the tree nor blasting it with a bullet ends the tree's status as a material object, nor does either act hamper its power to signify. Rather, it adds to it. The

scent of its life inheres in its death, and, like a photograph, it cuts across time.

2. *The Ice Gorge*: The third section of the poem returns to the photo album, beginning and ending with a photograph captioned "Ice Gorge at Wheeling / 1917." An ice gorge results from a snap of cold so fierce that it freezes the flow of water, not just the lapping waves of ponds and lakes, but rivers. It is a naturally occurring phenomenon, but one more common in subarctic climates. When it happens in more moderate temperature zones, it is catastrophic. No wonder, then, that the legal designation of "ice gorge" in the United States comes not just from the EPA or the DoA but from the Department of Transportation, which describes the occurrence in terms of halted traffic, as "a conglomeration of ice solidly packed from bank to bank which is obstructing the flow of the river and marine traffic" ("ice gorge"). The photo of the ice gorge in the old album resonates thematically, in that this frozen space echoes the snapshots of frozen time. But it also speaks to the power of the freeze. By all accounts the ice gorge of 1918 was a *force*. It held the Ohio River frozen, in suspense, and hence suspended its surrounding citizens. As such, it made an apt emblem for a nation recently engaged in the temporal suspension that results from war. As one local historian puts it, "as 1917 drew to a close and 1918 got under way, local newspapers were filled with news of two things: American troops who had joined the fight in Europe that eventually would be called World War I and the unprecedented snow and ice that was paralyzing the city" (Doane). The "paralyzed" city endured for an entire month, during which time the river remained "frozen shore to shore for 134 miles from Higginsport, Ohio, to Madison, Ind." But the frozen image of the frozen gorge is also consistent with another feature of "mechanism" at work in Gibson's poem. Like the others, this hyper-still image of suspension foreshadows a violent, cataclysmic release. This occurred on February 1, 1918, when the gorge melted into slabs of ice: "the fury of the river came in a 20-foot swell of water and ice that hit the Cincinnati riverfront. . . . At its height the river level downtown reached more than 61 feet." The consequence of this sudden rush of water was widespread destruction: "Steamboats, towboats and barges that were frozen in the river were crushed and sank. Many more were destroyed against the shore. It's hard to imagine the sounds of destruction that day" (Doane).

3. *The Shale Pit*: A third moment occurs at a shale pit, in the woods, where Gibson goes to practice shooting. He fires "down into a distant stream," but the bullet ricochets "off a round of river rock," narrowly missing him, instead "clipping walnut twigs from a branch / two feet above my head. So that I remembered the mechanism" (206–208). Gibson shoots downstream, and the river seems to shoot back. Of course, the stream has no intentionality, nor does the bullet, river rock, or walnut branch. Gibson initiates the causal chain—perhaps he is a poor shot; perhaps he doesn't see how the rock protrudes—but the ecology of the landscape delivers the memory of near-death. It alerts him to and clarifies this particular moment within his life, which echoes another (the bullet in the banister), which echoes another (opening the photo album), and so on. This encounter with the stream removes him, briefly, from the flow of time.
4. *The Highway at Night*: A similar moment of awareness occurs one night in his adolescence, as he walks home from the all-night bus station. Again, this moment is embedded in stillness: "so quiet I could hear the timers of the traffic lights a block away: the mechanism" (247–248). Here he shows a writer's sensitivity to the measure of time and the movement of others. He is no longer limited to his own internal clock but now attuned to the countless ways we measure out life as a species; the way we mark and control it so thoroughly that it becomes automated and integrated with landscape, hence naturalized. The only other event that registers is "the silence / spreading out to where the long trucks groaned / on the highway their vast brute souls in want" (249–250). His awareness of his surroundings is crystalline, so clear that it seems suspended in time, the "brute souls" of the trucks like beasts in the night, partners in an animate, technology-rich ecology.
5. *The Melting Snow*: A final example occurs when he arrives in Canada and looks upon his new home: "on the melting snow / of the city undreamed / and on the revealed grace / of the mechanism" (278–280). Like the god of the New Testament, the mechanism offers "grace" after the violent cognitive ruptures caused by the poet's awareness of it—no wonder the extant scholarship surrounding the work invokes the eschatological, the prophetic. It is not a divine grace, though, but a natural one, revealed by the melting snow. From it, the city emerges, announcing both seasonal change and its revelatory power. Schwenger writes that *Agrippa*'s performance of erasure

> forms a mini "apocalypse," in the sense of revelation, which he likens to the visions John recounts in Revelation, particularly his vision of a book that will trigger the apocalypse. His comparison to *Agrippa* is unambiguous: "*Agrippa* too is destroyed by being opened," but the consequence of that destruction, for Schwenger, is inaccessible: "Though the question of what comes to pass is ultimately beyond us" (69). *Agrippa* is no New Jerusalem; the enduring character of nature within the text seems to defer, perhaps infinitely, any final end of days.[28]

Each of these moments of illumination emerges from/within stillness. Each also presents a vision of nature as something that exhibits a transhistoric agency, in degrees of escalation, inherent in a variety of manifestations: the sap, the ice, the snow, the stream. These are not "agents" in the sense that Benjamin's angel of history is; neither is Gibson himself forced to look back in horror as he hurtles toward the future.[29] Natural objects instead function as constant witnesses and potent participants in historical progression.

If this reading and conception of nature is distinct from how Liu configures it in *The Laws of Cool*—there he argues that with "Agrippa" "Gibson cuts the tether to nature" (346)— then this is because we are defining nature in very different ways. Liu is referring to nature in its Wordsworthian, romantic sense, and in this sense, our readings of the poem concur. The nature of "Agrippa" does not cohere with a romantic conception of nature, neither in terms of how Wordsworth described it, capital N and majestic, nor of how it operated in the greater cultural sphere, as a "cultural artifact to be ruled by the recreational eye" (*Local Transcendence* 40). Romantic nature is peculiar: a source of a joyous emotional energy on the one hand and a source of political power in the form of property on the other. As John Berger puts it, the "enjoyment of 'uncorrupted and unperverted nature' did not . . . usually include the nature of other men. The sentence of poaching at that time was deportation. If a man stole a potato he risked a public whipping ordered by the magistrate who would be a landowner. There were very strict property limits to what was considered *natural*" (*Ways of Seeing* 108). Put another way, Liu once wrote in the context of romanticism that "there is no nature except as it is constituted by acts of political definition made possible by particular forms of government" (*Wordsworth: The Sense of History* 104). But "Agrippa" does not cut the cord of nature as I have been attempting to recast this term. It instead includes nature in all of its manifestations, in all of its technological alterity, which is more frightening than any steep cliff or lightning storm. More accurately, Gibson cuts the cord on the pastoral. In its place, a more complete, complicated, and encompassing nature emerges, and it is to this that the poet finds himself subordinate. Liu asks: "What is authorial inspiration? Fundamentally, Wordsworth and Gibson answer, it is obeisance to a terrifying, autonomous agency *without* that is somehow also a poetic agency *within*" (*Laws of Cool* 346). Liu points to a terrifying synchronicity between the self and system that "Agrippa" gestures toward, and that Gibson shares with Wordsworth: "Where Romantic Nature was the ghost in the machine that resisted iron mechanism . . . for Gibson the mechanism exposes the ghostly gears . . . undergirding contemporary life. . . . The only spirit rolling through the circuitry of all things is the dance of electrons that is the charm of contemporary technology" (347). As Liu states, these same electrons inhere in "the circuitry of all things": guns, wars, and human bodies, as well as tree sap, rivers, and typhoons. This is not a demotion from a romantic conception of nature. Locating the power of nature in the material world marks a promotion, perhaps even a cause for celebration. A material nature is more exciting and tangible than any phantasmagorical manifestation.

Between Cleansing and Eclipse: The Rain in Chiyoda-ku

"Agrippa" speaks to the natural ecology I'm defining, not only by presenting a dangerously vibrant, totalizing natural system of which the author is but one minute agent but also by *exulting* in that system. Steve Mentz locates such a moment in a more famous piece of literature, Whitman's "Song of Myself": "You sea! I resign myself to you also—I guess what you mean. I behold from the beach your crooked inviting fingers, I believe you refuse to go back without feeling of me, We must have a turn together, I undress, hurry me out of sight of the land, Cushion me soft, rock me in billow drowse, Dash me with amorous wet, I can repay you" (*Leaves of Grass* 22).[30] Mentz argues persuasively that this zesty encounter between Whitman and the Atlantic, with its frisky energy and sensual language, marks a moment upon which we might model a newly invigorated environmental ethos, one that rejects a pastoral sensibility and "cedes control while immersing the body in watery contradictions" (589). Like Whitman, Gibson "cedes control" to the mechanism and finds in it an occasion for laughter. Water appears throughout "Agrippa," in a diversity of forms, and in the poem's subtle yet steady creep away from Arcadia we can trace a rejection of the pastoral that Mentz urges.

The first section's series of photographs presents picturesque images of family life in the mountains. Here, father and son fish its ponds, a mother "strolls" around the water's edge, and the photographs capture idyllic scenes: "a flat-roofed shack / Against a mountain ridge" (25–26); "the wild flowers . . .

on the far side of the pond" (64–68). The following photograph of two ladies moves us away from the picturesque pond to the controlled waters of a fish hatchery, from the leisure of fishing to the efficiency of farming. The third section carries us completely into an urban landscape: "Iron bridge in the distance / beyond it a city" (140–141) with its "Hotels where pimps went about their business" (142). The fresh waters of the fishing pond recede. In their place the Ohio River and its attendants emerge: a steamboat's "smoke foul and dark . . . far bank overgrown with factories" (148–151). Part four introduces the stream at the shale pit that Gibson shoots at and that seems to shoot back, negating any sense of picturesque tranquility afforded by watching water. Yet it is in the last section of the poem that an encounter with water both reveals nature's mechanisms and offers a moment of joyous intersection.

This final moment of revelation, which occurs in the last stanza, speaks most clearly to Gibson's vision of an ecological system. The narrator is in Chiyoda-ku, Japan, a place with much historic import, both in its name, "field of a thousand generations," and its history, one of Tokyo's twenty-three central wards created as a part of Japan's reconstruction after World War II ("Chiyoda-ku"). Gibson walks outside in the violent weather of a typhoon; his "everted" umbrella indicates the strength of the wind. Yet he describes the rain that falls upon him not in terms of gusty torrents of water but more softly, as "Fine rain horizontal" (289), suggestive of mist, that emerges from the "storm's Pacific breath" (290). That the ocean air is likened to breath, a gentle, animating presence that connects all, suggests that it negotiates different levels of pressure; this creates an image of a tiny, fragile being suspended in a bubble within the storm's violence, aware and accepting that his memories and his art are subordinate to this larger system.[31] Yet this same storm propels him, and in this moment protects him—although it could destroy him at any other. In it, he finds occasion for laughter.[32] This is not an isolated moment in Gibson's larger oeuvre. In a key moment in *Neuromancer*, when the main character Case, mutilated and initially stranded in Japan, is able, finally, to access cyberspace, his ecstatic reaction echoes Gibson's own: "And it flowed, flowered for him, fluid neon origami trick. . . . And somewhere he was laughing . . . distant fingers caressing the deck, tears of release streaking his face" (52). Case takes his pleasure from a different sort of mechanism, the Ono-Sendai computer that grants him access to the matrix, but the "distant fingers caressing the deck" is a description that could be just as readily applied to writing. There are other parallels. That Gibson ends the poem here, in Japan, in a typhoon, is significant. Both historically and in science fiction, Japan has functioned as a site of apocalypse of every kind: "In sf literature and film, the nation has endured near-total annihilation by natural disasters, psychic teens, radioactive lizards" (Paulk 485). In a reading of the novel's tie to Japan, and the problem of Orientalism in general, Joshua La Bare writes, "The Japanese represent not only the apocalypse, but the fact of its transcendence: the finite, and through it, the infinite" (43). The final moments of "Agrippa" recall Japan's relation to this larger critical, historical, and natural ecology, as well as Gibson's role in shaping this space in the literary imagination.

The poet laughs in the moment, aware of himself within the throes of a violent system that contains cameras, guns, ice storms, world wars, and typhoons. All are part of the mechanisms of nature, a consequence of coming into contact with them. Cognitive and experiential estrangement occurs when one glimpses the organizing structure of the world, the *objects* by which organization and order are achieved, as well as the fact that one is precisely such an object. In other words, the poem presents us with a material model of nature that is holistic and inclusive, if not harmonious and romantic. It offers us a way to think of nature as a self-organizing system that includes these other modes of organization, illuminating several suggestive points of connection.[33]

To my mind, as powerful as such moments are, water needn't be the only natural force to which one must submit in order to foster the ecological model that Mentz has in mind. Any natural force might do, although each encounter will, of course, come with a varying rate of survival. Nevertheless, water offers a way to think about an ecological model that is at once joyous and dangerous. And, if Mentz is right, and we "need a swimmer poetics" of sustainability, then perhaps we already have one: catharsis. The term signifies a cleansing, both a literal wash and a spiritual ablution, as well as, in Aristotle, an emotional discharge and the balance achieved by its purgation. And yet the term is never quite settled in the *Poetics*: "The word *catharsis* drops out of the *Poetics* because the word wonder, *to rhaumaston*, replaces it" (Sachs). In the ancient world more broadly, catharsis is linked to prophecy, a different type of revelation. Consider the tragic cycle of The Oresteia. Cleansing, purgation, wonder, prophecy—we can trace the examples of catharsis throughout:[34] with Iphigenia's sacrifice to appease the wind and sea; with Clytemnestra's murder of Agamemnon on the "splashing floor"; with Orestes' murder of Clytemnestra; with Orestes' spiritual cleansing in the form of the blood of a suckling pig and his pardon in the *Eumenides*.

These grand, tragic moments do not align entirely with my current focus. But within them there are micromoments in which cleansing is suspended and the purgation deferred, moments that expand to accommodate a special type of emotional energy: frenzy, as with Clytemnestra's gleeful vengeance; guilt, as in Lady Macbeth's frantic hand washing; horror, as when Ajax's rage leads to slaughter. Neither the final lines of "Agrippa" nor the segment of "Song of Myself" expresses this energy to tragic scale, but each signals an immersion and suspension within water, as well as an energy that is positive and participatory. Whitman swims with it. Gibson laughs in it. Both express a joyous submission to its energy, because they are able to recognize their membership and complicity in the system.[35]

The default usage of catharsis refers to tragedy, and these modern texts are not tragedies. But neither are they instances of the sublime. The moment of laughter in "Agrippa" is not one of sensory abandonment but of pleasure resulting from a dangerous sensory indulgence. There is no suffering but instead an acceptance of the immensity of nature, our smallness in relation to it, and the strange, provisional correspondence that can occur between it and us. Instead of the consciousness-eclipsing moment of the sublime, the writer has the ability to stand suspended in the frenzy and report back. In the *Agamemnon*, the chorus asks the following question:

> —But once the blood of death is fallen, black
> And oozing at a slain man's feet, alack!
> By spell or singing who shall charm it back? (44)

Photographs are not the same as bloody corpses, but they nevertheless bare the traces of the beloved dead. And they ask a similar question: what can bring them back? In both cases the answer is memory, its arts and its agents, such as Aeschylus, Gibson, Whitman, and its technologies, such as writing, photography, and the blast of a gun. These are manifestations of a larger recursive system in which nothing is ever lost: nature. These technological mechanisms are complicit with natural ones because they emerge from them. Moments of heat inhere in the bullet, in the combination of sulfur, charcoal, and saltpeter we call gunpowder; the ice gorge of the Ohio is frozen water that freezes commerce; the rain in Japan is at once buoyant and monstrous, indicative of all manners of natural and technological devastation.

Agrippa, in sum, presents "mechanisms" of every kind: of biology, of memory, of code, of nature, all of which are more powerful than the human subject who, in fleeting moments of awareness, perceives them. These elements cohere as a system—and the past comes rushing to the present. Perhaps such a system seems antihuman. *Agrippa* as a whole erases human words, confuses and conflates memory, and distorts time, all within a technological-ecological matrix that is complicated and alienating. Even so, the work presents a picture of nature intertwined with the technological. This type of nature does not, however, exclude the human. Instead, the human experiences moments of agency and radical choice that become possible only when he is attuned to the greater system of nature that shapes him.

Coding the World

As in the dream of a universal language that Leibniz imagined, code not only describes worlds but also creates them.[36] Expressive code is always operational code. It always signifies. Because expressive code has the power to express the relation between abstractions, laws, and the world these laws create, it is also always a form of operative code for the human reader.[37] Expressive code is creative, generative, and world-building. By revealing the way the natural world is coextensive with computer code, such works suggest a world in which organic and inorganic entities—be they animal, vegetable, mineral, or digital—are one and all cut from the same fabric. The presence of code allows the subject to see how she is connected outward, to a world not limited to human components but dense with biological and inorganic elements. We are always already connected to nature, via the same chemical compounds and genetic structures that make up all matter, but we are rarely reflective about this fact. Code offers a way to rethink identity as something thoroughly stitched up with its environment, rather than as something somehow forged independently or existing outside of it. We should press the question of code's relation to aesthetics even further to see ourselves not as the authors or subjects of textual ecologies but as coproducers and coinhabitants of evolving systems. The next chapter discusses how key works of interactive digital art help us do just this. By collapsing the distinction between the human body and its environment, as well as between different artistic forms, such works allow us to view textual and artistic landscapes as coextensive with ourselves.

2
Collapsing
Challenging Boundaries of Bodies and Forms

> If any thing is sacred, the human body is sacred.
> —Walt Whitman, *Leaves of Grass* (1855)

> This oak tree and me, we're made of the same stuff.
> —Carl Sagan, *Cosmos* (1980)

Building Bodies

Digital art can help us play with the boundary lines between our bodies and the world, and even make these boundaries suspect. This is the aesthetic strategy of *collapsing*. By this I mean to signify ways that digital art works to challenge conventional assumptions about the physical integrity of the human body.[1] But it also challenges a taxonomic boundary that suggests that the human body is fundamentally different from the other bodies with which it shares the world.

The body is not a single thing but a multitude of different kinds of matter. Some of it is natally "ours," flesh, blood, organs, and bones, but much is not, bacteria, bugs, gut flora, and spores.[2] Of the many systems of functioning we think of as individually embodied and self-contained—digestive, respiratory, circulatory, reproductive, nervous, endocrine, and so on—all concern themselves with taking in matter from the outside and putting it to good use within. Early studies in anatomy are horrifying affairs; reading them requires fortitude, but they are worth the effort because they attest to this inside-out relationship; from them we learn that the inner organs were seen to have continuity with our outer parts—the Latin words for the parts of the heart include *ventricle* (little belly) and *auricle* (little ear). The word "capillary" comes from *capillus*, which means hair; the word "stomach" from *stoma*, which means mouth (Eckstein 123). Our bodies are porous and unruly; they *need* to take matter into themselves and push unwanted matter out. In this respect they are very much like the other bodies with which we share the world. Like Haraway's cyborgs and Deleuze's wasp-orchids, human bodies are conjoined with and depend upon for survival the objects of the world around them. Julien Offray de La Mettrie had an early insight into this in 1748 when he compared the lengths of our legs to the stems of his plants, in *L'Homme Plant*: "a simple analogy between the vegetable kingdom and the animal kingdom has shown me that the main parts of the one are found in the other" (77). This essay is less famous than his *L'Homme Machine*, but it is in many respects as important. When read side by side, the two texts provide an eighteenth-century concordance between men, machines, animals, and plants.[3]

I offer all this as a preamble because I have a concern. Ecocriticism and digital studies both question the disembodied model of subjectivity—that is, the Cartesian model—that was taken as a given in the understanding of both the natural world and the virtual one(s). Many in both fields (or in any field, for that matter) are no longer comfortable with thinking of identity as a self-sufficient intellectual kernel contained within an earthly, fleshy vessel. A rejection of a res cogitans model of personhood has proven crucial for both ecocriticism and digital studies, making way for exciting new ideas about "distributed" subjectivity, multiple selfhood, and networks of influence. It has created a space within which an object-oriented ontology might flourish. This is not my concern. My concern is that now that this problematic model has weakened, another seems poised to take its place. If Descartes' notion of a mind in a body bore some responsibility for divorcing the self from the world, the notion of the *body* as separate from the world is as problematic. As Latour reminds us, the human being is one object among many. We should remember, however, that the human body is itself similarly and multiply constituted. If early scholarship about digitality dismissed the body's connection to technology, current work perhaps overemphasizes the body's role in apprehending expressive works in this new medium.[4] This interest in "the body" manifests in cultural and literary studies as a whole. Mind in body has translated to body in world, with some of the same troubling rhetoric of separation, autonomy, perimeter, and boundary.

In this section I look at key examples that manage to call such boundaries into question through various levels of interaction, including *Kinectimals*, a children's game by Xbox's Kinect system (Frontier Development), and "You Are the Tornado," a free online game in Flash, as well as through the construction of avatar bodies in relation to natural features of landscape, as in Second Life's *Empress & Hierophant*. Such instances do not break with longstanding literary traditions of shape-shifting; they invigorate them. Yet the tradition of shape-shifting does not, in general, account for today's examples, because in older myths of metamorphoses, a being takes a final form, as in the myth of Laurel and Apollo.[5] The narrative itself achieves its telos through the settling of form. Nevertheless, a few important ancient precedents are noteworthy. The first is Proteus, the old man of the sea, who shows an affinity for the sea's creatures; it is his habit to sleep among the seals. In book four of Homer's *The Odyssey*, Proteus cycles through a myriad of forms before submitting, exhausted, to Menelaus' will. While Menelaus and his men prepare their trap, Proteus emerges from the ocean, approaches the seals, walks among them, counts them "and then . . . laid him down" among them "as a shepherd among his flocks of sheep" (398–463). Menelaus and his men lie in wait, however, disguised as seals themselves (a moment that prefigures Odysseus hiding with his men beneath the bellies of Polyphemus' sheep in book nine). This is a wonderful moment in literary history for its collapse of problematic bodily and species-based boundaries. Proteus, a god, emerges from the ocean in the form of a man before counting and lying down with animals, as men disguised as animals await him; they leap from their stinky seal hides and pin Proteus down, forcing him in and out of a variety of forms. He takes not only animal forms—in order, he appears as a lion, serpent, leopard, and boar—but also mineral, as "flowing water," and vegetable, as "a tree high and leafy" (lines 455–480). But the changes do not last. Proteus yields, finally, to Menelaus' pressure and assumes his original form.

Another example is Lucius in the *Golden Ass.* A lusty young man, Lucius sees a witch transform into an owl and desires to transform into this powerful bird himself. He sneaks into the witch's chambers and slathers himself with her magic salve, but he has selected the wrong ointment and the transformation goes awry. He changes into an ass. Lucius at the moment of his transformation fades into the background of the narrative and becomes an observer and recorder of the action. His agency is muted because he himself is mute. To the other characters in this protonovel, he functions as a silent feature of the landscape. But even within the first few pages of his transformation, this new asinine body starts to shape his identity. After a hard day of work he "indulge[s] in a refreshing dust-wallow in lieu of a bath" (91) and enjoys munching upon days-old vegetables. He cannot communicate with the other characters, apart from the base modes of communication he has at his disposal: braying, eating, and shitting. (This last one saves his life. When the thieves who have stolen him attempt to kill him, his "belly . . . suddenly let loose its burden . . . and . . . the liquid effusion squirted out rearwards" (90), deterring the thieves from their objective.) His identity as an ass allows us to think of the entire landscape as porous, filled with potential for witnessing and experiencing the world. Moreover, Lucius' story of bodily transformation yields a variety of *narrative* forms. The book has a sophisticated, nested structure, and its telling of the story of Cupid and Psyche, for example, is itself a tale about surprising bodily shapes: Cupid's invisibility is, for Psyche, evidence that he is a god; for her sisters it is evidence that he is a horrible serpent who wants to gobble her up. The tale is embedded in *The Golden Ass* within a variety of other tales: an old drunken servant recounts it to a girl held hostage by a band of thieves, while Lucius, trapped in the body of an ass, plots his escape.[6] Later, when Lucius and the young girl attempt to escape, the thieves catch them and intend to punish them by cutting Lucius open, gutting him, stuffing the girl inside, and sewing her shut within—a vivid precursor to Luke's tauntaun cocoon on Hoth in *Star Wars*. Embedded bodies reflect embedded narrative form throughout the entire text. Lucius' story, and all the others embedded within it, shows permeability between subject and object—or to put it more accurately, one object within a world of other objects, thinking, experiencing, or otherwise. Additionally, it speaks to the permeability between distinct modes of narration. But even as Lucius becomes mute, returning to "first nature," his central quest is to recover his humanity. He longs to find some rose petals to eat, which will transform him back into a human being. This is what shapes the plot.

A third example is Plato's peculiar description of the human soul in *The Phaedrus*, a remote ancestor to the contemporary notion of "cyborg." In the guise of Socrates, Plato writes: "Of the nature of the soul, though her true form be ever a theme of large and more than mortal discourse, let me speak briefly, and in a figure. And let the figure be composite—a pair of winged horses and a charioteer" (471). In various other moments, both in this dialogue and elsewhere, Plato likens the soul to an intelligible presence that can live beyond its physical body: "intelligible, partless and imperishable," much like the eternal forms that structure his philosophy ("Ancient Theories"). Here, however, Plato describes the soul as an amalgam of human, animal, and technological components: an assemblage. The charioteer is tightly connected to his chariot and team; together they form a cohesive, if unruly, unit.[7] As compelling an assemblage as this is, it is nevertheless clear that the human is at its center. The human is the *driver* of these other entities. It is worth noting that later in this section Plato uses the word "cybernete" to describe the mind as the "pilot of the soul." The word in Greek, which means "steersman" or "pilot," is the same word that Norbert Weiner, the founder of cybernetics, used to describe the system of feedback and control between man, animal, and machine in his research during and after World War II. The term "cyborg" itself, a portmanteau of the words "cybernetic" and "organism," signifies a body that is constituted by technological and organic components.

The term "cyborg" became popular in literary-critical circles due to Donna Haraway's "A Cyborg Manifesto," which imagines the cyborg as a creature that blurs the boundaries between human, animal, and technological categories. Haraway's insights inform our conception of the cyborg to this day, offering a powerful way to think about identity as always partial, always coupled, always already informed by the animal and environmental features that surround it. The term has two limitations in terms of my study, however. Firstly, the cyborg's materiality is as mythic as the goddess' is. This is not insurmountable; ichor flows through the single vein of the bronze proto-robot Talos just as it does through the veins of Hera. A second limitation, however, is more challenging. No matter how strong the position, no matter how convincing the manifesto, the cyborg Haraway envisions is still very much suggestive of a thinking, perceiving *human*-dominant organism. It may be useful to recall that the first cyborg, called "cyborg," was not a human at all, but a rodent, a white mouse hooked up to an osmotic pump. It was a part of an experiment by scientists Nathan S. Klein and Manfred E. Clynes, who in an article entitled "Cyborgs and Space" (1960) described their intent to determine whether or not a living organism could be hooked up to a device that would allow it to breathe oxygen in an extraterrestrial atmosphere. It might also be worth remembering that the first astronauts were not humans but dogs and monkeys: Albert I-VI, Yorick, and eleven mice were sent by NASA; Laika by the Soviets. All were blasted into orbit more than a decade before Neil Armstrong walked on the moon.[8]

Cyborgs as we commonly think of them remain recognizably human—not in all cases, certainly, but often enough. One might think of the music video by Björk "All Is Full of Love," directed by Chris Cunningham, in which a metallic assembler produces and fuses glowing white robotic bodies in a process of technologically mediated lovemaking and procreation. These robots, however, have human limbs and human faces (eerily, all Björk's). The technology surrounds them, informs them, and blends into them, but their form and features remain anthropomorphic. The same problem applies to the charioteer in Plato's *Phaedrus*. Although the chariot driver is locked within an assemblage of living and nonliving parts, he is still the central component of the amalgam. He is the *cybernete*, the steersman who controls the team.

The final example has less to do with human form than it does with the fluidity of artistic form. In *Windows and Mirrors*, Jay Bolter and Diane Gromala reinterpret an ancient myth that speaks to problems of mediation, transparency, mimesis, and artistic form. They return to Pliny's version of the competition between two artists, Zeuxis and Parrhasius: "In the story, Zeuxis is great because he could make his technique disappear—make the viewer unaware that . . . grapes were really smudges of paint on a wall. . . . But . . . Parrhasius is even better, because his painted curtain becomes transparent even to Zeuxis himself" (35). The story of Zeuxis and Parrhasius is foundational, but Pliny's is not the only version. In Lucian's account, the painter Zeuxis is obsessed with pushing his art into new terrain:

> The great Zeuxis, after he had established his artistic supremacy, seldom or never painted such common popular subjects as Heroes, Gods, and battle-pieces; he was always intent on novelty. . . . One of these daring pieces of his represented a female Centaur, nursing a pair of infant Centaur twins. . . . The picture of the picture I have seen, and the best word-picture I can manage of that I am now to give you. . . . On fresh green-sward appears the mother Centaur, the whole equine part of her stretched on the ground, her hoofs extended backwards; the human part is slightly raised on the elbows. . . . Of the cubs she is holding one in her arms suckling it in the human fashion, while the other is drawing at the mare's dug like a foal. . . . At the point of junction which blends the two natures, there is no sharp line of division, but the most gradual of transitions; a touch here, a trait there, and you are surprised to find the change complete. . . . Zeuxis imagined that when the picture was shown the technique of it would take visitors by storm. Well, they did acclaim him; they could hardly help that, with such a masterpiece before them. . . . [but] Zeuxis saw that they were preoccupied with the novelty of his subject, art was at a discount, and truth of rendering quite a minor matter. "Oh, pack it up, Miccio," he said to his pupil, "and you and the others take it home; these people are delighted with the earthy part of the work; the questions of its aim, its beauty, its artistic merit, are of no importance whatever; novelty of subject goes for much more than truth of rendering." So said Zeuxis, not in the best of tempers. (203)

This gem is consistent with Lucian's overall style and attitude, which is satiric. Yet the image he conjures is fantastic and *absurd*. He shows in this moment a dexterous skill for literary ekphrasis that manages to poke fun at Pliny, as well as, no doubt, members of the artistic crowds through which he circulated; and his emphasis upon the fact that there is "no sharp line of division" between the centaur mother's human and animal parts is suggestive. But Lucian is more interested in satirizing this type of formal experimentation than he is in exploring its potential, even as he manages to conjure, through words, an arresting visual image of various overlapping natures (human-horse, mother-dam, infant-cub) and literary forms (narration, ekphrastic description, artistic experimentation, and satire).

These ancient instances of collapsing are important precursors because they gesture toward an elastic notion of the human body and, in Plato's case, the human soul; but they do not account for new modes of expression in two important respects: In the first place, they are human dominant.[9] In the second, they *complete* the transformation or die trying. Instead of transforming to another form entirely—or swapping bodies or uploading identity to the digital ether—the works that I will turn to now offer a way to play with the boundaries that mark physical identity. We see in them an expression of the body's *permeability* that, as hyperbolic as it sounds, has never quite manifested in the same way. By definition, of course, these works make use of new technology, so the material apparatuses and conditions that are responsible for making them function are already very different, but this is not quite what I mean to suggest, although the material conditions are, of course, important. Instead of transforming into, say, a flower or a bird, one can transform into flower, bird, tree, human, rock, or the landscape as a totality, and then do it all again, without the demand for closure.[10] We can now turn to our examples to see how this is so.

Kinectimals' Cats

In a recent advertisement for Xbox's *Kinectimals*, two earthlings, a girl and a tiger, stand face-to-face in a living room, separated only by the glass of a flat-screen television. The girl jumps, and the tiger leaps; the girl falls to the floor, consumed by laughter, and the tiger falls into the green grasses that surround it, exposing its belly and squirming in pleasure. Recomposing herself, the girl reaches out to the screen, and the tiger reciprocates by pawing at the glass that separates them. While the game is in play, and the Kinect technology is operating, the actions of the girl and the actions of the tiger are causally linked. The girl's behavior determines that of the tiger and, insofar as the simulated tiger inspires the girl to react, the tiger's actions feedback into the girl's in a loop of interspecial interaction. And because the screen acts as a mirror-portal between the "wild" space that the tiger inhabits and the tame space of the girl's living room, the elements in each world mirror each other, as well, such that the space of the wild grasses becomes contiguous with the space of the home. By simultaneously collapsing and expanding the boundaries of the human body, and thereby effacing the borders between subjects and objects, such works offer an opportunity to perform environmental contingency and affirm our relationship with other members of our environment. The Kinect system marks a departure from the interactive technologies that led up to it, inviting reflection on the dramatic ideological shifts in thought that such technologies initiated.

Interaction is a correspondence between two agents. The word is so broad, so overused, and so contested that it will be worthwhile to tease out what it might mean in this context. Computers, we have been told since the days of the Commodore 64, are interactive. They respond to our input with state changes. I fire up Firefox and expect to be able to browse the web. I type lines of code into Oxygen, and I expect this code to validate. Yet all sorts of non-computational technologies are interactive: radios, television sets, film projectors. As Greg Costikyan puts it in an essay about game design, even light switches are: "A light switch is interactive. You flick it up, the light turns on. You flick it down, the light turns off. That's interaction. But it's not a lot of fun" (Costikyan). Entertaining or not, interaction, like computer code, has a history that did not start with Edison. We can think of the water clocks of Athens, the ballot counters, the mechanical equipment, the chariots, the looms, the potters' wheels, and the tools for mining, metallurgy, and prophecy. But to limit the discussion of interaction to mechanical objects or electronic objects is misleading. People are interactive, as are animals, as are any number of living things. Language itself, as well as any form of communication, is interactive.[11]

In *The Language of New Media*, Lev Manovich makes a distinction between cognitive interaction and external interaction.[12] All art, Manovich argues, is interactive, in that it requires the reader, viewer, or audience member to do some greater or lesser degree of cognitive work. He points to narrative omissions, cinematic montage, and experimental forms of visual art and cinema, as well as to the work of Dada, the futurists, and the avant-garde in general.[13] Such techniques require the cognitive and experiential work of the *reader*. But to equate interaction with cognitive action is a mistake. Not only does it ignore the myriad ways that interaction occurs externally, through the embodied actions of the reader, but it also neglects the fact that interaction allows us to put that interior effort into *expressive* action, in correspondence with the surrounding textual landscape.[14] Interaction is not merely something that requires cognitive effort or something that results in a beep or a click; it is instead something that changes its state as a result of your encounter with it, something that, in terms of a text, *emerges* from the very act of your reading it. With the Kinect system, the level of interaction is such that it collapses boundaries between distinct entities—girl and tiger—altogether.

From GUIs to NUIs

The Kinect system is highly interactive, both cognitively and textually. Its interactive capabilities depend upon its innovative interface, the so-called

NUI, or "natural user interface," a term that evolves from the more common "graphical user interface" (GUI for short, pronounced "gooey"). In their analysis of digital art and perspective Jay Bolter and Richard Grusin—and, later, Jay Bolter and Diane Gromala—critique a digital aesthetics that would strive toward transparency, invoking films such as *The Matrix* to suggest something about the way the technological interface can obviate its presence and, hence, assert its sinister authority by means of its invisibility. They suggest that "transparent" and "natural" interfaces operate in a similar fashion and relate "the myth of the natural interface": "Before there were computers—indeed, before there were any technologies—people were just in the world. They experienced the natural world in three dimensions and they moved around it with six degrees of freedom. They could touch and manipulate things directly; there were no keyboards and no mice. A good digital interface gets us as close as possible to that natural state, allowing us to interact by movement and direct manipulation" (Bolter and Gromala 53). I agree that transparency of this type is indeed a myth, for reasons I outlined in my introduction (see note 11), which have to do with the way that we are already and always mediating our sensory data. Bruce Sterling sums it up nicely in his preface to *Next Nature* when he writes that "as evolved beings produced by a biosphere, we're not capable of perceiving reality unassisted" (15).[15] But in the case of the NUI, although the interface seems to recede, even become invisible, it is because the human body itself has become the primary tool for engaging with the screen space. To understand how this works, it is helpful to consider the NUI in light of its relation to its forebear: the GUI.

The GUI is one of the most user-friendly technological innovations of all time.[16] In her influential book, *Second Selves*, Sherry Turkle makes the argument that the visual elements of the GUI offer nothing less than a complete reconfiguration of the modern subject. An extreme claim? Yes, and one that seems a bit ridiculous now, but it was appropriate and even understated for its time.[17] Turkle argues that this technology helps to foster fluid and multiple postmodern selfhoods. Rather than enabling an empowering state of mental coherence and intellectual purity, information technology offers the self a means of refraction, multiplicity, and subjective expansion.[18] For Turkle, the GUI interface challenges the central tenets of modernism, topples its entire subjective and epistemic regime, and inaugurates a new, postmodern era of fluid, multiple identity.[19] But more important than this is Turkle's claim that the GUI wipes out a rational notion of identity and instead encourages role-play and reformations of various kinds: bodily, gender, identity. How so? Her argument goes like this: The command line operating system, à la UNIX, which precedes (and underpins) the GUI, demands a rational skill set; it is a linear, rigid, and hierarchical system; ergo, it perpetuates a rationalist notion of the self. The GUI system, on the other hand, which creates a spatial representation of the computer's operations and contents, allows one to proceed along different pathways to operate the machine; hence, the use of the GUI interface encourages multiplicity and fluid notions of the self.[20] The GUI does provide a simple spatial metaphor for the contents of one's computer (here is your desktop; here is your trash can; here are your files).[21] Additionally, with the mouse arrow on the screen that the GUI necessitates, it also provides a sense of location, a "you are here" symbol that corresponds to your moves on this map. The Kinect's Natural User Interface—the NUI—explodes the modest mapping capabilities of the GUI employed on most personal computers and arcade-game interfaces.

In *Kinectimals*, through the NUI, the actions of the young girl and the simulated tiger are causally linked. With technology that measures your movements and feeds them back to you on an interface, it becomes very hard to see yourself divorced from the surrounding world. But the tiger is not real, after all; there is no psychic connection that the Kinect box can forge. So how does it work? It works by light. The Kinect box measures the movements of bodies as they pass through a field of invisible light. When the light hits the body, at all the different parts of the body, the Kinect calculates the difference in measurement between these body points and the Kinect light source, creating a sort of three-dimensional visual map of the body in motion. It does so in real time, on the fly, so as the body moves, the Kinect keeps calculating and creating a map of your movement, not just an individual snapshot of your body. What this allows it to do is take all of that information about your body and match it against the game you are playing, which will measure your body movements in response to the objectives and rules of the game. The games are all context specific, the makers of Kinect note, so if you're playing a game that requires you to ski, Kinect will be measuring your leg motions, the tilt of your back, the distance between your ankles, the angle of your knees. Unlike other body-sensitive games that are out there (think Wii), the Kinect is distinct in that it maps your whole body.

In some ways, this measuring and mapping of the human body is an extension of the rationalist, Enlightenment ideal of simulating, observing, and therefore controlling or exhibiting some sort of mastery over the world and the bodies and other objects within it. Without too much of a leap of imagination, we could think of any number of sinister applications of making such a body map—think surveillance, think incarceration, think physical control. We levied a similar critique against the grids in Char Davies' *Osmose*. The same principle applies here, although the grid is invisible. In terms of fostering a sensibility about one's relation and connectedness and embeddedness within a larger ecosystem, such works present some phenomenally powerful tools. With that said, it is my hope that Kinect will up its game, so to speak. The very idea that one can have a connection to a wild animal is enticing, exciting, and ridiculous. *Kinectimals* fosters an idea that tigers are cute, furry animals that want to play with and submit to their human playmates, and reviews of the game have tended to focus on this aspect. As a reviewer on Qisahn, a game store based out of Singapore writes, "How cute is your cat? Stop, it doesn't matter, because your cat will never be as cute as the cubs in Kinectimals" ("Kinectimals," Qisahn). As another reviewer writes: "Let's get one thing straight: Kinectimals is the cutest game in existence. This is just a fact. It's Cute Overload: The Video Game. Frontier has put over 30 great looking felines in here, and they all animate well and look soft enough to reach out and pet (which is kind of the point)" ("Kinectimals," IGN). The emphasis on cuteness promotes an absurdity—a dangerous one at that, not just for the ridiculous idea that a tiger wants to roll over and have its belly scratched by a four-year-old, but by the more dangerous idea that the natural world is a site of cuteness and entertainment, something to be domesticated and cosseted like a pet kitten or an animal spied on a Disney jungle cruise. *Kinectimals*' emphasis upon the cuteness of animals is also very much in keeping with several popular television programs that market themselves as documentaries, in which outdoorsman chase down exotic animals in their hidey-holes and hold them up, squirming, for the camera. Such a mode of narration is clearly problematic for the animal being "shot," but it also has ramifications for the humans doing the shooting. The *Crocodile Hunter*'s Steve Irwin was felled by a stingray in 2006; in 2012 a Florida airboat captain lost his arm to a gator he was tantalizing with a fish. As unfortunate as these instances are, they point to a larger problem in our culture: treating wild animals as exotic pets rather than as viable coparticipants in a much larger ecosystem can have terrible ramifications. Consider another example from Florida (there are many): the pythons that people have kept as pets that have escaped or been released and flourished in the Everglades. In 2013 the state granted hunting licenses for the snakes, but there's been little progress in keeping their numbers down.

Setting these concerns aside, however, the fact that a causal relation exists between the girl and the tiger offers a powerful aesthetic tool that is ripe with potential. In particular, the game is more about cultivating the relationship between the child and the tiger than it is concerned with amassing quest objects (although this is a part of it). This seems promising. In this, *Kinectimals*—for all its flaws—offers a departure from the telos-obsessed, object-oriented quests that have dominated the gaming industry and instead celebrates the collapsing of boundaries between human and nonhuman beings.

You Are a Tornado

Contrast *Kinectimals* to the free online game "Tornado Button Smashing" by mausland.de, a German-based gaming company that specializes in Flash-driven games, hosted by gaming hub sites such as *newgrounds*, *gamemonkey*, and so on. In it, you are a tornado, swirling through a small town in America. It is your job to destroy everything that you see. The game presents an absurd take on natural disaster, starting with its initial interface. The font, perhaps Adobe Impact, has been stretched, given depth, and otherwise modified so that it is reminiscent of the opening credits of Mel Brooks' *History of the World* and *Monty Python's Flying Circus*. The other string of text—"Press 1 to Insert Coin"—although written in an extremely common font, Arial or Helvetica, also signals something amusing, namely, the idea that pressing the number one key is the same as slipping a quarter into an arcade game slot, something rarely done anymore, and definitely not through one's personal computer.

The instructions of the game make use of cartoon fonts, a picture of an old-fashioned joystick (if the 1980s now count as old fashioned) as well as simple commands: Smash ENTER rapidly to expand tornado; W, A, S, D, or Arrow keys to direct tornado. Coupled with these instructions is a visual list of items that players should attempt to smash so as to garner extra time and speed. To get more time, you must destroy cars, trees, and teepees. To get more speed, you must destroy cop cars. Clearly, players are not dealing with any kind of politically sensitive reality. Targeting Native Americans and law enforcement at the same time as plants and cars lacks any kind of coherent vision—although we might read this as a whirlwind of American spectacle, as envisioned by the German developers who created it.

There is no attempt to create a real world, nor is there any attempt to model anything remotely similar to an actual town, or an actual tornado. Gas stations, grain silos, and farmland signal that we are perhaps in the Midwest, although the appearance of teepees and palm trees undercut any sort of geographic unity. It is the player's task to hammer away, as fast as possible, at the enter key, in order to make the tornado grow so that it will have enough force to knock down houses, churches, and teepees. At certain points in the bottom right corner, a frazzled man appears, pulls at his hair or grabs his face in surprise and fear, and disappears. Dead center, the tornado swirls, somewhat unconvincingly, appearing more like a Frappuccino blizzard than a deadly wind tunnel. In terms of its interactive capabilities, this game pushes no envelopes. It is in keeping with any number of simplistic shoot-'em-ups in which the sole object is to wreak as much havoc as possible. Such games do not, at least not intrinsically, do anything to promote ecological awareness. In fact, the game quite consciously is not forward thinking in terms of its aesthetic choices but instead looks backward. The references to the coin slot, the picture of the joystick, the giant red doomsday button, and the clunky point scoreboard on the screen take up a good 25 percent of what is already a very limited space and hearken back to early arcade games.[22]

But paired against the more lighthearted fonts mentioned above, a final script is dead serious, Palatino or Bookman Antigua, and well suited to the message it conveys: "The universe swayed and swirled / And the monstrous horn of a unicorn / Gored the world." These lines are taken from the final stanza of May Williams Ward's short poem about the violence of a tornado in her Kansas home. Here is the poem in its entirety:

> Leaves stood still, and our hearts stood still,
> But the sky was a-boil with clouds,
> A coppery wrack, and the greenish black
> Of shrouds.
>
> We dove for shelter and none too soon.
> The universe swayed and swirled,
> And the monstrous horn of a unicorn
> Gored the world.[23]

Ward's "Tornado" describes the powerful goring of the earth that occurs when a tornado strikes. By employing imagery such as unicorn and horn, coupled with the assonant sounds of "gored" and "world," Ward creates an almost biblical, eschatological picture of the cyclone's power. Here, in this ridiculous game, the verse is superimposed against the image of a twister, a white tunnel of wind against various shades of grayscale. The words above it are carved as if into a gravestone. The giant red button in the bottom center of the screen provides a telling, if not subtle, counterpoint. We're many years out of the Cold War, but the red button's association with, in the words of *War Games* WOPR, "global thermal nuclear war," has stuck. The button of Cold War–era destruction, instead of being tied to a missile or a silo, is hardwired to natural catastrophe. The red button signals the power of the twister. And you are responsible for making that power grow, by blasting away the other figures that surround the button: houses, trees, cars. You determine your flight path, as well as the intensity of your strength. In some ways, the act of identifying with one of the most powerful forces of nature speaks to the argument that I am making in this chapter, namely, that through interactive digital technology, users have the potential to collapse the distinction between self, system, and ecosystem by performing or taking on nonhuman attributes.

There is also a mild attempt at verisimilitude. Before the game starts, a newscaster appears in the bottom of the screen and gives a status update about an approaching tornado. The recording is well done. The voice has just the right combination of urgency and clarity to be convincing. Real (or real-sounding) place names—Hattica, for example—add some suggestion of real-world locations and serve to remind us of real place names—of Joplin, of Ohio—that have been devastated by violent weather patterns, including cyclones and tornados, in the past few years, as well as the rise of violent weather and anthropogenic global warming. The newscaster fades to static, suggesting, perhaps, the interruption of a television signal because of the tornado, and the game begins. This simple game collapses the human into a nonhuman avatar that borrows its form from nature.[24] The game tornado bears little resemblance to a real-world tornado, but there is something interesting about the way the tornado functions here. You are it, and, as it, you do what tornadoes do: you destroy. You wreak havoc upon small Midwestern towns. In this sense, "Tornado Button Smashing" is well timed, and its reference to Ward's poem is apt. The poem is difficult to date; it does not appear to have been anthologized in her books of poetry, but it seems likely that it refers to the "Tri-State Tornado" that hit Missouri, Illinois, and Indiana on March 18, 1925. Ward, although claimed as a Kansas poet, was born in Missouri and may well have witnessed its devastation up-close (Myers). This tornado killed 695 people, making it—still—the most deadly tornado in U.S. history. Yet in the past years, the level of damage and power of tornados has been catching up to the devastation of 1925. The year 2011's tornado outbreak was the largest rash of tornadoes in recorded history; they swept through Alabama and the southern states before making their way to the Northeast. The epicenter of devastation was, as in 1925, Missouri. Of the 348 killed in the outbreak, 158 were from Joplin. In the year 2013, there was another record-breaking twister, this time in Oklahoma, that killed 8 people in their cars, injured 115 more, and at 2.6 miles in breadth, now holds the record for the widest tornado in world history ("Tornado records"). Such instances speak to unstable weather patterns. We are now, in our highly measurable contemporary moment, seeing patterns of severe weather emerging and escalating at a very rapid clip. In this sense, Ward's poem and its invocation on this video game speak to the way that nature's agency endures across time, transhistorically, as in Gibson's "Agrippa."

But in the act of taking on the attributes of the powerful force of nature that has wiped out people, places, and things that are familiar to us, things we cherish and want to protect, there's something that gestures toward catharsis in a way different from "Agrippa" and its natural mechanisms. It does not achieve it, but in terms of the history of avatar-based interaction, "Tornado" is important, in its aesthetic potential to complicate the distinction between subject and object, self and environment.

You Are a Shark

Games such as *Kinectimals* and "Tornado" can be traced back to the ancient shape-shifting sources mentioned earlier, but they also emerge from gaming conventions. Taking on the role of another being during game play is an ancient tradition dating back to the Greek game of stones, dice, and any number of strategic board games comprising rules, players, and pieces. Chess, for example, is both a strategic game of logic and a political microcosm composed of pawns, rooks, bishops, and knights, as well as kings and queens.[25] Role-playing expands, however, with the tabletop games of the twentieth century,[26] even though such games are still focused upon a successful telos or endpoint of a game, that is, the game's objective. In *Monopoly*, the objective is to be the last capitalist standing. In *Clue*, the objective is to solve a crime, that most satisfying end point of epistemological puzzling. In role-playing games, however, which are often quest oriented, the object of the quest is on equal footing with the pleasure taken in exploring different identities. As opportunities for subjective exploration expand, the need for a quick telos gets deferred—not always, to be sure, but often.[27] Once the quest is identified, there is still a telos, a clear trajectory, but it might not be as important as the twisted, tangled, hilarious, bawdy narratives that emerge as a result of group interaction pitted against cold statistical reality. Role-playing paired with deferred telos also enjoyed a popular run in young adult/children's literature in the 1980s. Consider the Choose Your Own Adventure (CYOA) franchise, along with Zork, Endless Quest, which-way books, and so on. *You Are a Shark* (#45 in the CYOA franchise) is especially noteworthy because the deferred narrative telos is complemented by a deferred *bodily* telos. The book begins with transformation: "Your hike through Nepal leads you into a forbidden temple. As punishment for your intrusion, you must survive in the forms of several different animals in order to earn your freedom." You cycle through various animals (very rarely as a shark), exploring different animal identities.[28] As we shall see, this has something in common with some of the more radical works of digital art that confuse the distinction between human bodies and the world of objects. Yet the telos is also always there, even in the most intelligent conversations about games and role-playing. According to convention, a game is not a game without an objective. There has been some important resistance to this line of thinking, fortunately, especially in the work of game designers and critics, such as Mary Flanagan, who in *Critical Play* points to such children's games as "house," the object of which is not to amass as many gold coins as possible, or to hack apart a sulphur-spewing dragon, but to take on different household roles—mother, brother, sister, father, baby—performing and exploring identities that are different from one's own. These are important distinctions, and I want to align myself with Flanagan's work in order to stress the playful quality of works that allow their players to explore and perform rather than seek and acquire and win something, even something as alluring as dragon gold. Instead of transfer—*You Are a Shark* (or a tornado)—it is about diffusing one's self into a larger system, without ever settling on another, final shape, collapsing the boundaries between bodies and forms. We can see this at work in our next case study, a simulation located within Linden Lab's Second Life.

The "Sublime" Nature of *Empress & Hierophant*—Or, Remixing Romanticism in Second Life

It never stops raining in a certain section of Second Life, the online virtual world operated and owned by the American company Linden Lab. Rather, the rain beats ceaselessly upon a craggy landscape reminiscent of the coast of Cornwall. Lightning flashes across a steel-gray sky, and churning streams flow to sea, creating together a prismatic display of light and refraction. Coupled with the vertiginous cliffs and a sense of isolation, the simulation as a whole offers a continuous performance of the sublime power of nature. This virtual landscape, whose name is *Empress & Hierophant*, borrows heavily from romantic tradition yet offers a new way to think about the human body's relation to landscape, not only within romantic discourse but also within contemporary environmental and media aesthetics. By providing a place where users can, in effect, perform and explore the subjective blurring of sublime experience, without seeking its closure or a way to dispel the confusion it creates, *Empress & Hierophant* offers a complex ecological model in which the boundaries between human and landscape mingle, overlap, and collapse.

Such Great Heights

Highlighted as one of Second Life's top destinations and featured in the "Nature and Parks" version of its "Destination Guide," the virtual prospect of *Empress & Hierophant* is the popular creation of two artists of an entrepreneurial bent: Alchemy and Immortalis Cyannis.[29] Self-described "dream merchants," the Cynannises have developed *Empress & Hierophant* as a part of a larger commercial mission that includes, in addition to the simulation, a boutique on Second Life's commercial avenue, xStreetsl, which sells incense, candles, jewelry, sigils, and magical items, all of which conform to the overall aesthetic that underpins the simulation (sim). On their Internet homepage, they describe their "purpose and passion": "Together we believe in embracing virtual reality as a canvas for our dreams and locking hands with other seekers of beauty and the unseen. . . . we create props, scenes and experiences that invite suspension of disbelief and help you to live a more magical life. Life is not still, nor one dimensional. We provide tools for helping us all grow into a life of our own choosing. We infuse our work with magical intentions using sigils, rituals, phases of the moon and planetary hours. But if you're not into that. . . . We make everything pretty" (*Alchemy and Immortalis*). This writing is effusive and promotional, but it is difficult to deny the charm of the *Empress & Hierophant* simulation. In terms of the last sentence of their mission statement, especially "We make everything pretty," Alchemy and Immortalis can claim a measure of success. With its swollen waters and rugged cliffs, their simulation is lovely in a way that invokes a whole philosophical and aesthetic discourse about what it means to engage with natural spaces, especially in terms of the romantic tendency to express the sublime power of nature.

References to romanticism cover the surface level of the simulation—in the rain, the sheep, and the quaint huts that look so much like Dove Cottage replicas. More interesting still is how these surface details stir emotional experiences for visitors. A section of its landscape that has engendered more instances of expression than any other: its cliff-line. An assortment of portraits that visitors have created during their visit to the sim share striking similarities. Several feature young women, their backs turned to the camera, who stand on the edge of a cliff, overlooking a mist-filled void. These images, which can be found on the *Empress & Hierophant* Flickr pool and the Koinup user group, recall an iconic painting from the romantic period: Caspar David Friedrich's "Wanderer above the Sea of Fog."

Friedrich's "Wanderer" expresses the connection between emotional interiority and the powerful features of the natural landscape. A wanderer stands on the edge of a precipice, overlooking a rocky, mist-filled void. The wanderer confronts the chasm, and there is a strange way in which the two—chasm and man—are intermingled: his individual identity is signaled not by familiar features (we do not see his face) but by the fog that he confronts, the rocky chasm, the foggy void, the stretch of sky that points to some transcendent realm or the end of days. The painting is a vivid interior portrait as much as it is an external landscape. This is what makes it such a powerful exhibit in the history of environmental awareness. The man and the landscape are mutually informing sites of engagement: self as ecosystem. Yet this depiction is laden with the cultural and social values of its time. Carole Fabricant comments upon the craggy features of romantic landscapes, such as the ones Friedrich's "Wanderer" surveys, suggesting that they do more than cohere as a pleasing vista: "[They were the] central features of aristocratic landscapes—and later important features of the landscape toured and described by those who aspired to replace the nobility in the newly emerging social order. From such heights the eighteenth-century spectator, like a lord overseeing his creation, was able to 'command' . . . a view of the country stretching out beneath him and thereby exert control over it in much the same way that the aristocratic class . . . ruled over those on the lower rungs of the social hierarchy" (56). Friedrich's "Wanderer" is male, privileged, and entitled. The landscape speaks to a rugged and compelling interiority, but his posture is one of surveillance and mastery.[30] The landscape-cum-portraits of *Empress & Hierophant* are similarly complex and expressive of the Friedrich's conception of nature. Both present majestic vistas of cliffs, steep drops, and textured rocks; and although the wanderer in Friedrich's original does not look at a body of water directly, the "sea" of fog that surrounds him flows and unfurls like ocean currents beneath him. Similarly, the images of *Empress & Hierophant* capture the simulation's rainfall in sheets of white, which blur against the horizon like dense fog. Yet the two landscapes are not identical, and the portraits taken by *Empress & Hierophant*'s visitors are not merely imitative. In contrast to Friedrich's "Wanderer," visitors' portraits take pleasure in the sublime encounter's ability to eclipse and hence reconfigure the self. In the avatars within *Empress & Hierophant* the gender—and, in fact, any aspect of identity—is unknown. The sim grants its visitors the ability to choose how they want to represent themselves in this landscape, as well as how they want to document their encounters.[31] While many of the subjects who have recorded their experiences within *Empress & Hierophant* choose to represent themselves as female avatars, we cannot be sure whether they are women in real life. Second Life encourages this type of self-exploration and representation through object building and avatar customization.

Editing Trees, Highlighting Sheep

Second Life allows its users to create objects and landscape, to toggle between the disparate orders of expression and production, between a surface level of experience and the larger organizing structure that makes the experience of these moments possible. These two orders manifest as 1) the area of representation, which is what appears to the user on the level of the interface and 2) the tools that shape and make this visible layer. Dispersed across the landscape of Second Life are sites called sandboxes, which refer to open spaces where inhabitants can build objects, revise them, and destroy them without worrying about any long-term consequences: "Built into the software is a three-dimensional modeling tool based around simple geometric shapes that allows a resident to build virtual objects. This can be used in combination with the Linden Scripting Language . . . to add functionality to objects" ("Sandbox"). Members can save these objects, import them to their inventories, or let them fade into the sim's "lone and level sands." Once a user becomes familiar with these modeling tools, she can edit the landscape directly, provided she has the permission and access to do so. To see the construction and editing of objects at work within *Empress & Hierophant*, let us consider another of its features that has its parallel in many romantic landscapes: its sheep.

As Uvedale Price writes of sheep in his late-eighteenth-century treatise, *Essays on the Picturesque* (1796), "No animal, indeed, is so constantly introduced in landscape as the sheep . . . so suited to pastoral scenes, of which they are the natural inhabitants" (59). They are, as Price suggests, the picture of the picturesque; their presence is so harmonious with the pastoral scene that it is one of the indicators of a peaceful if rather boring manifestation of nature. Sheep are not sublime. The sheep of *Empress & Hierophant* are no exception. One can see sheep attractively and more or less realistically dispersed across the lush green grasses, but one also stands a good chance of seeing the sheep stacked oddly on top of each other and/or on the side of the rocky cliffs like woolen Legos. It is hard to know if this stacking is accidental or intentional, but it doesn't matter: the consequence of calling attention to the simulation's constructed nature is the same in both cases, pointing to a discrepancy in the order, a glitch in the system that signifies a mismatch between production and expression. In this sense the sheep gesture toward the sublime as a formal category rather than an experiential one. In a sublime encounter of the "experiential" kind, there would be no recourse for such a mismatch—nor would sheep be used to signal it, at least not in Price's schema. Second Life, however, offers a bridge between production and execution. Because

Second Life allows users access to the code that structures the environment, if one highlights the sheep as objects one can see their outlines, which one can manipulate if one has the permission and knowledge do so.

The highlighted sheep call attention to the peculiar coding of the simulation even more overtly than the stacking of the sheep, and while the emotional result they engender is more comic than sublime, they nevertheless reveal a rupture in the "natural" order by calling attention to their own material construction and organizing structure, as well as by inviting the user to bridge these two orders, to add to it, edit it, or otherwise shape it. In addition to the editing tools, Second Life offers a variety of features for changing and experimenting with three-dimensional perspective. The default mode positions perspective from behind the user, while the other modes allow peripheral and frontal engagement. There is also camera mode, which allows one to film what is happening in the world, as well as an option to remove individual perspective from the picture. One can also fly, viewing the world as an object from above. The same perspective options apply to objects. When creating them, one must attend to their arrangement on x, y, and z axes.[32]

Because one can take on first-person perspectives *and* see one's self as an object, as well as explore diverse views from multiple vantage points, one can also destabilize the idea that first-person perspective possesses ultimate subjective authority and control. Along these same lines, a powerful example of the collapse between subjects and objects that Second Life affords comes from avatar construction, which allows various—and variously embodied—"Wanderers" to survey the prospect. Each avatar is customizable; the simulation provides a matrix within which the boundary between self and system, body and world, and subjects and objects can unfold and refold. The boundary line is not so much a boundary as a perimeter that signals one potential instantiation from a powerful field of flux—Proteus unpinned. Instead, the avatar is a porous space of representation without ever requiring a balanced bottom line. My avatar, for example, is named Robot Evans. She is silvery-white, with a shock of pointy hair, and wears a tuxedo with a top hat. She could just as easily be male, purple, long-haired, and naked. However, there is only so much "built-in" (i.e., "free") customization available to me. If I wanted to take the form of other objects and entities—one friend is a rubber ducky; another is a faerie; I would like to be a tree; and so on—I could do so but would have to learn more about the Linden scripting language. This might be doable, but I would also have to shell out Linden dollars at a fluctuating exchange rate (currently this is at one U.S. dollar to fifty-five Linden dollar: 1$=55L$), which is not (Virwox). I mention this fact to stress that *Empress & Hierophant*, like all spaces within Second Life, is a *commercial space*.

As such, every object, avatar, location, and entity within it is also a piece of property and a site of ownership. Even so, investing in Second Life can have a profound pay off in terms of collapsing the boundaries of the human body as they are traditionally and problematically conceived—according to gender, race, and ethnic identity, as well as in terms of species.

"Becoming Dragon"

In 2009 Micha Cárdenas, then a graduate student at UC San Diego, spent 365 hours in Second Life in a project called "Becoming Dragon," "a mixed-reality performance that questions the one-year requirement of 'Real Life Experience' that transgender people must fulfill in order to receive Gender Confirmation Surgery" (Cárdenas). She wore a head-mounted display that projected the Second Life spaces to her and updated them as she moved through them; at the same time, a motion-capture film created a map of her movement, and a stereoscopic recording of her perspective in the simulation appeared for an audience as she performed. To heighten her sense of immersion when she performed, she saw images of real life only "through a video feed." To put on a head-mounted display is to immerse one's self in the screen space and to collapse the distance between the simulation and the sensuous experience one has of it, since the avatar is traditionally—still—something that appears on the screen, controlled by mouse movement, touch pad, or arrow keys. As Jochen Venus writes in *Beyond the Screen*, there is traditionally a fruitful tension between subject and object positions when one takes on an avatar: "The remotely controlled pictorial element is our avatar, the representation of our self in the virtual world. . . . We encounter a performative paradox: we simultaneously feel ourselves remotely controlling and being remotely controlled" (436). If I am on Second Life I see it on my computer screen; if I want to look outside my window for news of my "real" world, I can do this. Cárdenas' approach pushed the limits of the avatar to new levels. She opted out, choosing instead to see the real world *only* through the virtual one—through a "video feed," as she performed. Cárdenas' headgear and the video feed, in other words, changed the avatar's provisional tie to real life.

Her custom-designed dragon avatar was magnificent, red, and massive—perhaps four times the size of the pre-packaged avatars that Second Life offers—and her progress through Second Life as that dragon swiftly revealed how the hetero-normative and consumption-driven culture of the real world had, like a virus, replicated itself within many places within the simulation. She recounts, for example, visiting a Second Life night club, as the dragon, and being harassed for not blending in: "The bouncer warned me that I could stay, but only as long as I didn't cause any trouble." When she started dancing, the bouncer kicked her out, but not before "a neko, a cat-woman hybrid, came growling and crawling around me, making sexual suggestions about what she would like to do with my horns." This encounter yielded an important insight. Second Life might provide a place for experimentation and body-crafting, but Cárdenas' valuable critique of such spaces highlights its built-in constraints. As she puts it: "'Your world. Your imagination,' is the techno-utopic marketing slogan of Linden Lab, but this only applies if you own the land in question" (Cárdenas). In other words, Linden's economic framework of ownership, commerce, and laissez-faire economy subsumes desire and identity to a capitalist framework within Second Life, just as it does in the "first" one. Even so, Cárdenas' performance reveals how this same framework also creates opportunities; she comments on the "heterogenous" nature of Second Life and argues that provided one does own a parcel of Second Life's "land," there are real possibilities for "social, visual and embodied experimentation with . . . new configurations of gender and sexuality," which can "open the mind up to new demands for everyday life in the physical world" (Cárdenas). As an example, she recounts her encounter with members of the "Otherkin" community, which occurred on the ninth night of her project: "A huge-tiger striped dragon and a small glowing fox with butterfly wings visited me and told me about the Otherkin community. Alynna Vixen considers herself to be truly a fox and helps to organize spaces for Otherkin people. . . . She told me that she has known since she was seven that she is a fox and that she has a phantom tail which causes her pain when she sits on it. For Alynna, Second Life is the only place where she can be her 'true self' and she says that she would get species change surgery in a second if she could. Given the rapidly advancing pace of biotech and emerging do-it-yourself (DIY) practices like body hacking and more extreme forms of body modification, it would seem that possibilities such as fur and tails are not far away from our grasp" (Cárdenas). While Cárdenas' project is not about re-thinking natural ecologies, it has everything to do with an approach that does. By demonstrating how avatar construction enables a fluid sense of physical identity, as well as how that fluidity might transfer into real-world practices in terms of social behavior, individual identity, and, perhaps, even bio-technological re-formation, "Becoming Dragon" enacts the very concept of collapsing that I am attempting to articulate. Every formal feature of the simulation in general allows/encourages/demands precisely this kind of performance. Where *Empress & Hierophant* differs from "Becoming Dragon," however, is in its engagement with the tropes of romantic nature.[33]

Let us return to the example of Friedrich's "Wanderer" and the Second

Life portraiture it has inspired. Friedrich's work is still. It is a painting. The prospects within this section of Second Life are animated and interactive. Users can enter into them and correspond with them. Like the examples of "first nature" they emulate, the ecosystems of *Empress & Hierophant* go through cycles of rain and lightning, rainbows and refraction, sunrise and sunset. But they are, at their material base, numerically encoded pieces of information that can be read and operated on by a computer and its user. What this means, in effect, is that it is not only human bodies that can push up against their conventionally defined limits. The boundary lines between artistic *form* are also shown to be unstable. While the portraits in the style of Friedrich's "Wanderer" are impressive, they represent just one form of engagement, a sliver of the overall artistic expression that the simulation has inspired. Most of these—not all, but most—are also self-reflexive riffs upon romantic tropes in a variety of forms. One of the most detailed reports of interaction with the *Empress & Hierophant* sim was written by a Second Life avatar named Siri Woodget. In the blog entitled "My Life in Second Life," the author describes her encounter with the simulation in the following terms:

> I was craving the smell of a peat fire and the bleating of sheep and searched all day in sl for some virtual gorse and an Irish view. . . . I logged on. . . .I made my way to the *Empress and Hierophant* sim, currently under construction by Immortalis and Alchemy Cyannis. The tp landing presents a stunning view over rolling hills and rock walls. . . . Immortalis was busy building, holding a sheep in his arms. . . . Rambling up a hill I got those butterflies in the tum when standing too close to a ledge. The waves below churned bright and blue and I felt compelled to walk and walk along the worn paths winding 'round the island. Instead I tp'd my fellow intrepid explorer Wyatt and we sat among the blinking sheep, totally absorbing the countryside. In this kind of place, your mind goes meditative, and we let our minds wander and ramble like our bodies had done, contemplating our environments, both inner and outer. *Empress and Hierophant* is extraordinary. (Siri Woodget)

The entry demonstrates that *Empress & Hierophant* both invokes the expressive tropes of romanticism and marks a destination spot for those who seek them—Siri Woodget is "craving" a rustic experience of a north Atlantic, north-west European flavor (the "virtual gorse," the "Irish view") and seeks out *Empress & Hierophant*. The entry overall couples sublime experience with natural spaces, which, in turn, illuminate the interior spaces of the self. The account contains many terms that refer to geographical features of the natural landscape. The "rolling hills," "rock walls," "churning waves," and "totally absorbing countryside" figure prominently. Such features demonstrate a kind of agency, conspiring collectively to "compel," "absorb," and otherwise trigger an emotional response, which elicits a "meditative" contemplation of "both inner and outer" worlds. This contemplation feeds back into the landscape via the writer's expression of it. Finally, although a minor point, the contraction (aphaeresis) of the word "around" to " 'round" and the elision (syncope) of "teleported" to "tp'd" are consistent with the romantic tendency to elide syllables for rhythmic effect. This record also resonates in terms of the sublime as an experience of transport (Longinus), heightened sensation (Burke), and sensorial abandonment (Kant). The "buttlerflies in the tum" indicate a heightened sensory reaction, while the "absorbing" nature of the countryside and the "meditative" contemplation that allows their "minds to ramble like [their] bodies had done" suggest both the abandonment of sensation and a transportive emotional experience. This blog entry is telling for the way it casts the encounter with the virtual landscape in a romantic light, especially in terms of the landscape's ability to generate a passionate response—to stir emotions that feed back onto the prospect. Indeed, "Siri Woodget's" blog entry as a whole, in its description of the pleasure that one can take in the association of one's self with nature, is in some ways consistent with Dorothy Wordsworth's *Grasmere Journal.*

Consider, for one example, this excerpt from an entry in the *Journal* dated December 12, 1801: "Helm Crag rose very bold & craggy, a Being by itself, & behind it was the large Ridge of mountain smooth as marble & snow white . . . beautiful, & so good!! . . . The moon shone upon the water below . . . Wm lay with his curtains open that he might see it" (48). This entry is filled with references to natural spaces, such as the "craggy" crag, the "smooth mountain," the "large ridge," and the "bowl-shaped moon." These features cohere into a single agent or entity, that is, "a Being by itself," which inspires the reposing Wm (William) to open the blinds so he might drink in the prospect. Dorothy describes these moments in her journal, and her mediations have been coupled with the Grasmere prospect and the Lake District ever since. In light of responses to *Empress & Hierophant* such as these, it should be clear that the simulation quite deliberately appropriates the tropes of romanticism and that, furthermore, these tropes help shape—and perhaps even determine—the experiences of visitors.

Empress & Hierophant offers a venue for the performance and exploration of these motifs of a powerful, transportive nature, but it is not a perfect parallel. There is clearly a gap that exists between such conventional, print-based texts and the spaces of Second Life, which are so hard to codify according to literary and artistic tradition, yet emerge so clearly from this parentage. Yet there is an important way that the site enables an unfolding and performative mode of expression, a productive energy that is unleashed in the emotionally charged fusion of self and system. This is through the way it performs—and sublimates and defuses—the sublime.

Digital Sublimation

In his book *The Digital Sublime*, Vincent Mosco uses the term to signal the use of the sublime after the Industrial Revolution and technological change. He charts a genealogy of the sublime through Leo Marx, David Nye, James Carey, and Ted Kaczynski (23–25). His work offers insight into digital culture, but in terms of the sublime and its aesthetic history, it takes too great of a departure from tradition to shed light on places like *Empress & Hierophant*. When I use the term "sublime," I mean to indicate the way digital technology complicates—by negating—the issue of incommensurability during the sublime encounter. Instead of hinting at some larger organizing structure, *Empress & Hierophant* illuminates that structure and, as a result, sublimates it, that is, "divert[s] the energy associated with (an unacceptable impulse or drive) into a personally and socially acceptable activity" ("sublimate"). I also differ from the formulation of the sublime that Joseph Tabbi constructs in relation to technology. In *The Postmodern Sublime*, Tabbi writes that "Kant's sublime object, a figure for an infinite greatness and infinite power in nature that cannot be represented, seems to have been replaced in postmodern literature by a technological process" (ix). His convincing readings of Joseph McElroy and Thomas Pynchon, among others, clearly illuminate a trend in literary expression of using technological progress and processes to stand in for an awful, incomprehensible alterity. This is not, however, what happens in places like Second Life. Precisely because the coding is accessible and part of the process of interaction, and therefore a part of the narratives that unfold within this virtual world, the technological processes no longer function as the metaphoric "figure representing forces and systems that the human mind and imagination cannot hope to master or comprehend, but for which we are nonetheless responsible" (Tabbi 20).

But there *is* a traceable genealogy back to Tabbi's conception of the sublime in *The Postmodern Sublime*, as well as to Alan Liu's notion of transcendental data, that is, the notion that "revelation is never immediately available to consciousness lived on the interface" ("Local Transcendence" 324), which will connect us directly to the concept of collapsing that I have been limning in this chapter. Moments that allow us to do this sort of tracing occur throughout Pynchon's *The Crying of Lot 49*. Both Liu and Tabbi approach this text in terms of the sublime, singling out moments in which Oedipa can sense the perverse organizing structure of Tristero. Liu points to the moment in which Pynchon likens Oedipa's moment of revelation to an epileptic who remembers only the trigger or the "signal" of the attack, but "never the central truth" (qtd. in *Local Transcendence*, 324), while Tabbi points to "the way revelations, for Oedipa, 'come crowding in exponentially,' as if the more she collected the more would come to her" (Tabbi, *Cognitive Fictions* 43). Another instructive moment of (obscured) revelation in Pynchon's novel occurs when Oedipa looks over the San Narciso Valley, which Pynchon locates in proximity to Los Angeles, so that it might be comparable to the San Fernando or San Gabriel Valley: "a vast sprawl of houses which had grown up all together like a well-tended crop, from the dull brown earth; and she thought of the time she'd opened a transistor radio to replace a battery and seen her first printed circuit. The ordered swirl of houses and streets, from this high angle, sprang at her now with the same unexpected, astonishing clarity as the circuit card had. Though she knew even less about radios than about Southern Californians, there were to both outward patterns a hieroglyphic sense of concealed meaning, of an intent to communicate . . . a revelation also trembled just past the threshold of her understanding" (24). In this scene, Oedipa surveys a housing development in southern California—"Wanderer above a Sea of Smog." Like Friedrich's "Wanderer," Oedipa's moment is sublime, but in a different way. Her trigger does not signal a "natural" order, only an organizing structure. This presents itself but remains, ultimately, inaccessible. As in the moments that Liu and Tabbi highlight, her transcendent or sublime experience is dependent on inference. She senses her connection to a powerful order that is unknowable in its totality. In *The Postmodern Sublime*, Tabbi argues that such moments have emerged in our era not as a result of a natural, divinely designed order but of technological excess. In *Local Transcendence*, Liu argues that such moments point to the way data parameters, rather than precise selections of data, manifest on the computer interface. In each of these instances, the sublime experience occurs, as when Oedipa M. shudders at the circuit-like structure of the suburban housing development she surveys. In Friedrich's "Wanderer" and the Second Life portraits it has inspired, the experience of the sublime is negated, at least in its Kantian sense. In his third *Critique*, Kant writes of the sublime: "We found our limitation when we considered the immensity of nature and the inadequacy of our ability to adopt a standard proportionate to estimating aesthetically the magnitude of nature's domain" (120). Ruth

Ronen's translative gloss on the above quote is helpful: "That is, displeasure, when facing the sublime, is not the displeasure of threat or danger but rather the suffering, when safely secured, from the inability to sensibly grasp the magnitude of nature. It is the impossibility to contain what the subject cannot grasp sensibly, the impossibility to control the magnitude of the Other of nature" (74).[34] The portraits in Second Life do not express a sublime experience in this sense. They are rather smug in that they have managed in effect to "control the magnitude of the Other of nature" within this medium of a simulated environment. Indeed, they have controlled every aspect of their appearance and behavior and have inserted themselves into the system voluntarily—and taken a picture to prove it.[35] In such immersive landscapes the appearance of the larger organizing structure allows the subject within the environment to change the environment. Using these tools, the relationship between reader, spectator, and text becomes very fluid. Not only does the environment shift and reshape itself in relation to its inhabitants but the inhabitants of these environments also have their connections to these spaces literalized. They can reshape their bodies and insert them as they see fit into appropriate landscapes, which are equally malleable. This capability, not unique to the digital medium, has a strong history independent of romanticism. The "making strange" of language so as to create a feeling of distance or alienation and the "laying bare of the devices" of production—what the Russian Formalists called *ostranenie* and what Bertolt Brecht dubbed *Verfremdungseffekt*—is a familiar feature of high-modern aesthetics. It would be quite natural to situate works such as *Empress & Hierophant* within these traditions, especially given its hyper-mediated status. Lev Manovich, for example, has situated his new media poetics within the tradition of the avant-garde, if the avant-garde can be said to have a tradition,[36] while Sandy Baldwin has considered digital media and their poetics in terms of Virilio's explication of the modern fascination with the experience of speed. Jessica Pressman has aligned select pieces of digital art and electronic literature with the New Critical practice of close reading, as well as with the high-modern aesthetics of difficulty and speed. The reason I situate this feature of "laying bare" not within high modernism but romanticism in general and discourse about the sublime power of nature hinges on a related disjunction between digital texts and romantic expression: a certain type of excess.[37] While the sublime is traditionally configured in terms of emotional, experiential, and subjective excess, the sublime might also be thought of as a category of *medial* excess. In "No Preexistent World," Peter Gendolla offers a reading of contemporary works of electronic literature that points to what I mean. He connects the idea of the universal totality expressed in German romanticism—in the writing of Novalis and Goethe, in particular—to ideas about new media art. Both artistic periods, he argues, in spite of differences in terms of the cultural and historical milieux that foster them, share the goal of "not simply dissolving the separation of genres and of the arts alone [but] deleting the difference between art and nature, transferring art into everyday life and thereby transforming it aesthetically so that it finally can become 'universal poetry'" (375).

My argument is complementary but not identical. As I see it, sublimation provides an important link between romantic aesthetics and digital technology not because it functions as universal poetry but because it demonstrates the same medial excess found in romantic expression. It appropriates and plays with this excess; it *balances* it. *Empress & Hierophant* cannot contain itself. It has generated several different meditative responses to its spaces, in a variety of media. A video brochure by Lainy Voom, "Dramatic Celtic Landscape," for instance, offers sweeping shots across the island of *Empress & Hierophant*, highlighting its attention to "natural" detail, while in another video clip an avatar named Lukee performs an "Ode to Nature" on his violin (Lukee). There is also a group that has featured images of the island on its site, "Evocative Landscapes"; and on the *Empress & Hierophant* Flickr picture pool, there are 292 still shots from the simulation. The denizens of such virtual worlds can act in correspondence with the world, as evidenced by the multitude of verbal, visual, and musical responses that *Empress & Hierophant* has engendered. Across all of these responses, and in spite of great differences in terms of authorship, medium, technique, and artistry, visitors to *Empress & Hierophant* who take the time to share their experiences there attest to the power of nature to inspire introspection, exploration, meditation, and repose, and all offer readings of the simulation that offer productive engagements with the simulation's medial bounty.

Just as the sublime encounter overwhelms and exceeds the subject who experiences it, the expression of the sublime often eclipses the medium that attempts to contain it. While it would be daunting to catalog the various instances in romantic expression in which the sublime exceeds its medial form, William Wordsworth's "Elegiac Stanzas" provides an economical example that not only weds nature to the sublime but also seeks recourse in another medium to do so. Consider the following excerpt from the poem:

So pure the sky, so quiet was the air!
So like, so very like, was day to day!
Whene'er I look'd, thy Image still was there;
It trembled, but it never pass'd away.

> How perfect was the calm! it seem'd no sleep;
> No mood, which season takes away, or brings:
> I could have fancied that the mighty Deep
> Was even the gentlest of all gentle Things.
>
> . . .
>
> And this huge Castle, standing here sublime,
> I love to see the look with which it braves,
> Cased in the unfeeling armour of old time,
> The light'ning, the fierce wind, and trampling waves. (5–12, 49–52)

Wordsworth's poem offers a powerful yet restrained meditation upon the landscape that claimed the life of his brother. Yet it does so by describing a painting of this place that offers a discrepant representation of it. The subtitle of the poem, "Suggested by a Picture of Peele Castle in a Storm, painted by Sir George Beaumont," pairs Wordsworth's recollection of the same space in more tranquil times against the sublime depiction of the Castle in the painting. And while each work—poem, painting—has its own integrity, the full horror of the sublime encounter to which Wordsworth refers can be stood only in relation to the painting. Similarly, the painting offers a lurid beauty but superimposed upon its troubled skylight is the knowledge of Wordsworth's brother's death, which heightens the work's already charged atmosphere. Indeed, the two discrepant experiences and expressions of this landscape align to create a haunting portrait of the sublime power of nature.

These depictions of a powerful natural event acting as the catalyst for sublime experience permeate romantic expression and speak to one formal feature of sublime experience that all definitions have in common: an incommensurability between what is perceived and the organizing structure that makes perception possible. Longinus, Burke, and Kant all describe the sublime as an effect of discrepancy between what is presented and how it is perceived. In general terms, this gap opens as a result of a transcendent encounter, which reveals something else. We might not know exactly what that something else is, but we feel transported (Longinus), terrified (Burke), or abandoned (Kant) by its effects. This incommensurability is a striking feature of romantic expression, not only in painting, poetry, and prose but also in how these different art forms reimagined the power of nature to create such discrepancies, even, as in the case of Wordsworth's "Elegiac Stanzas," contrasting one expressive instance with another. The sublime bleeds outside its mode of representation by seeking recourse in another medial form of expression: painting to poetry, picture to song, sculpture to theater, story to novel. One medium cannot contain or express the sublime encounter.

We see the same thing at work with *Empress & Hierophant*. The space generates meditative responses in a variety of different medial forms—writing, photography, music, film. At their material base, however, due to the dedifferentiated nature of the digital medium, these responses and expressions of the sublime nature of *Empress & Hierophant* are indistinguishable from the landscape of the simulation itself. Of course the *output* is different, but as digitally encoded pieces of information, all are processed and expressed in the same language of production: machine-readable binary code. On the commonsense level of reception, this distinction is meaningless. Even though the same computer code underwrites all these medial forms, to the human user who interacts with them, the integrity of each form remains. Song is clearly song; images are clearly images; photographs—however photoshopped—are photographs; video is video; and words are words. Humans do not always (if ever) consciously interact with the computer code that produces the digital texts and images they read.[38] Granted that human users do not read binary code, the way that the spaces of Second Life are constructed nevertheless foregrounds the dedifferentiated nature of the digital.

In that the simulation refers to its own materiality and grants its participants access to its processes and tools of construction, users can bridge representation and production, inserting themselves as they like. If romantic expression of the sublime at times defers this problem of incommensurability by pointing outside itself to another medial form, the spaces of Second Life, such as *Empress & Hierophant*, resolve the problem of incommensurability by offering a way to span the gap between what is experienced and the larger organizing structure that makes the experience possible. The interactive text puts its processes of production in the hands of its users: they can add to the world, edit the world, take from the world, and in all these ways shape the world and the overall poetics and aesthetics unfolding within the world. They can create stories, poems, landscapes, artworks, narratives, and other, less codified, forms of art. Most importantly for the purposes of this section, they can reshape themselves, insert themselves within the landscape, and thus reshape the troubling narrative that divides the human body from natural spaces.

All of Nature, Animated

In the landscapes of *Empress & Hierophant*—as strange as these places might seem—the presence of an organizing structure has positive effects. Such environments offer a way to think about the idea of incommensurability between what is perceived, the subject who perceives it, and the organizing structure that makes the experience possible. The landscape literalizes how one is connected within a system that extends to but is not limited to human components, biological components, and nonliving components, in some ways fulfilling the vision of nature that Samuel Taylor Coleridge expresses his "Aeolian Harp" (1795).[39] But the implications of such a network of relations extend beyond romanticism. In works such as *Empress & Hierophant*, the categories of "nature" and "self" collapse, and the human body marks the site and celebration of this breach.

Empress & Hierophant is only one site within a vast, mutating world, and Second Life itself is only one virtual world among many. The futures of both are uncertain, but other sites and virtual environments are emerging that may well offer further opportunities for exploring how both virtual spaces and natural places are mutually information fictions. In the meantime, *Empress & Hierophant* serves as a case study, opening up questions we have about virtual worlds, natural spaces, and the complex relationships that exist between them. They also allow us to rethink the way we position ourselves in relation to the natural world by calling attention to how we are similarly embedded within and organized by its fabric.

3
Corresponding
Communicating with Natural Agents

> The men of old, unlike in their simplicity to young philosophy, deemed that if they heard the truth even from oak or rock, it was enough for them.
>
> —Plato

> The leap from living animals to humans that speak is as large if not larger than that from the lifeless stone to the living being.
>
> —Martin Heidegger

> Today was a sunny day and I was able to sunbathe a lot. . . . I had quite a bit of fun today.
>
> —Midori-san, the Blogging Plant

Nature's Agents: Chreods, Code, Plato, and Plants

In a restaurant in Kamakura, Japan, a *Hoya kerrii* plant named Midori-san ("honorable green") has its own blog. The "Sweetheart Plant" is hooked up to sensors that record the levels of light and moisture it receives throughout the day, and an algorithm translates this information into complete sentences in Japanese that indicate the plant's "emotional" state of "mind." These sentences are then posted on the plant's blog. Restaurant patrons can approach the plant, touch it, and interact with it. So can users of the blog. At Midori-san's weblog, one can click a button that gives the plant a flash of light. After doing so, one is rewarded with a brightly colored "Thank you!" since, as an article about the plant on the Pink Tentacle Blog testifies, "Midori-san seems to really appreciate every chance it gets to photosynthesize" ("Midori"). After a long day of satisfying chloroplast creation, Midori-san might reflect upon her experience in the terms expressed in the epigraph above: "Today was a sunny day and I was able to sunbathe a lot. . . . I had quite a bit of fun today" ("Midori").[1]

Bracketing temporarily the thorny, stubbornly human associations we have with terms such as "agency," "emotion," and "mind," I argue in this chapter that entities such as Midori-san perform what I am calling the aesthetic strategy of *correspondence*. Put simply, correspondence occurs when artists pair digital technology with objects, entities, and features of the natural world, allowing them the ability to communicate in human terms, a process that occurs through the translation of raw data into readable signs. The consequence is that avenues of natural agency and aesthetic agency, terms that are related but signify different modes of experience, broaden substantially.

Such works mark an evolution in the history of environmental aesthetics that has the potential to intervene positively in the way we conceive of natural spaces. I begin with Midori-san, the blogging plant, as an example, and although I will refer to "her" throughout this section, in the following pages I turn to two other projects in greater detail, both of which translate the voice of the natural world into human terms in more subtle ways. The first is a living art installation by Doug Easterly and Matt Kenyon, *Spore 1.1*, which uses rubber tree plants to "speak" about problematic cycles of consumption and unsustainable growth. The second is *slippingglimpse*, a piece of electronic literature by Stephanie Strickland, Cynthia Lawson Jaramillo, and Paul Ryan, which reveals the patterns of ocean waters as powerful, aesthetic agents. Before delving into these examples, however, it will be useful to discuss the vexed notion of "agency" itself, especially as it relates to nature, in order to see what and to what extent works like Midori-san, *slippingglimpse*, and *Spore 1.1* manage to communicate.

Nature's Agency

The peculiar status of agency remains a central point of contention within ecocritical discourse. In her succinct explication of this matter, Linda Nash provides a summary of the stakes in an article for *Environmental History*, arguing that the discussion hovers around two distinct lines of thought. The first concerns the provisional intentionality of the natural world; the second concerns the problematic notion of agency itself. Because the question of agency is central to the aesthetic strategy of correspondence that I am explicating, it will be useful to review—albeit briefly—these two lines of approach. Prima facie, the notion that any nonhuman entity possesses "agency" is suspect, yet Nash writes, "recently, environmental historians have argued that nature too has agency. This claim often has been met with skepticism. . . . Although nature may resist and complicate human actions . . . nature has neither the intentionality nor the choice that humans do" (67). Put another way, if agency is defined by intentional action, to what extent can nature be said to act? It seems preposterous to think about the "intentional actions" of a tree apart from a few examples within children's literature; even there, the messages such trees deliver don't really speak to the tree's power to act. The eponymous main character of Shel Silverstein's *The Giving Tree* continues to support its human companion, even after he has ground it to a stump. The story packs an emotional punch, but when compared to a full-blown depiction of agency, it seems—forgive the pun—sappy. Even the Lorax speaks for the trees, not to them. The very question of nature's agency appears as a hyperbolic expression of the pathetic fallacy. Even if nature possessed something approaching intentionality and agency, there still seems to be a large gap between human language and the ways that nonhuman life-forms communicate. A tree doesn't act in any way that speaks to intentional decision-making. In fact, it doesn't seem to "act" at all. And if it *were* to possess agency, how would we know?

The second line of approach that Nash outlines attacks the premise behind the questions raised above. Put bluntly, does agency—that revered human ability to choose how to communicate one's desires, to exert one's will freely, and, even in the face of the most dire obstacles, to *act* after careful, calculated reflection—even exist? And if we insist that it does, that it must, and if we persist in defining it as "the ability of people to act intentionally to shape their worlds" or as the potential to enact individual, autonomous decisions based upon a "free" will, then where can we find a demonstration of this power in action (Nash 67)?

Most of us would agree that human agency isn't as autonomous an affair as we might like to think. Our decisions are contingent on circumstances, private and public, one of the most pressing and influential of which is the reality of our environs. If I go for a hike in the wilderness, I might think that I am doing so in order to breathe clean air, to enjoy beautiful vistas, and to share an experience with others. Yet my decision would also be shaped by cultural notions about what constitutes wilderness, how I feel personally and politically about this term, and the public sphere that has instituted it as a category subject to legal policy. A related example illustrates another aspect of the contingent nature of agency. Consider the actions of Julia Butterfly Hill, who lived in a California redwood tree named Luna for two years, 1997–1999, in order to prevent the Pacific Lumber Company from cutting it down. She was successful, astonishingly, and Luna still lives, in spite of threats, bad press, and an attack by an anonymous chainsaw-wielding vandal. Here is human agency in action: a rational choice made by an individual sovereign subject who speaks and acts on behalf of the tree, who cannot. Right? Not so fast. She did not act alone. She was a social activist, a member of Earth First!, and a part of a group of protesters who, in fact, elected her to her lofty position. Does this fact undermine her singular achievement?

Not at all. It does, however, point to the social, provisional nature of free will and individual action.[2]

Nash's article demonstrates how vexing this question of agency remains, both in terms of defining "natural" agency and calling attention to the limitations of "human" agency. As Richard Grusin writes in his analysis of the Yosemite Valley's origins, which are in many ways also the origins of the national park system, "We need to understand the way in which natural agency differs from other forms of cultural agency. Or, to put it yet another way, we need a truly ecological criticism, one which understands that the cultural construction of nature circulates within what we could call a discursive ecosystem" (334). But there *is* an example of intentionality that all life-forms, at least, share: survival. Survival is both an individual and collective objective. There are countless examples of the nonhuman desire for survival coalescing into goal-oriented action. Is this the same as human intention? Perhaps not, but they occupy the same spectrum. To return to the example of a tree: if we think of a single tree, the question of agency continues to seem far-fetched (the Ent of the *Rings* and *Guardians of the Galaxy's* Groot aside). But does thinking about a stand of trees change this? Common wisdom about trees in forests dictates that trees compete for light, for water, and so on. ("Compete" may seem an anthropomorphic way of terming it, but labeling competition as a singularly human drive is not at all consistent with reality.) A sapling in a densely populated forest has a poor chance of survival, because the upper foliage of larger trees spread a canopy that simultaneously absorbs sunlight from above and blocks light from reaching the floor below.

Balance against this knowledge the findings of Dr. Suzanne Simard, a researcher at the University of British Columbia, whose team discovered "Networks of mycorrhizal fungal mycelium . . . [that] connect the roots of trees and facilitate the sharing of resources in Douglas-fir forests of interior British Columbia" (Simard). Put simply, Dr. Simard's team has discovered that trees communicate, not to us, but to each other—via mushrooms. As odd as it sounds, specific types of fungus grow into the roots of the fir trees and connect these roots to the roots of other firs, "bolstering their resilience against disturbance or stress and facilitating the establishment of new regeneration" (Simard). In other words, Simard's trees "talk" to each other all the time. They share information about their resources and transmit these resources to each other in order to survive. In her study of these systems, Simard has identified a dense communication network of interlinked roots and fungus, all which share water and nutrients. And after careful examination of the larger system, one of her graduate students "has found that all trees in dry interior Douglas-fir (*Pseudotsuga menziesii* var. *glauca*) forests are interconnected, with the largest, oldest trees serving as hubs, much like the hub of a spoked wheel, where younger trees establish within the mycorrhizal network of the old trees" (Simard).

The example of the fir trees suggests how difficult it is to define agency with any sense of finality. Nash offers no solution, perhaps because none exists, but her article leans toward rethinking agency as a whole, by way of Latour's Actor-Network-Theory. "Latour," she writes, "in his studies of modern scientists and engineers, has maintained that agency is better understood as something that is dispersed among humans and nonhumans in what he terms 'actor-networks'" (19). I am persuaded by this model, as I mentioned in this book's introduction. Yet I would now like to elaborate upon the hesitation I discussed in that section: Latour's method of flattening natural, human, and nonhuman agency to the same horizontal line. The problem with Latour's model is not that it demotes the specialness of human agency. This needs to be done, and Latour does it well—too well. One is, according to Latour's model, a mere member of a "parliament of things" (Latour, *We Have Never Been Modern* 142), a subject who is subject to the objects that surround her. Yet this approach razes all agents to the same level of importance—all subjects are objects, all objects are subjects, and agency is merely a byproduct of their collective, amalgamated action. As such, all things deserve legal standing, that is, rights. Latour "holds that we can come to recognize the rights, the autonomy, the agency of the object" (Lash). The term "rights" is sensitive within environmental activism, which has pushed for a more expansive notion of rights to include the creatures and life-forms of the natural world. But it is not always clear what that might mean. As Roderick Nash puts it in his *The Rights of Nature*, "the belief that ethics should expand from a preoccupation with humans (or their gods) to a concern for animals, plants, rocks, and even nature, or the environment, in general . . . has created considerable confusion" (4).

Outside of the sphere of environmental action, the question of rights is even more fraught, laden with histories of injustice and power struggles, such that the claim that we should seek to outline a rights of objects seems a gross injection into a sensitive historical unfolding. Latour might make the counterargument that the very notion of subjective autonomy has been responsible for the subjugation of people and violation of human rights in the first place. He may well be right. Nevertheless, while we may accept that we have never been modern, it is much harder to pretend that we never believed we were. But Latour's model provides a way for thinking about agency as distributed across human and nonhuman agents, and two high-profile legal precedents have occurred that complicate the confusion regarding who and what is worthy of rights. In 2008 Ecuador granted to its "tropical forests, islands, rivers and air similar legal rights to those normally granted to humans" (Kendall).[3] And in 2012 New Zealand bestowed rights upon the Whanganui River (Postel).[4]

It will be exciting to see how these landmark legal precedents unfold. In the case of Ecuador, it is unclear if the language has any teeth to it, how offenses against nature might be prosecuted, or—crucially—how the rights will apply to foreign investors whose tendency toward pollution has a decades-long history, as seen in the seemingly never-ending case between Chevron and Ecuador, which is still in litigation about events that occurred in 1992, the so-called Amazonian Chernobyl (Kendall). And in the instance of New Zealand, perhaps it should not go without saying that the river didn't earn this privilege on its own. It was a hard-fought case between the local Maori (the iwi) and the government, and the final decision of the court to assign to the river two custodians, "one appointed by the iwi and the other by the Crown" speaks to that division still (Postel).

Despite accepting Latour's notion of distributed agency and Actor-Network-Theory, animals and objects—human, plant, rock, computer—all have, I would insist, some kind of agency *in and of themselves*. These agents can and do act with varying degrees of volition within a given network. This signals a hierarchy of sorts, but of action, not essence; potential, not mandate. It is no Great Chain of Being, with angels on top, earthworms below, and human beings just three rungs down from God. This hierarchy is multifold, provisional, and messy—in flux and on the move.[5]

The word "agency" denotes the ability to act. I grant that this is a broad concept. But the type, manner, and extent of action that an object or network of objects can exert depends on the abilities and capacities of each object. In this sense agency is not singular. It is instead more like a box of TinkerToys combined in different ways to produce different objects to achieve different objectives—in this sense more Minsky than Latour, in that the potential of each object is not flattened to equivalence. As mentioned in my introduction, I'm not alone in my concern about Latour's flat ontology. Jane Bennett questions it in *Vibrant Matter*, as does Ian Bogost in *Alien Phenomenology* and Levi R. Bryant in *The Democracy of Objects*. Bennett voices her objection but provides no alternative, while Bogost's problem with Latour's flattening is that it does not go far enough to demote the human from its privileged position. Levi R. Bryant's concept of "onticology," however, helps to find a way out of this bind. This abstract-sounding philosophical word, Heideggerian of hue, is worth exploring because it signals the way that human objects have particular capacities that contribute and react to the networks that include and constitute us. Here is what Bryant says about it: "The democracy of objects is the *ontological* thesis that all objects . . . equally exist while they do not exist equally" (19). Bryant qualifies this counterintuitive statement with a follow-up: "The claim that objects do not exist equally is the claim that objects contribute to collectives or assemblages to a greater and lesser degree" (19). Instead of Latour's total flattening, Bryant offers a framework that attends to the capabilities and potentials of various objects: "Within the framework of onticology—my name for the ontology that follows—there is only one type of being: objects" (20). Yet Bryant concedes that there are many types of objects. A result of this is that "humans are not excluded, but are rather objects *among* the various types of objects that exist or populate the world, each with their own specific powers and capacities" (20).[6]

Agency lacks the symmetry and beautiful order of an ant—or ANT—colony. But if we treat an object's agency in terms of Bryant's "onticology," neither as a Kantian exertion of one's freedom of will nor in terms of Latour's level playing field, but simply—and less dramatically—as its potential to act within a larger network, the issue of agency becomes less problematic. To dispense with the hard-to-swallow notion of rational sovereignty, one might allow that the "animal" or the "vegetable" or the "mineral" object has varying degrees of the "power to act," even within an assemblage. This is not the same as assuming that the objects are irrelevant. Instead, it suggests that agency is always partial but an actor still has the power to act according to its particular capacities within a system.

Aesthetics illuminates this problem. The aesthetic agency of nature in romantic terms configures the relationship between human and nature as a one-way street (I, the subject, view nature, an object—or array of objects). Well-meaning people speak about the "wisdom" of the forest, but this wisdom usually refers to the way the human being feels in the presence of the forest, not to any special cognition or agency that the forest might possess. Aesthetic indicates *experience*. This ought to include the entire sphere of how nature is expressed and experienced, as well as how *nature itself* expresses and experiences. This second type of experience, made explicit, is only beginning to be incorporated into contemporary artistic practice. As Richard Grusin writes in his history of Yosemite, the ability of natural spaces to move viewers with their beauty instantiated an idea of natural agency as an outward-turn aesthetics capable of stirring *human* emotion: "Environmentalism became possible in mid-nineteenth-century America only by thinking of nature as art, an aestheticization of nature that operates according to the double logic of aesthetic agency exemplified in Olmsted's report" (348).

The double logic he refers to is that of an aesthetic potential that emerges not by its own volition but within its viewer. Yosemite, Olmsted writes, "is for itself and at the moment it is enjoyed. The attention is aroused and the mind occupied without purpose, without a continuation of the common process of relating the present action, thought or perception to some future end" (Olmsted). This agency is not an agent. Yosemite might be "for itself," but it exists more importantly at that "moment it is enjoyed," measured according to the experience it generates. The Olmsted Report locates nature's agency within human experience, echoing some troubling aspects of religious (Christian) idealism. In Ronald Knox's amusing pair of limericks, used to explicate the idealism of the Bishop Berkeley, there is an exchange between a young doubting Thomas and God that speaks to this tendency:

> There was a young man who said God,
> must find it exceedingly odd
> when he finds that the tree
> continues to be
> when noone's about in the Quad.
>
> Dear Sir, your astonishment's odd
> I'm always about in the Quad
> And that's why the tree
> continues to be
> Since observed by, yours faithfully, God

In Berkeley's idealism, "the great mover and author of nature constantly explains himself to the eyes of men, by means of perceptible arbitrary signs that have no resemblance or ·necessary· connection with the things signified" (*Alciphron* 60). Signs in nature speak to God's design, his will, and are best viewed as a concordance between sense data and reality that might have been arranged in any other way God saw fit (Downing). The transcendent natural value moves from the mind of God to the mind of man in the Olmsted Report. It is a step in the right direction, maybe, even if it maintains its human-centered bearings. Contemporary trends in computing and media studies—cybernetic experimentation, artificial intelligence, and algorithm-driven systems—have made us more comfortable with thinking about non-human intelligence within computational systems, but this type of thinking has not yet strongly influenced environmental discourse. Instead, the idea of "experiencing" nature to this day shines with a transcendent gloss.

In *Ecology without Nature*, Morton refers in a critical way to attempts to "re-enchant" the world in this transcendent manner as the practice of using the "aesthetic as an anesthetic" (10). This term is Morton's response to John Daniels' assertion that "you shouldn't teach kids about the dire straits of the rain forest. You should take kids out to the stream out back and show them water striders" (qtd. in Morton 10). This type of thinking, Morton writes, is "to use the aesthetic as an anesthetic," that is, to focus on the beauty of nature instead of its ecological fragility is to numb one's self to larger experience. Morton's is an amusing turn of phrase, but it too readily dismisses the power of aesthetics, not just to numb, but to nudge, push, and compel action. To be sure, Daniels' second sentence promotes a hackneyed vision of nature that I am trying very hard to avoid—serene, pastoral, cut off from technological intervention. How many of us have a "stream out back" with picturesque water striders prancing on its surface? The closest "stream" to me was cut by the Army Corps of Engineers and is much more hospitable to alligators and pythons; these often eat each other. And yet it is still a thing of beauty, and my experience of it and my connection to it does not numb me to the plight of other troubled ecologies. Far from acting as a numbing agent, it helps foster larger concerns.

Recognizing that nonhuman systems of communication abound in the natural world may well have an effect upon how one experiences that natural world and may help shape how one interacts with it, treats it, and corresponds with it, not in some vague metaphorical way, or some ambiguous new-age way, but in ways that recognize it as a literal coinhabitant and coconstitutor of a shared material space. The works I turn to now amplify these networks of communication and patch them into our own. By expressing in human terms data experienced by nonhuman agents, data from the manifold of existence (although Kant did not think we had any direct access to this, he averred that it existed), such works perform a natural form of agency. They also go beyond the notion of aesthetics as something involved with artistic practice. Correspondence complicates both uses of the term "aesthetic"—as an artistic category and as the experience that that art is supposed to engender—by bringing in nonhuman patterns and "experiences" to the table.

Digital technology allows nature to speak. By this I mean a mingling between nonhuman activity, raw data, and human signs, which together complicate problematic notions of agency and point to the agency and volition inherent in nonhuman things. The first, like Midori-san, achieves this through a solicitation of empathy; the second does through a process of remediation that is at once elegant and eerie. Both, however, express their material conditions in human terms. *Spore 1.1* has much to do with cycles of consumption and global capitalism. *slippingglimpse* speaks to the natural cycles of ocean currents, of patterns in the water called chreods, juxtaposed against lines of verse.

Spore 1.1

The top half of Matt Kenyon and Dave Easterly's living art installation, *Spore 1.1*, is a common rubber tree plant, *Ficus elastica*. The plant's stalk is straight and thick, its leaves glossy and green; each oval offshoot is like a handheld fan, purple-veined, with soft umber undersides. Its soil appears dark and moist, the area around its base manicured and clean—a bit oversanitized but in keeping with the fashion of our time, a nod to the antiseptic white aesthetics made popular by the apple computer chain. In short, the top half of this project reveals a plant that is healthy, a rubber tree plant in its prime.

Zooming out, however, yields unanticipated data. The rubber tree's planter is larger than usual. Its roots do not terminate within a terra cotta pot. Instead, a large glassy box, divided into chambers, provides not only a house for the plant but for an entire technological ecology of which the plant is but one component: circuit board, wires, cords, tubes, and a shallow pool of water, spiked by siphons. These items manage *Spore 1.1*'s automated watering system, and many suburban lawns are laced with PVC piping that does the same. But the data that determines the timing and duration of the plant's water constantly fluctuates, not according to a conventional irrigation system but to the New York Stock Exchange—specifically, to the performance of Home Depot, the company from which Kenyon and Easterly purchased the plant. *Spore 1.1* calculates a weekly average of Home Depot stock, and, if the stock has done well, the plant is watered. If the stock has underperformed, the plant goes without. If the plant dies, they replace it, hook the new one up, and *Spore 1.1* lives on.

The rubber tree plant both conforms to and departs from Latour's "parliament of things." As *Spore 1.1* it is the entire apparatus, a mini parliament, but an assemblage of things nonetheless—a system that takes as a given one's relation to a larger system, family, or cooperative: an ecology. The plant, however, is the central "agent" in this collection because it generates empathy. Through empathy, *Spore 1.1* demonstrates correspondence in action. Like Midori-san, the plant elicits an emotional response from its viewers. Whereas Midori-san speaks in short, emotive sentences, *Spore 1.1* expresses its data in a more direct fashion, through the health and robustness of its leaves. Empathy is not the same as the solipsism of viewing nature as a mere object or even a majestic object or a source of inspiration. It is reciprocal and requires identification and acknowledgment that the object of empathy is like one's self in some meaningful way. *Spore 1.1* elicits a new form of empathy that transcends human experience and has potential to overcome human exceptionalism, heighten sensitivity to the natural world, and demonstrate the way human, animal, vegetable, mineral, and digital are mutually constituted. This transcendence is not otherworldly. Instead, distinct modes of experience have an opportunity to come into contact across the gap between that normally exists between them.

Spore 1.1 takes the data produced by the natural world and renders it into human terms. Instead of simply having the power to produce powerful aesthetic experiences within the human who observes them, it "talks" back and shakes up the subject-object hierarchy of aesthetic agency. This is not to say it overturns it. Instead, it makes the relation visible and explicit, and allows access, however provisionally, to a nonhuman mode of existence. We never know how long the plant within *Spore 1.1* will last before the fluctuating stock market causes it to go without water. We don't know exactly what Midori-san will say or how she will say it. But the not-knowing fosters curiosity. These positive reactions hinge upon empathy. These types of works trigger an empathic response, allowing the human subject to take on the perspective of something that is not human and yet has some kind of reciprocal potential to respond.

Once hooked up to the data of the stock market, *Spore 1.1* reacts in active correspondence with a stream of socio-economic data. On its blog, Midori-san translates its natural conditions into affective human language. In both cases, these entities perform for us their own biological conditions in terms we can understand. When I heard about *Spore 1.1* I felt equal parts amusement and dismay. It was amusing to me to see an innocuous houseplant hooked up like Frankenstein's monster to a technical apparatus. On the other hand, I felt sorry for the plant. How unfortunate, I thought, to buy something living, just to let it die. How awful not to intervene in an attempt to thwart its demise. This was overemoting, perhaps. But I am not alone in receiving an emotional trigger from the art project or projects like it. When I asked Matt Kenyon, one of the artists who made *Spore 1.1*, whether or not others had expressed similar reactions, he had the following reply: "Yes, Doug and I found this surprising. People have expressed a great deal of empathy for the wilting plant. This empathy helped the direction of subsequent works" (S.W.A.M.P., Skype interview).[7]

After thinking it through, I begin to think not of the plant itself but of the entire apparatus as *Spore 1.1*. With the tie to the stock market I begin to think about what really controlled the lifespan of each rubber tree plant. Home Depot was responsible: the management and shareholders, the cost of raw materials and distribution, the consumers of Home Depot goods. Had I not just purchased packing tape and bubble wrap from Home Depot? Was I not responsible on some level? Weren't we all, to some extent, culpable in the exploitation of the rubber plant? The answer is yes. *Spore 1.1* performs this paradox, criticizing and participating in a troubling system of consumption. Perhaps it participates in order to criticize, and I wondered if S.W.A.M.P., its creators, had any thoughts on the idea of complicity in relation to *Spore 1.1*. Their answer was superb: "Doug and I think a great deal about this issue. We feel that today it is difficult if not impossible to be 'outside' of the system of consumption. We can't simply wall off art from the world, and try to lob our critiques over the wall. We try to construct an artwork as a system that intervenes within the system it is critiquing. After all, it is our everyday actions that produce the system of what is often called consumer culture" (S.W.A.M.P., email). At the same time, *Spore 1.1* clarifies the culture of consumption. The plant died and was replaced several times, free of charge because of Home Depot's year-long warranty. Yet in each of its reincarnations, it died, not from lack of water but too much of it. *Spore 1.1* debuted during the height of the housing boom, when Home Depot stock went through the roof, at a gain of roughly 100 percent from the previous year,[8] which meant that *Spore 1.1* drowned as a result: "Home Depot's stock ratings varied the whole time of the project. In November and December, however, *Spore 1.1* received water on 8 consecutive weeks. Its health seemed to steadily deteriorate after that, as its roots became rotted, and eventually died in January 2004. This was an unexpected result, as we assumed a weekly 1 minute watering would not kill the plant, rather only a lack of water would kill it. But it somehow seemed appropriate that the plant would die because of an overabundance of Home Depot stock gains" (S.W.A.M.P., "Postscapes"). Why appropriate? The rubber trees' deaths and resurrections speak to balance, a central problem within ecocritical discourse. Ecosystems maintain a balance. Whether intentionally or not, agents within a given system tend toward equilibrium. *Spore 1.1* is a system gone astray, destroyed by its own gluttony. There is something here we might learn from this, unless we are, as Agent Smith suggests in the *Matrix* film franchise, "a virus": "Every mammal on this planet instinctively develops a natural equilibrium with the surrounding environment; but you humans do not. Instead you multiply, and multiply, until every resource is consumed" (*The Matrix*).

Thinking about how one is always a participant in the system that one critiques is useful, and recognizing one's contingency with the social and natural world leads to a rejection of human exceptionalism, particularly in terms of empathy and agency. Empathy is the ability to take on the perspective of another; such works engender an aesthetic experience of this type. The word "empathy" emerges from the German term "einfühling," a term that first appeared in German romanticism, especially within the writing of Novalis and Herder, who argued that the ability to "feel into" nature provided a remedy for the cold rationalism of scientific objectivism, a "vital corrective against the modern scientific attitude of merely dissecting nature into its elements; instead of grasping its underlying spiritual reality through a process of poetic identification" (Stueber). In the work of Herder it was a call "to feel into everything, to feel everything out of [one's self]" (qtd. in Stueber). For Novalis, it was a way to reconcile one's self with the majesty and mystery of the absolute. In a curious parallel to Kant's "secret mechanism"[9] of the intellect that recognizes in the sublime moment an organizing, rational totality, Novalis identifies an innate talent for appreciating the wonder of nature: "No one will fathom nature . . . who does not with an inborn creative joy, a rich and fervent kinship with all things, mingle with all of nature's creatures through the medium of feeling, who does not feel his way into them" (106).

Empathy did not refer to nature for long.[10] It became instead a term to identify the way humans imagine other human minds. But in these early passages, it is explicitly tied to all natural objects. And even though Novalis' larger objective is to "re-enchant" the natural world with the magic that he believed technological progress was in the process of robbing from it, he nevertheless "adopts the new view that natural things are in themselves meaningful and inspirited, and that, in the right culture, we could all directly observe and experience these qualities in natural things" (Stone 143). Novalis offers a wonderful insight: nature offers access to such puzzling concepts such as "spirit," "enchantment," and even the "magic" of the absolute. The signs of nature illuminate the nature of the self. His views are complex and consider a wide variety of ways that nature operates coextensively with humankind.

"Feeling in" is an apt way to describe the type of empathy that occurs when one comes into contact with *Spore 1.1*. This empathy is at once tied to nature, to objects, and to other human minds. The artwork provides an access point to a whole network of relations—indeed, it not only acts as a portal for thinking about such relations but embodies them. *Spore 1.1*, considered as one plant, does all the normal things that a plant does, but it is tied to a larger commercial system and expresses, in the material bloom and demise of its living parts, the vagaries of the stock market and the larger system of consumption that drives it.

Empathy allows one to imagine other human experience, to shift one's center out of bounds, to think and feel one's self as something outside the boundaries of one's own body. In an essay on landscape, Allan Wallach writes similarly of our relation to landscape as something that exists "between subject and object." Romantic landscapes function in relation to the human subject who is imagining them in relation to his own inner life, his past, and even to a remote eschatological future. In contrast, when looking at *Spore 1.1*, one's self is shaken up, understood not as a divine manifestation of divine soul, spirit, or intellect but as a related entity. It becomes, in the words of Novalis, a "*You.* (Instead of non-self—You)" (qtd. in Stone 157) and grants access to an entirely different realm of experience.

Midori-san, like all plants, "enjoys" photosynthesis, but unlike other plants, it writes about it on a blog. It expresses in language the way that its environment participates in its quality of life. As one customer reported to Reuters after reading the plant's journal, "I now believe plants have a type of consciousness." I am not sure that I do, yet hearing about the conditions affecting a plant's health translated into human language has allowed me to empathize with plant life in a new way.[11] *Spore 1.1* communicates on its own. Instead of being spoken through or spoken about, it speaks for itself. It displays a startling agency—again, if we can think of agency in complicated terms, neither as a subject nor object but as something that communicates about itself and its conditions. *Spore 1.1* allows access to nonhuman, and in some cases nonliving, experience. When one "feels in" to one of these works, one becomes a part of the project. The art is "living" and collective actions determine its lifespan. The empathy it triggers invites one to reconsider one's role as an active, responsible participant within a larger social system.

There are some who argue that we do violence to the environment by anthropomorphizing it in language. It is possible to see these works as nothing more than anthropomorphic personifications; if they have anything to "teach" us, it is about how problematic and persistent the pathetic fallacy is—an accusation that I at times make to myself. As it often does, a history of a word opens to the history of the world. The term "anthropomorphic"—literally, "man-shaped"—originally worked "in reference to . . . gods . . . having human form and human characteristics." It is not until 1858 that it refers to "animals and other things" ("anthropomorphic"). This first instance of anthropomorphism referring to features of the natural world occurs in a new type of writing, a study of marine life by George Henry Lewes. Why should it happen then, in 1858? It was part of the exciting frenzy of knowledge about transmutation and natural selection that was emerging as a result, in part, of the writing of Charles Darwin. In 1858, Darwin presented a paper to the Linnaean Society in which he outlined his ideas on natural selection, which he'd been refining since his *Voyage of the Beagle*; in 1859, he published *On the Origin of Species.*[12] Lewes' usage, while innovative, is symptomatic of an exciting intellectual milieu. In his discussion of anemones and mollusks he writes: "But as we are just now looking with scientific seriousness at our animals, we will discard all anthropomorphic interpretations, such as point to 'alarm,' because they not only confuse the question, but lead to awkward issues; among others, that the Anemones have highly susceptible souls, as liable to emotions of alarm as a fine lady" (153). This sentiment—not that anemones have emotions like fine ladies, but that they do not have any at all—has persisted. Any time we read emotions or will in anything that is not human, any number of cultural spheres—religious, scientific, poststructural—stand ready to reprimand. In *A Thousand Plateaus*, Deleuze and Guattari make a trenchant argument about anthropomorphizing animals, arguing that men should not put human characteristics onto animals, although the reverse, "becoming animal," is a fundamental aspect of their argument (262). This powerful statement suffers from a unidirectional way of thinking.[13] In her analysis of Darwin's rhetoric, Gillian Beer offers a convincing way to recast this term: as reverse anthropomorphism. Viewing animals in human terms is not wrong, she suggests; it is instead the distinction between the two terms in the first place that is misguided. The "man-shape" of anthropomorphism assumes a man-creature with inviolable boundaries and, as such, implicitly accepts that humans and animals are fundamentally distinct. Beer argues that when Darwin comments upon how the horse must enjoy his lazy basking in the sun, it is not anthropomorphic but an overt *rejection* of anthropocentrism that provides an example of how taking a sensuous pleasure in sunbathing is something many mammals, including humans, share.[14] We *are* animals. Empathy may be one of our most noble features, but it is also one we share with many other species, well documented within the animal kingdom (Preston), and we may well find evidence to support empathic networks within the plant kingdom. The mycorrhizal networks discussed earlier seem to be one small part of a larger tendency within the plant kingdom.[15]

Although *Spore 1.1* and Midori-san have been severed from their natural environments, assuming some sort of primordial forest where rubber tree plants and green sweetheart plants flourish side by side, there is a way they also act as emissaries from the natural world in a way that is different from how technologies have been understood in the past. In *The Machine in the Garden* Leo Marx describes the noise of a train's "sudden entrance into the landscape" as something that disrupts the tranquility of the Garden (343). The intrusion of the machine upon that pastoral scene expresses a tension between natural spaces and technological progress. Such works as Midori-san and *Spore 1.1* perform a reversal: they, the natural, intervene in an increasingly dominant technological aesthetic. If before the *machine* surprised with its shocking contrast to the quiet natural world, it is now the natural that disrupts technological continuity. The cyborg is not in the garden; it *is* the garden.[16] Perhaps this is troubling in the same way as a token ficus wilting in a doctor's office is troubling. Yet *Spore 1.1* calls attention to the diminishment of natural features by speaking out. A translation occurs between the hyper-technological and the seemingly natural. Rather than excluding each other, the representative worlds speak to each other, and hence communicate with us and elicit empathy from us. There is no longer a frightful or sublime dialectic, but a dialog.

This provides a sharp contrast to how nonhuman language appears in many works of science fiction. In Grant Morrison's graphic novel *We3* a secret military organization kidnaps three pets—a dog, a cat, and a rabbit—and creates out of them a networked weapon. They communicate in simple, disjointed commands that are as heartbreaking as they are humorous, and the syntax of their language borrows from computer code. In William Gibson's story "Johnny Mnemonic," the dolphin Jones, a heroin-addicted ex-military operative, "speaks" in a similar manner; his words appear as encoded information on a screen. These animals elicit empathy, to be sure, and encourage a healthy fear of the military industrial complex, but neither We3 nor Jones is capable of stepping outside of the system of language that has imprisoned them. To be sure, lacking legs, neither Midori-san nor *Spore 1.1* can "step out" of the systems that contain them either; but here's the crucial difference: they are real. Their material conditions are our material conditions. Their language is public, accessible, and spoken, not only spoken through them. Jones and We3 are cyranoids of a system that has appropriated them and made puppets of them. Midori-san and *Spore 1.1* "speak" about the conditions of their environs in a way that forces us to acknowledge that we share these environs with other species.

Such works are well poised to act as messengers from the natural world, even if the message of our own extinction is the only one we hear. If every time there was a drought, we had to contend with messages from the "earth" that said it was dry and thirsty, we might be less able to ignore the parched land around us. If every time there was a cloud of pesticide sprayed on some fruit we heard, "help, I'm being poisoned," we might not be so willing to douse our food with airborne toxins. If every time we went for a walk in the woods, the trees said, "thanks for not driving!" we might have some positive reinforcement for making hard changes.[17] I am being dramatic here to make a point, which is this: the fact that we speak English (for example) and animals, vegetables, and minerals do not has provided a convenient excuse for separating ourselves from the land that sustains us. I am suggesting that by using digital technology we have the potential to translate natural patterns into language that makes sense to us, and that this could be a powerful tool for conservation and environmental awareness. Digital technology makes it easier to make the earth speak to us in our own terms. Whether or not we would listen is another matter.

slippingglimpse

Off the coast of Maine, the water of the Atlantic hits against the shoreline. Sometimes it does so violently, in wide-sweeps of spume-crested waves. Other times it flows softly into rocky strands, forms shallow pools, and disappears with the pull of the tides. In each instance a pattern emerges that speaks to the water's current state—calm, stormy, churning, serene. This pattern provides a map of the "necessary path" that the water must take: a chreod. Coming from the Greek words for necessity (chreos) and road (hodos), a chreod signifies an exigent pathway, a necessary route that natural phenomena take ("Chreod"). Given this definition, chreods already speak to agency, although not a directly intentional form of agency; rather, they speak to a pattern that repeats so often it seems to be willful. Chreods can be found in weather systems, wind patterns, river flows, and ocean currents. The pattern of chreods off the coast of Maine, some of the most ruggedly beautiful coastlines in the United States, motivate both the form and content of Stephanie Strickland, Cynthia Lawson Jaramillo, and Paul Ryan's elegant piece of electronic literature, *slippingglimpse*. As Paul Ryan, the project's videographer puts it, "water takes so many different shapes, such as billows, droplets, back curls, waves, fantails, and cascades. Each of these shapes exhibits a different pathway in which water can flow, a different chreod" (Ryan, "Earthscore").

slippingglimpse has received a generous amount of critical attention for its peculiar form and its multiple media. N. Katherine Hayles' analysis of it in terms of the collaborative concept of "Three-ing" offers an ecological reading that pays equal attention to its human, technological, and natural elements. Building from Hayles' reading, my analysis focuses on the work's sole natural feature—the ocean waves. The waters within *slippingglimpse* demonstrate the kind of agency I have spent the previous pages outlining, as well as how that agency manifests itself in human-readable terms.[18]

slippingglimpse takes data from mercurial water swirls within the ocean and translates that data into something readable. The home page of *slippingglimpse* presents ten images of the sea, each a different section of the Atlantic off the coast of Maine, depicted in small thumbnail-size rectangles, arranged into a larger rectangle. The images are laid against a black backdrop, interrupted by minimal text, which includes the title, written in a form somewhere between cursive and calligraphy. There is also a link to an introduction that orients the reader and two links to the same essay about the work, also by the main authors, Strickland and Jaramillo.

The center of the rectangle holds simple instructions: "Select one to start." This arrangement recalls a jukebox or nickelodeon, one a device designed to play a piece of music, the other a site of early cinema, peep shows, and illustrated songs. *slippingglimpse* offers similar, additional enticements. By placing on display images of water in widely differing states, it employs digital technology to offer up samples and snapshots of natural signs. These include, from left to right and up to down, the following images of water: choppy, serene, green, aquarium-like, brown-and-white, crashing, churning, storming, sun-shot, and autumnal. Selecting any of these leads to something altogether more revealing and puzzling than a peep show: a video recording of the volition of water.[19]

Superimposed upon this water, lines of Strickland's poetry begin to appear on the screen. Each of the ten videos, rendered in Flash, is coupled with a segment of Strickland's poem, which can be read only in pieces, not simply because the segment is a fragment of a larger piece, but because the placement of the words on the screen depends on the movement of the chreods. *slippingglimpse*'s software tracks the motion of the water's movement that occurs in each video and uses this to animate phrases and lines from the poems so that they move in correspondence with the chreodic patterns. The words of Strickland's poem respond and are subject to the structure of the chreodic patterns in the water.

Again, this brings us back to the problem of agency, although not, again, agency as a manifestation of a Cartesian cogito but as purposeful action or intent. What I would like to suggest with *slippingglimpse* is that there is a kind of agency revealed here seen most powerfully through the images of water. The poem, the code, and the reader are all very important, to be sure, especially within the context of media studies, which has tended to fetishize the technological at the expense of the natural. For this the chreod offers a powerful lesson: the water's pull powers the text.

The "voice" of the water is paramount when it comes to thinking about environmental fragility. Communicating the contingent nature of ocean water is, according to *Poets for Living Waters*,[20] one of the central intentions of the poets: "*slippingglimpse* is a collaborative interactive Flash piece using videos shot off the coast of Maine. This poem is based in the profound conviction that we need to be in conversation with the waters of the world." The authors have a special concern for pollution and contamination: "Needless to say, pouring oil on, over, or through their self-directed motions is the act of a speaker who does not listen" (Strickland et al., *Living Waters*).

Each chreodic pattern, recorded by motion capture, is coupled with these pieces from a longer poem. The reader of the text is allowed to view this intimate exchange but not allowed to intervene. The water churns according to its pattern, which determines where the text of the poem appears on top of it, as well as how the text's features (font size, movement, and duration) appear and move across the screen. This calculation was determined by sampling different changes in color values: "Cynthia wrote video tracking software in Flash that allowed us to track water movement by looking for changes in pixel color, every 10 pixels. Every time there was a change above a certain threshold, that location was saved in a matrix of pixels. This procedure was carried out every 10 seconds for the duration of the video. These lists of pixels are then put into each individual ActionScript program to serve as the locations into which the words will need to travel" (Strickland, email exchange). Software defers the act of "reading" the poem to the water. For the human reader, this may well render the poem illegible, "because in this mode language is undergoing physical movement imposed by the 'chreod' pattern of the Atlantic waves" (Strickland et al., *slippingglimpse*, *ELC*). This tactic of excluding interaction is a powerful tool for thinking of nature not as an object of consumption or even admiration but as something imbued with its own drives and impulses.

The reader is invited to click the "scroll text" button that initiates the legible text; it comes into view as black text on a mostly white background lightly laced with shadows that look like the veins of leaves, twigs on a forest floor, or blades of grass, all saturated so only the palest outlines remain. The reader can control the speed at which the text scrolls but cannot affect the chreodic performance above the scroll. Words from the poem will float on top of the water in mostly illegible clusters, coming together in clumps, spilling outward, at times falling outside of the video frame entirely. Sometimes the words shrink to points until they look like stars; at others they expand until they become enormous and uncontainable. The video disappears at the beginning or the end of the recording in eight out of the ten recordings (the clips at the bottom left corner [left light green] and bottom right corner [green] are exceptions), so that only the strangely cursive-like script will remain, floating against a black backdrop, clustering and growing like a tangled, willful bramble, unfurling and colonizing the spaces around it.

On a purely visual level, this makes language look organic: these pieces of verse, in the tradition of the concrete poets, crawl out of the sequential nature of written language in order to explore different forms. They remain words and phonemes using English syntax but also become part of a larger natural sign system comprising water currents and chreodic patterns, algorithms and data flows. What the chreod does, in effect, is to colonize human language, subsume it to its own structure. And by bookending each video with words, the piece suggests that language and natural phenomena work as crosscurrents, contaminating each other in the best possible sense—feeding back into each other and changing each other as a result. It is nevertheless the water that drives the piece. In their introduction, Strickland and Lawson Jaramillo go so far as to say the water "reads" the poem: "we model a ring in which the roles of initiator, responder, and mediator are taken by all elements in turn. . . . Water reads text, text reads technology, technology reads water, coming full circle" (Strickland et al., *ELC*).

This claim that the water "reads" the text is provocative. The water is not curled up with the poem and a cup of tea. Yet reading has always been more than a self-absorbed and solipsistic affair. And as more and more texts become multimodal, social, and tactile, the stereotype of the solitary reader has been, thankfully, challenged. Reading is a way of parsing, organizing, and making sense of the world, and reading in *slippingglimpse* embodies the reading process in a variety of its forms as a performance that reveals the patterns and impulses of the natural world. As Strickland notes in an email exchange: "I think a deep meaning of reading the water and the water reading comes from my early experience on boats with my father. He would read the color of the water as relating to the depth as we moved over reefs and shoals, and of course he would read/interpret many aspects of the wind and water as any sailor will. It seemed clear to me that the water was also reading/interpreting the depth using color to signal, as the wind interprets/reads/signals temperature. In other words, I never restricted reading to a symbol system. Reading was a way to wade and proceed in an environment, whether of literary symbols, mathematical symbols, or physical signs" (Strickland, email). If we think of reading even more broadly, as a way to organize the world, the idea of reading water becomes more clear. In one moment from *slippingglimpse*, taken from the bottom right corner of the opening rectangle (scroll six), we see images of green-tinted water crashing up against a rocky shoreline. Superimposed upon this water are lines from Strickland's poem.

In this moment, the phrase "the air lives" emerges in the upper left corner of the screen. The phrase is one line of the poem that scrolls below, of course, but it also signifies within the context of the image alone. Here, the living air brushes against the spume of the wave. The writing brightens, becomes obscured, and then fades. There is a relation between the text and the organic—the air "lives"—made possible by the underlying code, which has put the two into correspondence, text and water. When the poem begins to scroll, we can see that the line emerges as its own single stanza:

> the air lives
> by turning green
> not struck from stones
> not blossoming out of twigs.

The lushness of the water and the wetness of the air perform the words of the text. The reference to fire, "not struck from stones," suggests obliquely that humans are not involved in this sparking of energy that unfolds throughout the chreodic motion. There is a definite translation process from one sign system to another—natural, digital, visual, and linguistic. As in all translations, however, there is never a pure transmission from the original to the target. Instead, there are sign systems at play, each of which seeps into the other and changes the message entirely. There is the natural (the water), the textual (the poem), the rushing water (recorded, manipulated), and the coding (the algorithm). Each of the other pieces follows this form. But it is the natural sign system that dominates. The water drives—and reads—the text.

In the seventh segment, the waters are calmer, perhaps, but the colors are marbled, intermingled, and have the appearance of segments of stone. The poetry that forms on the surface of this section complements the darker color tones:

> thrown in the ditch
> pulled out by the hair
> skinned heckled broken scorched
> washed in lyes worried
> to pulp
> as flax is hackled with a comb of thorns
> grapes are ripped from stalks
> with the comb of the fingers.

Again the water collapses with the words of the poem and the cursive-like writing blends into the surface of the water—expands, comes into focus, and disappears. The transcript that scrolls below tells the story of a violent harvest, and the dark, contusion-like colors of the sample speak to an intermingling of human pain, harvest pain, and an unreliable and vulnerable surface upon which to record it. Beneath it, the insistent pattern, the chreod, mixes with other signs, rearranging them. Strickland has indicated that inspiration for this poem comes, in part, from "The Passion of the Flax," a folktale about the harvesting of flax and the spinning of linen that appears in Western mythology, explicated most thoroughly by Robert Eisler in an essay of the same name. In all its forms, the "passion" refers to the uprooted plant, which rivals the passion of the Christ in terms of its stages of torture, not on the road from Gethsemane to Golgotha but in its journey from a plant in the soil to pulp in the paper mill. In the Silesian version that Strickland draws from, the plant recalls its time in the ground, in contrast to its violent day of harvest: "As flax, I stood in a broad deep bed / Blossoming blue in a lush green field, / Thus I grew up where they sowed me . . . / Billowing like the sea's great waves, / Blown about by changing winds . . . / All too soon came the harvest. / Ripped out from my mother's womb, / Root and branch they tore me" (120). A "harrowing" tale, this, but one that also speaks to the flax's enduring status as a material object. After being cut, bleached, and laid out to dry—only fleetingly "refreshed by the dew"—the flax is covered in lye, cut into a shirt, pressed, and worn to rags, "which are then worried to pulp in the paper-mill and rolled and pressed into sheets upon which poets may scribble their fancies" (121).[21] This inspirational source is significant for several reasons. First, the flax's preharvest state of "billowing like the sea's great waves" echoes the motion of the chreods and speaks to the plant's patterns of movement and its own particular agency. Second, the original story speaks to empathy, in that it considers and imagines the experiences of nonhuman things. However, Strickland's poem does not engage empathy in this way. Instead, the words of the poem take on the chreodic patterns, at times becoming illegible to the human reader: like the ocean, the flax dances, too, and not to human sign systems. As Robert Eisler's etymological excavation of the word "linen" in "The Passion of the Flax" suggests, this same process of mourning at the time of the harvest appears in the *Iliad*, in book eighteen's famous description of Hephaestus' forging of the shield of Achilles. The scene of harvest's reapers and "sharp reaping hooks" includes a song to Linus, who (Eisler speculates) is the god of flax in human form (here is anthropomorphism in its original state), since the word for flax in Greek (and, as Eisler enumerates, any number of Indo-European tongues) is "linon." If so, this is important. While the shield of Achilles is held as the example, par excellence, of ekphrasis, linking as it does a variety of artistic forms—poetry, metalwork, sculpture, images, dance, and song—it has just as much to say about ecology. On the shield a rich, vibrant ecology in which animal, vegetable, and mineral entities circulate and acknowledge each other, even as they commit violence in the form of harvest, battle, and sacrifice. Homer's poetry creates not just a shield, in other words, but a world, before Achilles' mother comes, "like a hawk" to collect it, "sweeping down from the snows of Olympos" (615).

In another segment (the bottom left of *slippingglimpse*), a bright, almost lime-green pool of water swirls, funnel like, repeats itself, merging and floating with the words on the surface: "I finally learned to see / beyond the retinal / experience / eighty-five percent— / which I liked." This, a specific reference to Duchamp's "retinal shudder"—that is, Duchamp's desire to remove the visual arts from the tyranny of the eye's mode of organizing it, so that art would instead come to the viewer not as a mere object of vision but a system of apprehension—speaks to the organization and subsequent experience of *slippingglimpse*. As the videographer Paul Ryan states, "I would avoid the term visual to describe video. You can see a bottle of perfume, but sight is not the sense it really affects. . . . Video is about perceiving events with the nervous system, not visualizing in a pictorial way" (Ryan, "Interview").

Paul Ryan, inspired by the writing and work of Charles Sanders Peirce, Rene Thom, and C. H. Waddington, summarizes his system in terms of Waddington's desire to imagine that we might be able to "evolve an information transmission system based on shared perception of environmental realities rather than language" (Ryan, "Earthscore"). This line of thinking emerges, in part, from the linguist Derek Bickerton, who "reasons that despite the vast powers that language has conferred on our species, some of the consequences of modeling reality with language threaten the continuation of our life on earth" (qtd. in Ryan, "Earthscore"). To challenge the dominance of language, Ryan imagines an environmental aesthetic that strips language away from the equation.[22] One sympathizes with this rationale, to an extent, but the word "language" is just as vexed a term as "agency." Language is the assertion of power, he writes. It stunts us and functions as a tool of domination. *Human* language is rule-bound, syntactical, baroque in its complexity, to be sure, but it is not the only game in town. Language of various kinds permeates the world. With that said, it might seem ironic that *slippingglimpse* superimposes lines of poetry, via lines of code, on top of Ryan's visualizations. Instead of selling out to language, *slippingglimpse* plays a "round robin" with it. And instead of having one mode of signification dominate—image, text, code, water, chreod—the work cycles among them, each mingled with the other. The work is not about mimeses or presenting a pleasing or accurate rendering of the world, although the images are lovely. Nor is the work about translating the natural world into language. *slippingglimpse* effaces the authority of language by showing its dependence upon visual, natural, and computational sign systems. The water, the words, the coding, the authorial and poetical "I" merge into one funnel-like ecosystem. In a telling passage, the work as a whole speaks to its own title. In this section, a lone leaf revolves and warps on the surface of the water. As it does, the following line emerges in the scroll: "a realm / (. . . to come / of slipping glimpse." In this moment and throughput the poem as a whole, *slippingglimpse* offers a peek into a possible future in which all natural entities are coconstituted, structured by each other and our environment.

As a whole, *slippingglimpse* recalls the myth of Echo and Narcissus, suggesting the echo of words on the surface of the water, and the futility of mimesis. In places it seems as if the writing tries but fails to imitate the water so as not to become erased by it. As such, this speaks to another lesson of the myth: one entity's incompatibility with the other. Yet to read the piece in this manner would be a mistake. This is not mere reflection; neither is it a wholly mimetic form of representation. The work doesn't merely repeat or parrot information; dynamism is at work in each segment. In her recent assessment of the ecological turn in media aesthetics, Rita Raley mentions this myth in relation to the field in general. She identifies a move away from the notion of the "'narcisystem' to an engagement of the ecological system . . . comprised of human and non-human actors and lively, vibrant, animate matter" (889).[23] For an example of this tendency, she refers to *Verbiage Végétal*, the digital artist Cyrill Henry's series of beautiful, algorithmically generated trees: "a complex arborescence made of alphabet letters . . . of tens of thousands of words" (Henry). Each of these trees "finds its origin in a text file. Each branch is generated by a chosen word in the text. . . . Each tree draws a path, a possible voyage through the text. The constituent words come from the text author's word field" (Henry), as well Alison Clifford, who in *The Sweet Old Etcetera*, inspired by e. e. cummings' poem of the same name, uses Flash to animate his verses so that his poems take various forms—a branching tree, a flitting bee, a spreading valley, a hillside of prose, and, of course, the crowd-pleasing r-p-o-p-h-e-s-s-a-g-r—and in doing so makes the work her own.

These projects overlap in an important way with *slippingglimpse* and *Spore 1.1*, in that all use digital technology to illuminate natural signs and show a continuity between digital and natural ecologies. I locate *Verbiage Végétal* and *The Sweet Old Etcetera* squarely within mimetic tradition, at least in terms of their treatment of natural objects.[24] These works suggest, through imitation and simulation, the parts and processes of the natural world.[25] As Raley suggests of contemporary new media poetics in general, *slippingglimpse* demonstrates a move away from technological navel-gazing, a rejection of the "narcisystem." Yet both *slippingglimpse* and *Spore 1.1* press past mimesis and metaphor, as well. While *slippingglimpse* does engage with some aspects of the myth of Echo and Narcissus (images, reflections, water, frustrated desire, the relation between the reflection and the original source of the emanation), it *translates* it: turns image into word, word into water, water into text.

Socrates and the Cicadas

Naming nature, addressing nature, and ascribing agency to nature is nothing new, but during the modern period it became taboo. Heidegger, who decried the way modernity trapped the power of nature into standing reserve, was himself swept up in all the worst aspects of modernism. His unwillingness to let anything but man serve as the measure of being is reflected in his "three theses" about the world and its worlding: "[1.] the stone (material object) is worldless; [2.] the animal is poor in world; [3.] man is world-forming" (*Animal Philosophy* 18). The distinction rests on human language, by which communication is made through verbal sign systems. So important for Heidegger is language that it forms the condition for experiencing the world. If Heidegger is correct in his assertion that "the leap from living animals to humans that speak is as large if not larger than that from the lifeless stone to the living being" (18) and that it is the ability to communicate that instantiates this gap, then what are we to make of plants, animals, water, and soil that do?

One might recall that for many writers there was never any question of their capacity for speech, even in the face of technological progress. As Thoreau writes in a journal entry in 1856, "If a stone appeals to me and elevates me, tells me how many miles I have come, how many remain to travel,—and to the more, the better,—reveals the future to me in some measure, it is a matter of private rejoicing. If it did the same service to all, it might well be a matter of public rejoicing" (*Journals*). In *Walden* he writes, "the most innocent and encouraging society may be found in any natural object. . . . There was never yet such a storm but it was Æolian music to a healthy and innocent ear" (5). Yet these messages are always about and for the exquisite, private world named Thoreau, who is the center and origin of this act of communication even as he shares his insights. A predigital, pre*modern* communication model in which the landscape participates within a larger circuit of information exchange and meaning—the correspondence I am pointing to here—can be found in Plato's *The Phaedrus*.

The Phaedrus is frequently read as a warning about the dangers of the new technology of writing: "This invention will produce forgetfulness in the minds of those who learn to use it, because they will not practice their memory. . . . You have invented an elixir not of memory, but of reminding" (563). This passage is often invoked in media studies to frame the discussion of any new or emerging technology. We are told that for Socrates, and therefore for Plato, writing is bad. It denigrates the integrity of the soul's "present," more "truthful" expression, and is a copy of what is "written on the soul." Yet Plato's dependence upon writing inheres throughout the dialog. Through this medium he is able to present multiple perspectives via various personae. Plato (1) uses the voice of Socrates (2), who recounts a story to Phaedrus (3) from the perspective of an Egyptian God (4), who speaks to Toth, inventor of writing (5). Even so, this argument that writing is bad is furthered by a condemnation of all of the mimetic arts, which, like writing, are shown to be mere copies of an external ideal form. It is an effective passage and a powerful scene, but what is less frequently emphasized is the manner in which the dialog is saturated with evidence that runs contrary to its conclusions. In "Plato's Pharmacy," Derrida reveals some of these contradictions to demonstrate how shaky the ground is upon which binary oppositions rest, playfully teasing out the multiple significations—both poisonous and medicinal—of the word "pharmakon."

But other passages in the dialog speak in interesting ways against the strong argument that Plato (through Socrates and Ammon) makes. The powerful notion that natural signs can act as fluid intermediaries between different modes of existence, by speaking simultaneously for themselves, to us, and to a higher organizing power, is something Socrates laments in *The Phaedrus* as already lost: "The men of old, unlike in their simplicity to young philosophy, deemed that if they heard the truth even from 'oak or rock,' it was enough for them" (565). Yet the dialog itself suggests that natural objects continue to signify, powerfully. Instead of supporting a "pure" system of communication between an inner self and the world of forms, such moments reveal a much larger system of correspondence, comprising human animals, nonhuman animals, and the divine, all mediated through features of the landscape.

The dialog occurs beneath a sycamore tree. Socrates expresses his pleasure to Lysias, commenting on the singing of the cicadas. He is enchanted by the location Phaedrus finds, beneath the shade of a tree on the edge of a stream on a hot summer day:

> By Hera, it is a charming resting place. For this plane tree is very spreading and lofty, and the tall and shady willow is very beautiful,

> and it is in full bloom, so as to make the place most fragrant; then, too, the spring is very pretty as it flows under the plane tree, and its water is very cool, to judge by my foot. And it seems to be a sacred place of some nymphs and of Achelous, judging by the figurines and statues. Then again, if you please, how lovely and perfectly charming the breeziness of the place is! and it resounds with the shrill summer music of the chorus of cicadas. But the most delightful thing of all is the grass, as it grows on the gentle slope, thick enough to be just right when you lay your head on it. So you have guided the stranger most excellently, dear Phaedrus. (423)

It is such a relaxing and idyllic locus that Socrates warns Lysias that they must not fall asleep lest the cicadas see them in their slumber and report back to the Muses what they have seen. Lysias does not understand what Socrates means, so Socrates goes on to explain that the cicadas were once men who lived before the Muses came. Upon their arrival, they were so enchanted with song and dance that they stopped eating and drinking and lived only in music. As a reward, the Muses gave them a gift: they can go through their entire lives singing and dancing with no need for food or drink; and when they die they will come before the muses to report to each one who has been honored by whom on earth: "They have this gift from the Muses, that from the time of their birth, they need no sustenance, but sing continually, without food or drink, until they die, when they go to the Muses and report who honors each of them on earth" (513).

The tree, the stream, the grass, and the bloom of willow cohere as a locus. Socrates dips his foot in its waters and immerses himself in the scene. But the song of the cicadas is startling. The presence of these insects and their song marks an early moment in literary philosophical history in which landscape acts as a messenger in a larger communication circuit that neither originates nor ends with a human subject. The cicadas report and inform on humans, who are the objects discussed in transmission and *not* the speaking subjects. Rather, the cicadas act as points of rupture between human, animal, and divine realms. In this moment, Socrates points to the importance of reporting, of transmission, of participating in a larger circuit of communication than that described in the passage about writing. He expresses his desire to share the gift of the cicadas (the Greek word is *tittex*, which is alternately translated as cicada and locust, but which Liddell and Scott define as "grasshopper") and therefore *approves* of mediation. Additionally, he points to elements of the real world—the charming space beneath the sycamore tree, the softness of the grass, the warmth of summer, the edge of a river—as participants within a locus of divine communication.

While few would want to recover a world system based on the peculiar logic of ancient mythology, many share Plato's lament that we have compromised our connection to the features of the natural landscape.[26] Works such as Midori-san, *Spore 1.1*, and *slippingglimpse* offer fresh opportunities to recover this rich circuit of communication, not within the divine context of augury or sacrifice or even new-age mysticism but within the context of living and reporting to each other about the conditions of our shared material world.

These examples emphasize the power and agency of the natural world in order to gesture toward a much more profound payoff: all emerge from a long tradition of pushing the limits of human consciousness beyond the confines of the human body, beyond the idea of a cohesive subjectivity, to acknowledge that our identities are constituted not only by what we experience from within but by a vast lattice of living and nonliving relations that affect us from without. This tradition is something we can trace through all of literary history. In such works the landscape is filled with hints of agency, with signs of presence. The rustling leaves mean something. As in Plato's *Phaedrus*, the flora and fauna, whether songbird, sycamore, or cicada, report something.

In works that combine features of the natural landscape with digital technologies, such features are not merely suggestive of agency. Such features act. They are not merely addressed. They respond. Similarly, the human being who "reads" these features is called on by the environment to act, to engage, to reciprocate. In other words, the features of the landscape, including human and nonhuman features, become co-communicators within a common environment. And it is this ability to respond, to speak, and to communicate decidedly nonhuman experience into human terms, to which we should pay attention. Full agency for these nonhuman beings need not be claimed, but their potential for correspondence—that is, active, animated nature made reciprocal, put into dialog with humanity via digital technology—should be. And that should force us to think long and hard about the very notion of agency itself.

4
Conserving
Saving Nature through Game Play

> Our vision is to leave a sustainable world for future generations. Today's society faces unprecedented challenges. Dwindling natural resources, declining economies, a rapidly changing climate and other threats require that all of us begin working together to reach common solutions. More than ever before, we must find innovative ways to ensure that nature can continue to provide the food, clean water, energy and other services our growing population depends upon for survival. Now is a time of opportunity.
>
> —The Nature Conservancy's Mission Statement (2013)

> [Is it] better and more good for the people of Athens that the Basileus lease the land that has already been cultivated within the bounds of the sacred meadow for the purpose of building a portico and providing additional equipment for the sanctuary of the Two Goddesses [or is it] better and more good for the people of Athens to leave untilled to the Two Goddesses the land that has already been cultivated within the bounds of the sacred meadow[?]
>
> —Petition to the Pythian Apollo via the Oracle of Delphi (352 BCE)

Saving Nature

Making the decision to conserve land has, since recorded history, been a contentious political undertaking. In the fourth century BCE, petitioners from the city of Athens traveled to the Oracle at Delphi to ask whether or not a portion of a "sacred meadow" (sacred to the Earth goddess Demeter and her daughter, Kore) ought to be further cultivated or left alone; the second quotation that forms the epigraph to this chapter is a citation from that petition. I include the story here to suggest something different from previous chapters. In those, I attempted to demonstrate that computational technology has premodern antecedents to shake it free from the conventional notion that technology is a modern monster. Here, I mention the ancient oracle to suggest that the history of conservation itself has a monstrous history that spans eons. The tensions and political interests inherent in it persists through premodern, modern, and postmodern epochs.[1] We might like to think that conservation is a modern invention—and in the sense of the environmental movement of the twentieth century, it is—but its politics have historical roots. But I mention the oracle for another reason, as well: the manner of consulting it has much in common with digital technology. Here is how it worked in terms of the petition cited above: "The secretary of the council is to write on two tin tablets, equal and similar, on the one: 'whether it is better and more good for the people of Athens that the Basileus lease the land that has already been cultivated within the bounds of the sacred meadow for the purpose of building a portico and providing additional equipment for the sanctuary of the Two Goddesses' and on the other tin tablet 'whether it is better and more good for the people of Athens to leave untilled to the Two Goddesses the land that has already been cultivated within the bounds of the sacred meadow'" (Parke 102). After composing these statements, the petitioner was instructed to roll each into a cylinder, cover each cylinder with wool, and place one in a jar of silver, the other in a jar of gold. Once this was completed, the petitioner made his way to Delphi to ask the god to decide whether the gold or silver jar contained the best solution. This process, in effect, "exclude[d] the use of human intelligence on the part of the priests or priestesses in determining their answer . . . [serving] to guarantee that the chairman would not know which of the two alternatives he was putting into which of the two jars" (103). Oracles in general made use of this sort of decision-making process, and this is in some aspects continuous with contemporary conservation practices that also rely heavily upon automated processes.[2]

In our age of ubiquitous computing, conservation efforts, like every aspect of our culture, are touched by digital technology. Works of digital art are imagining different ways to aid in conservation efforts and are contributing to the bottom-line of conservation in terms of how many acres are set aside for preservation. And there are just as many that speak to a different yet equally urgent concept of conservation: the conservation of energy and natural resources at global and local levels. At the same time, such works call into question the very notion of conservation, at least when conservation is tantamount to putting a bell jar over a parcel of land and excluding human beings from the spaces being conserved. Conservation aesthetics favors remote vistas; it celebrates the erasure of the artist that paints the picture or takes the photograph and perpetuates the very problem that has plagued the conservation movement from its inception, namely, the problem with claiming that human beings are separate from nature. It is a lonely aesthetics.

In *Alien Phenomenology*, Ian Bogost offers a critique of Actor-Network-

Theory relevant to conservation aesthetics: "In the networks of actor-network theory, things remain in motion far more than they do at rest. As a result, entities are de-emphasized in favor of their couplings and decouplings. Alliances take center stage, and things move to the wings" (7). In *The Pasteurization of France*, Latour puts this succinctly: "Actors do not stand still long enough to take a group photo" (qtd. in Bogost 7). "But yet they *do*," Bogost replies, "even as they also assemble and disband from their networks" (7). Both Bogost's insistence that things endure and Latour's statement that they do not are useful for thinking through the evolution of conservation. For an example of this, consider three important snapshots within the progression of conservation aesthetics: Yosemite in three acts.

The first moment is familiar. A stocky, khaki-clad Teddy Roosevelt stands next to a lanky, bearded John Muir beneath the roots of a giant sequoia (McFarland). The photo commemorates their three-day camping trip in Yosemite's Glacier Point, which will result in policy changes in terms of the reach of federal resource management. By taking control of state-owned land in order to put it under the federal aegis of conservation, Roosevelt inflected the discussion of nature conservation in America for a century. His relationship with Muir, as well as the tour they took together in 1903, helped initiate the American Conservation movement. Conservation, the practice of setting aside large tracts of public lands and limiting development upon them, is a cornerstone of broad-tent environmentalism. This first snapshot, frozen in time, simultaneously captures this foundational moment and makes possible the power of the second, "Clearing Winter Storm," taken by Ansel Adams as a part of his "Yosemite" series in 1944. The Yosemite Valley unfolds like a chiaroscuro painting with a diamond-cut finish. The clouds and mountains intermingle; El Capitan looks down upon Half Dome; Bridal Veil Falls gleams as it cleaves Cathedral Rocks and Spires; every tree in the valley confronts the storm, each with its own rough texture. This photograph documents the power of a variety of natural agents that cohere as a majestic and self-sufficient entity, one that has been allowed to unfold and thrive as a consequence of the conservation efforts that the first photograph documents. The third picture is less familiar but no less relevant: it is a snapshot of the park's Tioga Pass, taken in the winter of 2009 (California Nevada Applications). The picture captures the features of the land—the purple hues of the California winter, the mountains blanketed in snow, and the quiet flow of moisture-laden clouds overhead. On the whole it suggests a remote landscape untouched by human intervention. Appropriately enough, this photograph was not taken by any human hand but by a remotely operated and mostly automated Scripps Institute–owned webcam, stationed on a pole overlooking Tioga Pass. Although this webcam is now "indefinitely out of service," at least three others remain, offering views of the Ahwahnee Valley, the vertiginous heights of Sentinel Peak, and the rocky cliffs of Turtleback Summit.

The 1,190 square miles that we know as Yosemite National Park have endured over time, as have its natural objects contained therein. Half Dome still imposes; Bridal Veil Falls still falls; Mirror Lake still reflects. These pictures, however, demonstrate that very different networks of actors, at least in terms of conveying a message about conservation, have cohered, disbanded, and evolved. Conservation, as Muir envisioned it and as Roosevelt helped legislate it, opposes certain types of technological intervention. It prohibits certain types of technologies, including logging, certain types of irrigation, road development, housing, and so on. It might seem logical to conclude that digital technology would similarly run afoul of conservation efforts. Yet, as the third picture indicates, digital technology helps sustain vulnerable sites of land paradoxically, by interacting with these spaces on every level. Far from existing as separate from sites of conservation, digital technology intermingles with all aspects of conservation management. And it also allows the public to enjoy its spaces remotely. One hundred years after the famous Muir-Roosevelt summit, one need not fly to California to see the national park. By visiting the service home page for Yosemite National Park, one can check the weather from a remote sensor, view the air quality from online simulations, and enjoy beautiful snapshots of the Ahwahnee Valley or Turtleback Dome courtesy of multiple webcams. Children can explore various national parks online, learn about the history of each park or learn about current issues the park has to contend with, and play games related to floral and faunal conservation. Such digitally created images help demonstrate that networks can change over time, that methods of conservation and attitudes toward the preservation of natural spaces are not preordained. This is an important insight for conservation in the future, as well as for how digital technology might participate in these efforts.

Greening the Game: Community Conservation Efforts Online

SHALL WE PLAY A GAME?
> How about Global Thermonuclear War?
WOULDN'T YOU PREFER A GOOD GAME OF CHESS?
> Let's play Global Thermonuclear War.
—*War Games*, 1983

Ever since *War Games*, the film in which a pale, teenaged Matthew Broderick engaged DARPA in a game of global thermonuclear war from his parents' suburban home with little more than a dial-up modem and a push button telephone, the pairing of computer games and adolescence has been greeted with some suspicion. This is particularly true within the environmental movement, where video games, television, and other forms of popular media often provide a convenient scapegoat for environmental apathy. A book review on the Sierra Club's "Green Life" blog sums it up: "Collecting leaves, flying kites, looking for bugs, and playing tag may evoke fond childhood memories for many adults, but these activities are at risk for extinction in a world where television, video games, and computers compete for children's attention" (Sierra). Here the relation between online play and engagement with natural spaces is configured as a hostile one, where the computational threatens to hasten the extinction of the natural, the environmental version of "Game Over."

On the Sierra Club page alone there are over a hundred posts that couple playing video games with some sort of negative attribute, including indolence, apathy, and general malaise. Still, there is a trend, growing stronger all the time, of making use of games to promote social awareness, aid in conservation, and democratize activism. In this chapter I explore how video games are already contributing to environmental action, as well as how they have further potential to intervene more positively in the future. Such games appeal to a wide range of users. From Facebook-compatible applications that claim to reclaim endangered rain forests and educational "eco-quests" that inform children about global communities to green-powered search engines that provide game-like statistics for conservation efforts, online video games promise to make it easy—or at least easier—to be green.

The word "game" in my analysis is employed broadly, signifying both a general "amusement or pastime" and "a competitive activity involving skill, chance, or endurance on the part of two or more persons who play according to a set of rules, usually for their own amusement or for that of spectators" ("Game"). Some online games that claim to foster social awareness are ill-designed and sophomoric, tedious to play, and insipid. Yet whether they are games that can stand alone as art objects, while not entirely beside the point, is not my primary focus. I am concerned with to what extent online games offer a set of viable tactics for reframing environmental conservation as a collaborative network rather than an exercise in isolation aesthetics. The collaborative nature of such sites, I argue, offers incentives for environmental engagement and builds community. As a result, these games contribute to conservation efforts but also encourage questions about conservation, allowing community-driven action to steer the lonely, isolated aesthetics of conservation toward a more communal and distributed aesthetics.

Digital engagements with nature have flown under the radar because of the way past works of art, literature, and film have imagined digital/computational technology's relation to nature, that is, as opposed to a balanced relationship with natural ecologies. Such works have primed us to believe that digital technology and the art and objects it produces can have only negative consequences on the natural world. "Green games" already have two strikes against them in the popular imagination. Such game spaces offer very different expressions of conservation than have been imagined in the past, especially in dystopian fiction, where pristine spaces of land are often nothing more than monuments to human failure, sad and shameful epiphenomena of post-apocalyptic devastation.[3] In the annals of science fiction this is the rule rather than the exception. Secondly, narratives about games themselves are also often dystopian in flavor. Instead of connecting their players to the real world, they often foster alienation and cause them to withdraw from it. This retreat might lead to an engulfing, nearly inescapable game space, as in *Tron*; to warfare, as in *Ender's Game*; to outer space, as in *The Last Starfighter*; or to a tortured, psychotic form of inner space, as in *Mazes and Monsters*. But no matter where it leads, it has tended to leave the natural world behind.

But there are also several literary-aesthetic traditions that create a blind spot about digital-ecological convergence. The first is the pastoral. In her essay on the online game *FarmVille*, Alenda Chang offers an excellent overview of the shifting nature of the pastoral in relation to online gaming practices, suggesting that "in their reductive idealization of country work, *FarmVille* and games like it partake of conventional pastoral" (Chang 238). The second tradition is the so-called *novela de la selva*, that is, the "forest novel" or the "jungle novel." This has been a fundamental construct for priming expectations about the types of spaces we should wish to save, on which, more later.

The games I examine here offer a new and exciting path for conservation aesthetics, but mine is also a *critical* assessment. Such works offer positive engagement with real-world natural spaces, yes, but also they also highlight problematic issues about the ethics of online gaming and environmental practice. For example, in addition to acting as sites of engagement and play, such games function as places of inculcation into environmental communities with specific, and not unproblematic, ideologies. Additionally, although many players might feel a measure of virtue in playing them, certain that their efforts are helping to fund a greater good, many games that purport to be "green" have little or no connection to environmental action of any kind. Many of them are run by crafty entrepreneurs who can be likened to digitally savvy Tom Sawyers, in that they give members of the public buckets of paint in order to enlist their aid in the labor of corporate greenwashing. These sites are unapologetically commercially driven. Hence, I mean for "game" to work also in the way that the title of Richard Connell's famous short story "The Most Dangerous Game" does, as a play on the dual meaning of the word, which signifies both the game to be played and the quarry to be caught.[4] To show how this is so, I will begin with a case study of a very popular online game that no longer exists but that during its brief lifespan encapsulated many of these tensions.

Little Green Patches

"Here is a Venus Flytrap plant for your (Lil) Green Patch. Could you help me by sending a plant back? Together we can fight global warming!" Users of Facebook from 2008 to 2010 may recognize the origin of this message: the now-defunct *(Lil) Green Patch* (*LGP*). This was a Facebook-compatible app that bounced from company to company for three years. *(Lil) Green Patch* was created by a software developer named David King in 2008, who sold it to the company Playdom in 2009, which retired it in 2010.

Like many applications on Facebook (*Mob Wars*, *Vampires*, *Pillow Fight*, and *Poker Palace*), *LGP* was notable for low-resolution graphics, primitive design, and terrible grammar. Where it differed was in the unmatched sense of *virtue* it encouraged. Playing *LGP* had positive, real-world consequences, or so it claimed: "Together we can fight Global Warming!" The accuracy of this particular claim is hard to pin down with any certainty, a point I will return to momentarily, but for now, regardless of the fuzzy bottom-line, a postmortem of *LGP* offers a valuable lesson. By dissecting its peculiar two-part structure, we can determine how well it worked as a vehicle for environmental conservation. The first part of this structure is the user-end surface, that is, the diegetic level of the story where the players played—the so-called front end of designed screen space. The front end of any website signifies the part the user can see, click, read, and play, without interacting with or even being aware of the processes at work to make these effects visible. The second part, however, the so-called back end or code level, is harder to specify when it comes to *LGP*, in part because the term "back end" is so misleading, suggesting as it does that if one were to erase the first layer one would see a "real" level behind it. By clicking open-apple u, in order to view the source, one will see html, php, and so on. Yet such a peek will not reveal the whole picture, not only because there are any number of codes, protocols, and technologies that govern the surface appearance of any website, many of which are not visible because they are stored in separate files or generated on the fly in response to the user's input, but also because focusing on site-specific encoding obscures a whole group of processes and relations that are handled by outside sources: search engines.

In terms of the first part, the front-end space for playing the game itself, the rules and processes were straightforward. The application created a virtual garden for the user that showed up within the "boxes" section of one's profile page. The object of the game was to cultivate one's virtual garden, fill it with plants, and accrue credits. One accrued credits not merely by keeping one's own garden green but by interacting with other players. Although one could conceivably "play" *LGP* alone, the game was at heart a community effort. To accrue maximum points, players had to interact with each other by giving plants to other members of the community, by accepting plants offered in return, and by protecting each other from environmental "hazards." Every visit to the garden yielded an environmental update, such as "your (Lil') green patch is dry—can you water it?"; or "your (Lil') green patch has aphids nibbling on its leaves!"; or "your (Lil') green patch has been taken over by rabbits—can you feed them?" If one had the tools to address the problem (a watering hose, bug spray, rabbit food), one could simply click on these items and make use of them. If not, a visit to the "store" to trade in credits to purchase them would take care of it. If one left one's garden in disrepair, Facebook friends would be alerted when they visited their own gardens, where, instead of an environmental alert, they might have received something like this: "Elizabeth's Green Patch needs help. Can you help please?" If one chose to help, the application would take the user to her friend's garden, which she could tend to by spending her own credits and using her own tools to maintain order, even if the garden's owner had maintained a policy of gross neglect ("(Lil') Green Patch"). Overall, the front-end of *LGP* exhibited signs of a pastoral aesthetic, in a way that was interesting in terms of technology. As Alenda Chang writes in her analysis of *FarmVille*, to conceive of such games as if they were a "direct descendant of the pastoral tradition . . . is to miss the way . . . games like [these] naturalize technology so that it becomes an undifferentiated part of the agricultural landscape" (239).

This is a useful insight in light of discussions about the issue of *transparency* in digital art. As I note in my second chapter, Jay David Bolter has been quite critical of this tradition. As he and Diane Gromala write in *Windows and Mirrors*, "HCI specialists and some designers speak as if that were the only goal of interface design: to fashion a transparent window onto a world of information" (26). At times Bolter and Gromala even liken such an aesthetic to Platonic philosophy, and not in a good way: "Whether there are or aren't any atheists in foxholes, there should not be Platonists in digital design" (138). Their critique is valid. An aesthetic that privileges transparency tends to obscure the objects and processes that make the aesthetic experience possible—that make the network function.

But Chang's reading of *Farmville* offers a particularly apt way to think about transparency within a tradition of the pastoral. Works such as *FarmVille* and *LGP* enfold technological motifs, artifacts, and techniques within the pastoral tradition, naturalizing them. This is a different type of naturalization from the one that Bolter and Gromala criticize. As Chang writes, "the machine is present not only within the game (as tractors, combines, and even the genetic manipulation of seeds) but also as the game's framework: the infrastructure (computers, mobile devices, and networks) without which the game could not be played" (251). As simple as *(Lil) Green Patch* was, it, too, relied upon machinery, tools, and computational technology to cultivate its gardens, and this "naturalization" was effective for undermining the technological-natural divide.

Additionally, the game itself fostered a community-based conversation about conservation. With each gaming session, players were informed that they had "saved" a certain number of acres of rain forest. Players did not have access to how this was occurring, but two words will explain how it worked: incentive advertising. This is what drove the second part of *(Lil) Green Patch*, that is, the app's back-end. Patched into this network of little green patches, a complementary set of patches—square, but decidedly not green—appeared on the screen to make use of community action through a very different "gaming" mechanism: paid advertisements. Companies paid for the opportunity to hawk their wares within 250 x 250 pixel squares of the *LGP* game.[5] *(Lil) Green Patch*'s financial success was the result of sponsored advertisements appearing on the surface level of the screen. By clicking these, users generated significant revenue for the company. Search engines have become thoroughly intertwined with the front-end side of websites by interspersing outside content within willing websites to generate ad revenue. We are seeing more incentive advertising and profit skimming every day. Indeed, a related "farm" emerged part and parcel with games such as *(Lil) Green Patch*: the content farm, "a company that employs large numbers of often freelance writers to generate large amounts of textual content which is specifically designed to satisfy algorithms for maximal retrieval by automated search engines. Their main goal is to generate advertising revenue" ("content farm"). Collectively the users of *(Lil) Green Patch* were responsible for generating ad revenue, a small percentage of which was donated to the Nature Conservancy's "adopt-an-acre" program, which benefited conservation efforts on the Osa Peninsula in Costa Rica. According to the claims made by the developers, the more one used the application, the more ad revenue one generated, the more money was donated, and the more square-footage of rain forest was saved.

These two sides of the game were causally linked. On the surface level of the game's front-end, there was active plant trading, patch maintenance, and general custodianship of a virtual space. And as a result of the back-end of things, especially in terms of ad revenue, a *real*-world space was allegedly being aided by all of this activity, a lush green preserve in the heart of Costa Rica. From its inception in 2008 to its closure in 2010, the *(Lil) Green Patch* app had over 5 million installations, "350,000 monthly active users" (*(Lil) Green Patch*); the site donated over a quarter of a million dollars to the Nature Conservancy. The *(Lil) Green Patch* application proclaimed proudly that "The *(Lil) Green Patch* community, working together, was able to save 183,244,167 Sq ft of Rainforest so far! We are very excited about our progress and are confident we can make an even larger impact in the future!" (*(Lil) Green Patch*, allaboutfacebook). With all of the focus on the accouterments of play—including the messages and tools and gardening implements—it is easy to see how the connection to the actual site of conservation might have become obscured. The poor design did little to help, and the graphics used to represent the garden looked nothing like plants found in the real world. Rather, the plants in the garden had a 1980s 8-bit retro aura about them, as if someone was working with an aesthetic template that combined the worst features of Strawberry Shortcake, the Cabbage Patch Kids, and Space Invaders. Additionally, *LGP* lacked racial and ethnic diversity. In this it was consistent with many such works that obscure or downplay real-world agricultural business practices. As Alenda Chang points out, "ethnically diverse migrant workers constitute a critical but underserved segment of the nation's agricultural workforce," but "farm games, with their default cast of pale, cheerful faces, appear intent on ignoring such realities." Instead of portraying a culturally and racially mixed farm force, "an astonishing number of titles feature fair-skinned, redheaded heroines, who sport nary a freckle or sunburn even after toiling in the hot sun for months on end" (242). Although *LGP* did not have character avatars, it was in terms of its sprites (i.e., its visual gaming elements) just as guilty of this tendency, and perhaps even worse, in that it racialized its fruits and vegetables by making them white.[6]

Yet the plants that grew via this application were quite clearly meant to simulate organic life within garden spaces, and it is worth considering how this game managed to connect its players not only to the simulations of nature it represented but also back to the real-world spaces that inspired them.

So how did *(Lil) Green Patch* manage to do this? Its conventions, as primitive as they might have been in terms of gaming practice, fostered a sense of community, encouraged a sense of custodianship and responsibility for the environment, and offered tangible rewards for caring for the property of others, which in turn complicated a strict sense of ownership and supported real-world stewardship of environmental resources. By participating in this community "game," one reaped all of these benefits. This was aided by the fact that the subject of the game, while primitively expressed, was not arbitrary. The developers could have just as easily created the same type of revenue-skimming procedure in a game about alien invasion or a zombie apocalypse, both of which have, incidentally, come and gone on Facebook. And vice versa: the real-world cause could have been any number of charitable organizations. By having the game itself, however, be about stewardship, care, conservation, and cultivation, the developers instead created an intriguing, if tenuous, link between game play and the actual real-world benefit of rain forest conservation that the game achieved via its donations to the Nature Conservancy.

While we are seeing more and content farms run by for-profit and not-for-profit companies, *LGP*'s gambit of *causally linking* the components of game play and incentive advertising for environmental action—however schmaltzy the game and paltry the payoff—was unprecedented. When I last visited *(Lil) Green Patch*'s site statistics, I was impressed at the amount of Central American rain forest that the community had collectively been able to maintain, and I felt a small measure of virtue about my modest contribution to its total (twenty-seven square feet). The collective efforts were laudable, but the entire cash flow that the *(Lil) Green Patch* gaming network—which included its players, its advertisers, Facebook, and the Nature Conservancy—generated raises questions about the efficacy of such efforts, especially concerning transparency.

In the first place, all the data about *LGP*'s contribution to the Nature Conservancy was and remains a black-boxed formula. Second, the community was not given any input about where, how, or why the money would be used and diverted. Of all the countries that constitute the isthmus of Central America, Costa Rica is perhaps the least in need of conservation activism. It is a gorgeously well-maintained and forested corridor between Panama and Nicaragua, one of the few countries in the world to have instituted a ban on recreational hunting (Daniel). Its jungles are lush, its monkeys are raucous, and its sloths are lazy and plump. Part of Costa Rica's impressive environmental track record comes from a strong national ethos about the importance of natural spaces, but it also comes from a strong economic incentive. The nation's economy is dependent upon ecotourism. If players had been given a choice about where to target conservation in Central America, would they choose Costa Rica? Who can say? I personally would choose Panama, Nicaragua, or Honduras, although I would have been curious to know what the rationale behind the choice of Costa Rica was and would have been open to being persuaded. The *LGP* "community" was not given such a choice, nor was it included in any aspect of the decision-making process. Instead, the community generated profit, only a fraction of which was given for conservation efforts. This autopsy of *LGP* suggests that a future game that would allow for greater transparency by showing how much is generated and granting users input about where the funds should go might enjoy a greater longevity. Giving the users a sense of accomplishment by taking care of a virtual natural space, *(Lil) Green Patch* and other games like it have fostered collaborative conservation online, even if they also made it just a little too easy to be green. Playdom, which acquired the application in April 2010, shut down the operation in June of that year and has no intention of continuing any efforts toward conservation. Yet such applications are useful for allowing us to think through the means of collective conservation and activism that are already springing up in its place.

The Little Green Engine

Although *LGP* is no more, its method of skimming ad revenue for a larger philanthropic purpose has begun to gain popular momentum. In particular, this practice has given rise to a cluster of search engines that all purport to "do good" while searching for information. These include GoodSearch.com, Freelanthropy.com, and Helpuu.com, as well as several smaller-scale sites. There is one search engine whose explicit, singular focus is environmental action: Ecosia, the ecologically "friendly" search engine based out of Berlin, which was founded in 2010 by Christian Kroll, a German entrepreneur devoted to using ad revenue to benefit conservation efforts. To use Ecosia, a user visits Ecosia.org and enters a search term. That's it. On the surface level, it works just like any other search engine. Ecosia isn't a game, per se, or even a piece of art, but as a cultural object with a distinct aesthetic that has drawn in millions of users, it is worth considering within this context. And in that it patches people into a larger social effort and allows them to see the results of their actions, it functions very much like a game whose object is conservation. Like *LGP*, it uses gaming elements to foster conservation. But there are many illustrative *differences* between Ecosia and *LGP*. The main beneficiary of Ecosia's ad revenue has been the WWF, not the Nature Conservancy, although they have recently partnered with the Nature Conservancy's "Plant a Billion Trees" program. And the plot of land it has targeted is not Costa Rica but large tracts of Brazilian rain forest that are increasingly threatened by development. In terms of its business practices, Ecosia also departs from *LGP* in three important ways. In the first place, it gives much more: "Ecosia . . . gives at least 80% of its advertising revenue to a rainforest protection program run by the WWF" (Ecosia, "All about Ecosia"). We never knew just how much *LGP* donated, but given the wild popularity of the game (five million installations), measured against the alleged quarter million dollar payout, the numbers suggest a much lower ratio. As of July 2013, Ecosia has "raised over 1.5 million dollars for rainforest protection" (Li). More money translates to more acres "saved," and, so far, Ecosia has been up front about what these numbers signify. Second, Ecosia offers a self-reflexive assessment of its own energy consumption, as well as a clear description of the ways it attempts to make its consumption of energy "green": "All Ecosia servers run on green electricity, so they do not cause any CO_2 emissions. By using Ecosia, you can turn your web searches green" (Ecosia, "Ecoisa"). Finally, although not related to environmentalism per se, Ecosia guarantees the privacy of its users: "Ecosia holds your privacy in the highest regard . . . collected information merely serves to remove fake searches and are completely deleted within 48 hours. To protect your privacy, the data is not further analyzed, sold, or given to a third party" (Ecosia.org). Ecosia is generous, green powered, and protects the privacy of its users. What could be better? In many ways it stands as a paragon of the power of passive online environmental action. All of these are laudable objectives that speak to a progressive ethos, yet Ecosia has come under fire, not because the company lacks individual commitment to these objectives but because it depends upon high-profile and globally reaching partners to achieve them. Ecosia is a search engine "mask" powered by Yahoo and Bing, which is to say that it is powered by Microsoft, which owns both of these search engines and plans to merge them some time in the not-too-distant future. How can Ecosia claim to give 80 percent of its profits to the WWF without these search engines intervening? How can Ecosia claim to be green when the average search engine query—including Yahoo, including Bing—involves an enormous network of material and an enormous amount of energy (Schelmetic)? How can Ecosia claim to protect users' privacy, given the following promotional copy on Microsoft Advertising's information page? "We love data and we excel at interpreting it for our partners. We collect information from every campaign and mine it for insights" ("Microsoft advertising").

In response to these questions and concerns, Ecosia has changed as a company. In the first phase of Ecosia (2010), if the user downloaded a little piece of code from the Ecosia site, a status report would show up in the bottom bar of the browser window, which would provide information about how much rain forest had been saved, individually and by all Ecosia users. As of December 2010, Ecosia claimed to have saved "230,405,306 m^2" of Brazilian rain forest. Such a statistic suggests two bold, questionable claims: First, how could simply using a search engine generate enough money to save this much land? Second, how was Ecosia able so precisely to keep track of this effort, down to the meter? The answer to the first question is straightforward. Ecosia works in a similar way to *(Lil) Green Patch*, namely, the same way that other ad skimming, pay-per-hit organizations work: paid advertising. Advertisers pay to show up in search results. Advertisers pay to place ads on different web pages, and they pay the search engine that takes them there. Imagine that the advertisements on the Internet represent an ocean of money (they do). Dip a net into that ocean and skim the surface. Give 80 percent of what you haul out of it to the World Wildlife Federation (WWF), who will use it to preserve Brazilian rain forest.

The answer to the second question—how did Ecosia get such precise stats?—is even more straightforward: it didn't. The numbers functioned as "symbolic statistics," averages based on data from Ecosia's users. It did not tell each user how much she actually contributed, although, in theory, such a calculation would be possible. If a certain amount of income comes from each fraction of a cent earned by clicking on one ad or another, it should be possible to see exactly how much has been earned for my cause. We use the same types of samples as indicator species all the time, in our surveys, in our elections, in our public opinion polls. The same principle applies here. To address some of these concerns, however, and to be in compliance with the WWF's policies, the second version of Ecosia has changed the number of acreage saved to the amount of money raised. In response to the question about whether or not the number of acres saved referred to statistical averages, a representative for Ecosia provided the following telling response: "That's a place where we got a lot of criticism; you have probably noticed that they are gone now. They were symbolic averages. WWF International wants to present facts and facts alone to keep it that way just so that everything is as transparent as it can get with an organization of their size. We have a problem though in the sense that people love the statistics, whether they understood them or not. We got the criticism from the press as well. A lot of people just didn't understand how it would work out. And they were right to ask the question, so now we are looking at ways to maybe make those two separate things, like maybe create some kind of a personal statistics game" (Ecosia,

"Skype"). Ecosia has copies of its financial transactions available to its users, and that I was able to contact an Ecosia representative who took the time to answer all of my pointed questions along these lines speaks to their commitment to transparency. There are two other claims that Ecosia makes that are worth noting before moving on to its complex aesthetics. The first is that it manages to use only green energy in its energy consumption. This seems suspect, in that "one Google search is equal to turning on a 60W light bulb for 17 seconds" (Newman), yet the company is well aware of the problem and is working with the myclimate organization to offset its energy consumption (myclimate). Second, in contrast to other search engines that gather, harvest, reap, and sow personal information from their users, Ecosia promises that it empties its search caches every two weeks. All of this sounds like the very best in terms of making use of online technologies in order to "green the game"—or at least a much better step in the profit-sharing process that *LGP* initiated. Yet both Ecosia and *(Lil) Green Patch*, for all their innovative approaches to community-based conservation, bring into relief several issues in relation to the aesthetics of conservation in general.

The first is this term "saved." What does it mean to "save" these meters squared? Most reasonable people agree that the fragile ecosystem of the Amazon rain forest is fundamental to the health of the planet and, consequently, the species of plants and animals, including human beings, who reside on it. But things are never this simple, and the monitoring of acreage "saved" calls attention to the complexities inherent in what it means to save something in the first place. What does "saved" mean for the local people in this area? Does Ecosia save jobs? Did *LGP* save lives? What is the social impact of conservation on the area? Does the WWF's version of "saving" equal "saving" for the people who live in Brazil and South America? The two should not be incompatible, but there is very little mention of Brazil, its people, or its politics on this website. There is a paragraph about the Juruena National Park, the Tumucumaque region, the history of these places, and the efforts of the WWF to educate the public about them. Yet apart from the mention of a "government official" who works with four German members of the WWF, it is almost as though the national borders of Brazil do not exist. Instead, some mythical land—what name could be better than "Ecosia"?—is superimposed upon its national boundaries and somehow manages to supersede them. The aesthetics of the first phase of Ecosia only compounded this disconnect, and I shall now turn to this aspect of the site.

In its first year of operation, the image on the Ecosia home page was always the same, a dense green jungle with absolutely no trace of human activity. Set against an antiseptic white background, this version of Ecosia's home page had the appearance of a sterile office environment with a small window that happened to look out at South American jungle. One could almost hear the monkeys, see the macaws. It was a lovely view, but not a wholly innocent one. Aesthetics never are. It fostered spectatorship but did little to encourage connection.

The evolving aesthetics of the search engine suggests that Ecosia is working to move away from this image. In the current second phase, a new design reflects new partnerships, a greater attempt at transparency, and a livelier home page. Yet its initial window is still synecdochic of a troubling power relation that has pervaded conservation aesthetics for a hundred years. Both *(Lil) Green Patch* and Ecosia, in that they offer Western interventions into Latin American spaces, perpetuate an aesthetics of colonialism. Second, in that the conserved space is quite separate from the users that are working to conserve it, it separates human activity from natural spaces, and hence falls prey to the alluring, lonely aesthetics of conservation. Rather than man and nature coexisting in an integrated whole, conservation aesthetics removes humanity from the picture. Here is the spectator, there is the observed. One is the viewing subject, the other the vulnerable object. For its genealogy in this context, consider the literary genre that, perhaps more than any other aesthetic form, brought the splendors of the South American rain forests to the global attention: *la novela de la selva.*

Green Mansions, Pixel Forests

The *novela de la selva*—Spanish for "novel of the jungle" or "novel of the forest"—is the name given to a cluster of novels written in the early to mid-twentieth century that take place in the Amazon rain forest. These works express a remarkable set of tensions between humanity and nature, colonizer and colonized, man and woman, civilization and "savagery," that can still be seen in conservation aesthetics today. Works in this genre include William Henry Hudson's *Green Mansions* (1904), Jose Eustasio Rivera's *La vorágine* (1924), Romulo Gallegos' *Canaima* (1935), and Alejo Carpentier's *Los pasos perdidos* (1953). Hudson's *Green Mansions* remains one of the most popular. Published in 1904, *Green Mansions* is the story of a white European man living in the jungles of Venezuela who stumbles upon the last survivor of a white, bird-like race of people. Her name is Rima. Rima's skin has an iridescent sheen, and her garments are spun from spider silk. The novel is both a mystery and a romance; it details the search for Rima's mysterious origins and chronicles the narrator as he falls in love with her and the world she represents, a fantastical world within which humanity and nature enjoy unity.

On first read, perhaps, *Green Mansions* is a compelling fairy tale, one that offers a delicious, eroticized portrayal of the jungle as a magic space whose sole "natural" inhabitant—that is, Rima—must be protected from industry, culture, and other signs of modern progress. And Rima herself, so mythic in manner and appearance, has much in common with the ancient notion of the genius loci, the spirit of a place embodied both in Roman mythology and in the verses of Alexander Pope: "Consult the genius of the place in all; / That tells the waters or to rise, or fall" (57–58). But the genii locorum in ancient times were also fundamental for solidifying property lines. They referred to spiritual guardians who dwelled in specific natural spaces, but they also took the form of statues, placed strategically as markers indicating who owned what, as well as where the boundaries of ownership extended. These figures marked property at every conceivable level of ownership, including the very small (one's garden), the less small (one's estate), the large (the region), and the Empire (Caesar's own genius loci, *genius Augusti*, encompassed all of the above [Woolf, 251]). And it is along these lines of ownership, trespass, and property rights that Rima, and *Green Mansions*, should be read.

Critics have situated *Green Mansions* within a variety of literary traditions, including romanticism (Fletcher), as a retelling of "Lady Morgon's novel, *The Missionary*" (Baker), and, most recently and in my view most convincingly, as a tale of postcolonialism and attendant problems concerning race, gender, and the way nature was and remains configured along these same problematic lines. Hudson himself embodies some of these latter tensions. Born in Argentina to European parents, he left South America in 1874, relocated to England, and wrote *Green Mansions* in English. In spite of the novel's problematic expression of Latin American "nature," it remains influential in our conception of jungle spaces. As Maria Helena Rueda eloquently asks of these "green mansions" of the *novela de la selva* in general, "How today can we talk about that imaginary and distorted jungle, in appearance so removed from the real jungle and yet nevertheless so determining in our perception of it?" (31). In spite of the difficulty inherent in sifting facts from fiction, especially when fiction has contributed so problematically to real-world exploitation, Rueda states the matter clearly when she writes that the *novela de la selva* "on the whole holds a very concrete and precise place and time in the history of the region: the slingshot exploitation of the Amazon basins and the Orinoco during the first years of the twentieth century. This is its setting and origin" (31). *Green Mansions* conforms to this fraught history of representation, offering, on the one hand, a compelling portrayal of the South American jungle as a site of beauty that must be protected and, on the other, a troubling suggestion about who must do the saving (the colonizers), as well as who, precisely, it must be protected from (its native inhabitants). Accordingly, such works function as sites saturated with late-nineteenth-century imperial impulse. As one critic puts it, the Latin American jungles in "W.H. Hudson's *Green Mansions* (1904) are the literary manifestation of a longed-for but never fulfilled desire centered on the lands not colonized by the British empire, and therefore even more mysterious and fascinating to British eyes" (Brazzelli n.p.).

It is tempting to write these works off as outdated conveyers of a tainted Western aesthetic, but to do so would be a mistake. The aesthetics that come from them are still with us today, even if residually, via accretion: "Composed in ever-widening circles, further and further removed from any originary 'essence' of what it is attempting to represent" (Wylie 179). It is important to be aware of these residual tendencies if we wish to see them challenged.

Journey to "Amazonia"

The tropes of *la novela de la selva* become especially conspicuous with educational games that purport to inform young players about natural resources and the importance of conserving them. Such games highlight the importance of natural landscapes and take pains to educate children about biodiversity. In *Journey to Amazonia*, a Flash-based game created by PBS, the object is to learn facts about animals and plants of the Orinoco basin. As the player learns the rules of the game, however, the narrative that frames the educational fact-finding mission reveals allegiance to the postcolonial aesthetics embodied in Ecosia and *Green Mansions*: "Welcome, adventurer! You are Sam Smith, natural historian extraordinaire. The American Museum of Natural History, based in Washington, D.C., is sending you to the Amazon on a mission of exploration. Scientists at the museum have been unable to answer pressing questions about the environment. It is up to you to explore the Amazon basin and return with the answers that the museum researchers need. Are you up to the challenge?" (*Journey*). The game favors the approach of the Choose Your Own Adventure! franchise, which features androgynous children on the covers of its books so as to appeal to both boys and girls. Sam Smith follows suit. With an androgynous look and a name common to both sexes, it might be difficult to determine if Sam is a girl or a boy, but he or she is certainly white, young, and North American. Amazonia Explorer follows the trope of the white explorer journeying to an unknown continent in order to glean information about its environmental treasures, down to the very common appearance of the red line of an airplane flying over a parchment map, from D.C. to Brazil in two seconds flat.

In the brief fact-finding mission presented in Amazonia, the explorer interacts with three parts of the jungle's ecosystem: its canopies, its rivers, and its forest floors. Each place offers appealing drawings of different creatures, and by clicking on these the young explorer gets valuable information. I did not know, for example, that the Amazon jungle sloth rests up to 80 percent each day, nor did I know that the harpy eagle is strong enough to fly away with—in order to eat—an adult monkey. Yet I do know that these animals, as appealing as their cartoon avatars make them out to be, do not exist in isolation from each other, the jungle, or the larger cultural context of the region, including the Brazilians and Amerindians who live there. This interpenetration between cultures is sorely missing in educational games that purport to teach children about conservation. While in some ways providing a laudable educational goal, such games nevertheless evoke the entire continent of South America as unknown, remote, and full of a frightening and uncivilized alterity. Conservation is not an outdated pursuit but the postcolonial aesthetic that informs it should be. It is important to save the rain forest, but not to retain postcolonial mythology about what this culturally and environmentally precious region constitutes.[7] Insofar as games such as *LGP*, search engines such as Ecosia, and educational online quests such as PBS' *Amazonia* and Green Peace's "Ecoquests" continue to separate conservation from human activity and to present natural ecologies as beautiful spectacles rather than as complex systems coextensive with different human civilizations and cultures, they fall prey to the troubling legacy of colonialism, a specter that still haunts conservation aesthetics today.

I have focused upon the conservation of land, but conservation also refers to a spectrum of environmental practice that focuses on energy conservation and the protection of limited resources. Green games are also turning up in this important sector of environmental practice. Digital technologies, drawing from video games or taking their cue from game-like environments, are also intervening in this latter type of conservation, which is to say consumer-side conservation within the domestic sphere.

Welcome to the Green House: Science Fiction, Conservation, and the Future of Domestic Space

In the realm of environmental activism, the commandment to "think globally, act locally" functions as a powerful and persistent mantra. What could be more "local" than the space of one's home? Energy-saving appliances, ecologically friendly insulation, and "green" electricity all promise to make the home a more efficient space for living. Yet these same labor-saving devices and processes have also been associated with the troubling side effect of social alienation. In the history of dystopian fiction the "smart home" has been envisioned as a model of conservation but has also served to disconnect its inhabitants from the real world. Instead of operating in cooperation with a larger global community for a greater, greener good, they can cut their inhabitants off from society—global, local, or otherwise. Smart homes in such fictions are linked to the conservation of energy and precious resources, but also to individualism, labor, and the dark side of liberal humanism. They have tended to pervert nature, produce anxiety about subjective boundaries, and isolate their inhabitants from the rest of the world. But that was then. In the following section, I argue that contemporary smart houses have the potential to turn this tendency around by democratizing conservation efforts. Shaspa's "smart home" and Byron Reeves' so-called *World of Greencraft* are concept pieces that imagine virtual gaming environments that would allow consumers to have more control over resource management remotely, through an interactive digital interface. Both works help us imagine an aspect of home-based conservation that has not yet been realized and that encourages individual consumers to make their consumption a matter of social action and common concern.

The Happylife Home

In *Welcome to the Dreamhouse: Popular Media and Postwar Suburbs*, Lynn Spigel analyzes fantasies of domestic spaces as they manifest in various forms within the post–World War II cultural imagination—advertisements, television programs, films, and cartoons. Her analysis includes some of the most iconic expressions of futuristic abodes, including Epcot Center and Tomorrowland. These postwar fantasies of future houses promise more individual freedom for homeowners, offering "a self-sufficient and sentient space that satisfies all the needs of its residents" (385). From the living rooms of the *Jetsons* to Buckminster Fuller's vision of the Dymaxion house as a "machine for living," what all such spaces hold in common is their promise to save time and energy. Even the Flintstones live in a dream house. Their prehistoric abode in Bedrock is equipped with pterodactyl-run can openers and other time-saving appliances because, after all, they are a "*modern* stone-age family." In other words, such houses speak to the individual consumer, configuring, as Spigel puts it, a vision of "technological progress based on nostalgic longings for privacy, property, and propriety" (385).

The troubling consequence of such devices, and the conservative architecture of the domestic structures that house them, is that while they might save *individual* labor, concerns for the community tend to go right out the (presumably automated) backdoor. Far from envisioning a societal approach to conservation, the structure of the "house of tomorrow" imagined in postwar America promises the opposite: "an insular design that fails to imagine a future for the community" (385). In addition to the real-world spaces Spigel describes, any number of science fiction narratives could be rallied to support this thesis. In the cinematic adaption of Dean R. Koontz' *Demon Seed*, an artificial intelligence takes over a networked house in a wealthy California suburb in order to impregnate Julie Christie with its metallic progeny. The film is a dystopian parable that warns about granting too much agency to the place where one resides.[8]

One of the most interesting aspects of Spigel's thesis is that the inward-turning architecture of the smart home pervades the domestic spaces of *both* utopian and dystopian narratives, fiercely guarding the boundaries between private and public without caring one whit for the community at large. She discusses the cultural expressions of alienation that such homes embody but does not touch on the way conservation aesthetics in general enters into the picture. Two stories not included in Spigel's analysis offer related lessons about smart house technology in the cultural imagination and help crystallize my claim that dystopian works have prepared a negative poetics for technology's relation to the environment: Ray Bradbury's "The Veldt" (1951) and "There Will Come Soft Rains" (1950).

"The Veldt" expresses the smart home's sinister agency, its ability to alienate its inhabitants from the outside world and each other. The process of estrangement is coupled with the house's conservative, energy-saving procedures. In the story, a couple of the future—as Bradbury in the 1950s imagined the future would unfold—named George and Lydia Hadley have recently moved into a fully automated "HappyLife" home that does everything for them. It cooks and cleans and raises their children. We quickly learn that instead of making the Hadleys happier, the house has made them feel ill at ease and restless. "Maybe I don't have enough to do," Lydia speculates. "Maybe I have time to think too much" (9). They recognize that the house is compromising their sanity and after some debate Mr. Hadley takes action: "He marched about the house turning off the voice clocks, the stoves, the heaters, the shoe shiners, the shoe lacers, the body scrubbers and swabbers and massagers, and every other machine he could put his hand to" (17).

This list of appliances suggests just how totally the Hadleys have turned themselves over to the mechanized order of the "HappyLife." The shutting off of the house comes with an epiphany for the adults: "We've been contemplating our mechanical, electronic navels for too long. My God, how we need a breath of honest air!" (17). This "breath of honest air" is exactly what the house deprives them of, and their isolation from the outside world is visited upon the reader. Readers never see the house from the outside or anything outside its walls at all. The third-person perspective also creates the feeling of watching the Hadleys within this space, rather than depicting them as free agents whose actions unfold via choices over time. Even though the Hadleys at this point seem well on their way to escaping the anxious atmosphere of their home, one has the feeling that the rivalry is not quite settled, that the house isn't done with them yet.

The children's nursery is attuned to the wishes of the children; it simulates their desires, however perverse. In terms of its functioning it predates, for example, the Holodeck and the "Project Genesis" from the *Star Trek* franchise, as well as any number of science fiction narratives that have cordoned off spaces *from* nature for the creation *of* nature. When they tell their children of the plan to turn off the house, the children balk. Even when George tries to persuade his son, Peter, that leaving the house will give him opportunities to do things for himself, to learn to be independent, Peter responds with a resounding negative: "No, it would be horrid. . . . I don't want to do anything but look and listen and smell; what else is there to do?" (14). Peter's sentiment suggests another sinister feature of the HappyLife Home. Not only does it cut off its inhabitants from the outside world, it acculturates them to its processes. Peter and Wendy have surrendered to its ministrations. The house has *naturalized* for the children the mechanical and artificial existence that the adult Hadleys find so *un*natural. Ironically, the children retreat instead to the house's simulations of natural spaces, which are contrasted to the real nature that the children refuse to visit. The house creates two disturbing visions of nature. The first is an African veldt where lions roam and violently feed. The second is a South American jungle: "a green, lovely forest, a lovely river, a purple mountain, high voices singing, and Rima, lovely and mysterious, lurking in the trees with colorful flights of butterflies . . . singing a song so beautiful that it brought tears to your eyes" (12–13). As with *Green Mansions*, the wild places that the nursery creates can be read as symptomatic of colonial desires, containing, confining, and making into a spectacle of entertainment places of colonial interest and expressing too a fear that the containment will not hold, that with the real lions the real Africa will emerge violently from within the modern space that contains it. But in the context of the Happylife Home's simulated natural spaces, neither the colonizer nor the colonized emerges victorious. The house itself comes out on top. By the time their parents are killed by the lions in the veldt, the children have already rehearsed their deaths many times.[9]

Bradbury's "There Will Come Soft Rains" offers a complementary set of lessons about domestic spaces. It details a day in the (non)life of another automated home of the future, which calls out each of its duties, regular as clockwork: "*Nine-fifteen*, sang the clock, *time to clean* . . . *Ten o'clock*. The sun came out from behind the rain . . . *Ten-fifteen*. The garden sprinklers whirled up in golden founts, filling the soft morning air with scatterings of brightness" (206). This initial cheerful tone of efficiency shifts quickly to horror: the inhabitants of this house have all died, their shadows burned into the walls as a result of a nuclear holocaust: "The entire west face of the house was black, save for five places. Here the silhouette in paint of a man mowing a lawn. Here, as in a photograph, a woman bent to pick flowers. Still farther over, their images burned on wood in one titanic instant, a small boy, hands flung into the air; higher up, the image of a thrown ball, and opposite him a girl, hands raised to catch a ball which never came down. The five spots of paint—the man, the woman, the children, the ball—remained. The rest was a thin charcoaled layer" (206). Stripped of its occupants, the house reveals its mania for repelling the outside. In the following passage the house anxiously continues to maintain control over its perimeter, keeping the natural world at bay: "How well the house had kept its peace. How carefully it had inquired 'Who goes there? What's the password?' and, getting no answer from lonely foxes and whining cats, it had shut up its windows . . . [a] self-protection which bordered on a mechanical paranoia" (206). The sentient house does not mourn; instead, it offers a lesson in humility in terms of humanity's provisional role within a larger natural ecology. The title of the story takes its name from a poem by Sara Teasdale of the same title, which describes how nature would "react" if humankind were to perish in such a scenario: "Not one would mind, neither bird nor tree, if mankind perished utterly; And Spring herself, when she woke at dawn / Would scarcely know that we were gone" (10–14). This poem illustrates how dystopian fiction, including Bradbury's story, imagines conservation's failure. As a species, we will fail, and only after our disappearance from the earth will nature take on its fullest potential. Then, and only then, will a new Adam and a new Eve enter into its green forests in order, most likely, to reclaim it, repopulate it, and reconquer it. There are many stories of such recovery, where the last remnants of humanity return after millennia encased in bubbles (*Logan's Run*), asleep in stasis (*Alien, Red Dwarf*), or underground (*THX-1138, Sexmission*). The powerful moments of emergence in science fiction are figured as entries into a new Eden, which is not a new Earth but an Earth finally healed after human-caused destruction. Such moments suggest that this cycle of consumption and human dominion will unfold in the same way as in the

Biblical tale, which is to say *badly*, and that this destructive cycle will continue, ad infinitum.

The Queen of Games

The tradition of the sinister smart house as a space that closes in rather than reaches out persisted through the twentieth century.[10] Given the poor marks that smart houses have received in these fictions past and present, it is no wonder that we might be suspicious of new technologies that claim to turn the smart house around—or, rather, inside out, to make it extend its effort *outward* instead of frantically attempting to control its interior. And yet several trends in digital technology are promising to do just this.

A pioneer in this arena is Jane McGonigal, the wildly popular cultural critic and game designer, whose sobriquet became "The Queen of Games" after her TED talk in 2010 on the topic of collaborative gaming practices and socially motivated problem-solving. In this talk she notes that "the planet spends 3 billion hours a week gaming" and suggests that "if we want to solve problems like hunger, poverty, climate change, global conflict and obesity . . . that number should balloon to 21 billion" (qtd. in Feiler). McGonigal's games foreground community. In her critically acclaimed *EVOKE*, for example, which was sponsored by the World Bank Institute, teams of players band together to fight social and environmental problems, including those mentioned above. In her post-mortem of *EVOKE*, McGonigal writes that the social aspects of the game were planned for and mostly successful: "We made it social. Early versions of *EVOKE* were decidedly unsocial. We amped up the engagement factor massively by employing social media . . . and social networking. . . . Players were never in it alone; they were in it together, and could be inspired and helped by others" (McGonigal, "blog"). But this popularity came with a cost. In the same document, she notes that "The 20,000-person social environment was overwhelming, and 'super-motivated' players drowned out other strong players who would have shone more in smaller social contexts. Furthermore, our completely open environment was too inviting for trolls and griefers" (McGonigal, "blog"). McGonigal's emphasis on social action is key. But what her games have yet to do is map gameplay directly upon real-world locations. In *EVOKE*, she targets Africa, but within the frame of a graphic novel. Similarly, in *World without Oil*, she outlines a scenario in which players need to figure out how they will survive when the oil shortage hits and catastrophe ensues. These are important, educational games that inspire environmental awareness and conservation in ways that are far more sophisticated, from a literary-aesthetic perspective, than either *LGP* or *Amazonia*. Yet playing them does not result in any clear bottom line in terms of real-world, *site-specific* conservation, at least not yet.[11] Several other games, however, are promising to do just this.

The World of Greencraft

In 2008, Stanford University sponsored a conference on the topic of "Behavior, Energy, and Climate Change." At a panel entitled "Multiplayer games, Virtual worlds and Energy Efficiency," Byron Reeves, a professor of communication at Stanford, introduced a small film with large implications for conservation in the domestic sphere. Just under two minutes long, the film documents a concept for a Massively Multiplayer Online Role-Playing Game (MMORPG) that would allow domestic consumers to compete against each other in a virtual gaming environment that looks something like a cross between *The World of Warcraft* and *The Sims*. Unlike other MMORPGs, however, the objective is not the fun of gaming itself, nor the glory of conquest, nor even, as it so often is with *The Sims*, the heady feeling of panoptic, God-like control over one's *Sim*-ian civilizations and subjects. The objective of Reeves' untitled demo is real-world, community-based conservation.[12] Given the massive popularity of online games, Reeves wagers that online conservation play has the potential to make saving energy a group effort: "There are known ingredients for great games and many of them can be seen in the video (for example; timely feedback, self-representation with avatars, transparent reputations, an economy with points and currency, and collaboration on competitive teams). The purpose of the movie is to explore the use of successful ingredients in virtual worlds and games that will change energy use behavior" (Reeves).

World of Greencraft (*WOGC*) begins with a nod to the global-to-local ethos of environmental action, starting with a picture of earth, a blue-green globe as seen from outer space, before we begin to zoom, Google Earth style, into the North American continent, to Michigan, and, finally, to the local, street-level surface of west-central Michigan, maybe Mt. Pleasant. We land before a two-story suburban home, complete with brick facing, white window treatments, and a two-car garage. Once here, in the heart of the American Midwest, the woman who owns the home appears in a corner window of the screen and begins talking about how she uses "smart meters" to keep track of her energy consumption. "Smart meters are like regular electricity meters," she explains, "except they can tell me just how much energy I'm consuming, any time online." In addition to smart meter interfaces online and through handheld mobile devices, the Smart Meter is hooked up to a virtual replica of the same home. "My smart meter connects me to a virtual home that gives me detailed information about how my house is consuming energy." At this point, the demo switches to a virtual world, complete with a virtual avatar of the real-world home. Here, the woman, now an avatar walking through her virtual home, demonstrates how the Smart Meter functions. As she walks through a large kitchen, little text bubbles pop up on the screen, filled with tips about energy conservation in the home: "save over $100 per year with compact florescent bulbs," "microwaves use 50% less energy than ovens." So far, this is fairly consistent with how one might imagine the Happylife Home to be marketed, which is to say as an energy- and money-saving technology for the individual consumer. Even the aesthetics are the same—once we are in the home we have no access to the outside. All of the monitors point toward individual consumption. Yet the next phase of the demo changes the game: "And then the real challenge begins, because the smart meters let everyone see just how much energy we're using and play a really fun game to compete to make our homes that much greener, because in this world the only way to improve your virtual home is to lower the energy usage in your real one. . . . When saving energy and the environment is this fun, everyone wants to do it" (Reeves). Now we leave the confines of the house and retreat to the street view, in order to witness how well other members of this neighborhood are conserving their energy. When someone does well, we see green status updates, complete with positive points attached. Conversely, when someone does poorly, red squares flag the screen, negative number points flashing within. In addition to the points updates, a game interface frames the screen, complete with conservation points, a tally of money saved via smart conservation choices, and shifting game ranks, which include "Global Protector," "Green Warrior," and "Eco Maniac." At this point the conservation potential, in terms of community, seems most palpable and most game-like. The spirit of community-driven competition comes through clearly, creating a vivid snapshot of what such a game could look like, as well as all the energy conservation it might foster. The game is easy to play, drives home a point, and offers clear incentives for lowering energy consumption in the home, and hence, like *(Lil) Green Patch*, affects a real-world location. It costs no money, and there is no reference to ad-revenue-driven content. It connects personal responsibility to a larger whole, encourages community play, and offers practical tips that yield financial incentives for conservation.

Yet intentionally or not, the game design suggests affluent denizens of suburban neighborhoods. The house is modestly appointed on the outside, but its spacious interior displays many signs of upper-middle-class existence:

a stainless steel refrigerator, endless counter space, the island table, the cappuccino machine, and something that could be either an espresso maker or an electron microscope. The halls of this home are empty, void of life, and strangely reminiscent of the way the Happylife Home of "The Veldt" was imagined both in Bradbury's short story and in 1960s television: antiseptic, white, slightly perverse. So far, this vision is not doing much to counter the idea of the smart house as something that isolates its occupants. Indeed, at the moment we transition from real-world space to virtual space, a curious event occurs.

In the virtual world, the neighbors disappear. As this is supposed to be a community game, one would hope that the real-world application would remedy this. A second troubling thing about the game is how it color-codes conservation. The neighborhood it virtualizes is predominantly white. We see one avatar of a darker hue who walks fairly quickly down the otherwise white-inhabited streets, even looking over his shoulder a few times, as if afraid to slow down.[13] Even more puzzling in a game about responsible resource management, the color green itself signifies success. In the real world, the xeriscaped house that uses native plants that work well with the natural vagaries of local climate and local weather is the one that should be awarded points, regardless of color. In this game, however, the greener one's plants, and the more of them one has, the better. At one moment, our narrator points condescendingly at her neighbor's house, which is barren, ill-kempt, and promptly awarded −14 efficiency points. Barren and ill-kempt it may be, but it is not using valuable water to keep it that way.[14] This conflation of surface appearance and conservation is problematic and pervasive within popular culture. A game that attempts to educate and conserve would do well to start by blowing such a problematic premise out of the water.

The treatment of water is representative of the larger problems with the game's aesthetics. No one seems to be getting negative points for driving cars. A well-known fact about cars and the expenditure of fossil fuels that is necessary to drive them is that they are a cause of global warming. Here in this world, however, cars drive along as a part of the background, not participating in the game. In a game that purports to be about energy conservation, this is a large oversight. Another troubling component about this prototype is that it lacks any self-reflexive reckoning of its own energy consumption. One can access the smart meter "online, at home, and on the go," which means that whenever the consumer looks at his or her conservation stats, he or she is using a whole network of costly technology to do so—not merely costly in terms of the financial price of maintaining them, which is significant, but in terms of the energy it costs to run them. As an article in the *Guardian* put it, although the precise energy costs of using the Internet are hard to pin down, we have a general sense of the order of magnitude: "A lot—although exactly how much is still not clear. . . . The energy footprint of the entire Internet is much more than data centres—it includes the devices we consume the Internet on (computers, mobile phones, iPods and more) as well as the telephone exchanges that deliver information" (Johnson, Bobby). Finally, it smacks of surveillance (watching each other, literally monitoring each other), of shame-based education (spotlighting underperforming houses), and of covetousness, in that it takes "keeping up with the Joneses" to a new extreme ("Finally," the avatar says triumphantly, "I can beat my neighbor Frank at something").

By highlighting these issues I don't mean to dismiss the game. Rather, this is a good time for critique, when the game exists not yet as calcified and mass-produced but as a prototype for the what-could-be. This is an entirely possible game. The desire to be green has never had more cultural cachet, the technology is here, and these efforts to take home energy conservation outside of the home and into the community are absolutely exciting.

Consider Shaspa, a UK-based company cofounded by Oliver Goh. Shaspa employs a suite of tools known as the "OpenShaspa Home Energy Kit," which consists of a remotely accessible interface, a customizable "bridge" between real life (RL) and virtually real (VR) homes, coordinated by an impressively extensive set of online schematics. Shaspa offers "monitoring, analysis, automation and smart control" home technology designed to "improve efficiency, lower costs and reduce environmental impact." A contender for the "Serious Games" competition in the United Kingdom, which "seeks for innovative uses of technology to address key social issues such as Climate Change, Health and Sustainability," the "Shaspa Social Energy Game" marks the next step in the evolution of energy conservation that Reeves' demo initiates. This game is more of a slideshow presentation than a full-fledged demo, but the technology that would run such a game is already in action: "While in Hong Kong on a business trip recently, Oliver Goh was on his laptop playing around in a virtual world when he realized he'd left the water running in his home back in Switzerland. He noticed this because the virtual world contained a recreation of his Swiss residence that pulled information about the home's energy and water consumption in real time. The gauge that measures water use was blinking. No problem: After his avatar hit the right button, the real-world water valve in Switzerland turned off" (Au). There are any number of smart home technologies that have emerged on the popular market that allow consumers to monitor and control their houses remotely. The android app for Rogers Smart Home Monitoring, for example, is viable and popular, and Google Nest is poised to do what Google does best, namely, take over an emerging market and crush the competition. Yet these applications lack the social dimension that *WOGC* and Shaspa offer. There's a financial incentive to conserve, to be sure, in terms of lowering the cost of energy, but there is no game if you are playing only against yourself. In some ways, as smart as they are, such companies are doubling down on a game of environmental solitaire, serving up yet another version of the Happylife Home with its attendant features of alienation and class-consciousness. A satirical vision of this technology appears in Chuck Palahniuk's novel *Damned*. In it, the main character, a teenage girl, reports from hell: "The closest way I can describe death is to compare it to when mom boots up her notebook computer and hacks into the surveillance system of our house in Mazatlan or Banff. 'Look,' she'd say, turning the screen sideways for me to see, 'it's snowing.' . . . Hunched over her computer screen, she'd sigh . . . hitting her Control and L keys to lock a maid inside a bathroom from three continents away because the tile didn't look adequately polished" (1–2). For the smart home to succeed, it must be communal. Consensus requires community dialog. What Shaspa offers, however, is an attempt to make the conservation of domestic energy a social affair. Like the *WOGC*, Shaspa offers remote access to a digital interface to control energy consumption in the home, refers to a real-world location, and gestures toward community. This angle is not nearly as developed as it is in Reeves' game, at least not yet, but it is possible. But for these visions to be successful, some kind of community needs to form around them. In that both *WOGC* and Shaspa target wealthy homeowners, both run the risk of ignoring a much broader audience that could include environmental activists, gamers, and technophiles. This is the audience that the popular cultural critic and game designer Jane McGonigal has been cultivating for the past decade.

Bringing Nature Home

Community-driven, digitally enabled conservation marks a new cultural strategy for environmental action. Through community building and game play, digital technology is already intervening, every day, in this discourse. Its intervention is often positive, often problematic, but always provocative. On the whole, such sites offer productive strategies for community action that have yet to be fully tapped for their crowd-sourcing potential. The games I have highlighted have a complicated relationship with the real-world spaces they attempt to conserve/preserve. Like many works of art, these games are mapped upon real-world locations. A key difference, however, is that in these works, the game map has the potential to become or confuse the territory it models. This may sound like a dystopian exaggeration that takes the postmodern prophecies of Baudrillard (via Borges) too seriously, and perhaps in some ways it is. Yet before dismissing the powerful influence digital maps wield over the territories they model, one might consider that in 2010 the neighboring Central American countries of Costa Rica and Nicaragua almost came to military blows when Costa Rican officials noted that the Google Maps' depiction of their borders favored Nicaragua's interpretation of a disputed boundary: "Costa Rica called on Google Wednesday to fix its satellite map, which indicates the disputed land belongs to Nicaragua. That prompted Nicaragua's foreign ministry to write Google on Thursday, telling the company the map is fine the way it is and not to touch a thing" (Rogers). In spite of judicial decisions in 2011, 2012, and 2013, the issue is not yet wholly resolved, awaiting further adjudication from the International Court of Justice in The Hague. The Google Maps–fueled land dispute is symptomatic of the increasing interpenetration between virtual landscapes and the real-world places they depict, as well as the confusion that such interpenetration can cause.

The games considered in this section see conservation as a community effort. They reconsider the boundaries between different nations and organizations, as well as the ontological realms of virtual and real. Finally, as a result of the first and second, they can offer an alternative model of conservation aesthetics. Although such sites are not a replacement for traditional, grassroots activism, they have the potential to extend the roots of the grass to a much wider field.

Coda

Self, System, Ecosystem

> Ones and zeroes bleeding mesa noise
> And when you're empty there's so much space for them
> You turn it off but then a still small voice
> Comes in blazing from some vast horizon
>
> —Josh Ritter, "Monster Ballads" (2006)

The preceding chapters have outlined four strategies of aesthetic engagement that bring together natural and digital ecologies: coding, collapsing, corresponding, conserving. Focusing upon each, one at a time, has allowed me to demonstrate its effects in clearer relief than if I had considered them all at once. If object-oriented ontology and Actor-Network-Theory teach us anything, however, it is that nothing occurs in isolation. These techniques are no exception; there is an important way that each work engages with all four, albeit to varying degrees. Char Davies' *Osmose* uses coding to create a world that is continuous with the natural world but also speaks to collapsing, calling into question any rigid sense of perimeter about the human body, since it is the body's breath that drives one's progress through the installation. In that legible signs form a part of this landscape (code, words, graphs, and grids), it also gestures toward correspondence. And in that it fosters a sense of inclusion and immersion rather than spectatorship and isolation, it challenges traditional notions of conservation as I have cast the term. The same applies for *Agrippa*. It, too, incorporates codework as a primary aesthetic motif, but the codework both expresses and hides its literary treasures, blurring the boundaries between medial forms—books, diskettes, aquatints—and resonates well with collapsing. In the poem, which highlights nature's power to signify with virtually every life-threatening epiphany, correspondence is key. Moreover, in that natural forces intervene in human affairs, both on private and public scales, the poem challenges the lonely aesthetics of conservation. The *Empress & Hierophant* simulation, which works so well to collapse the boundaries of human—and literary—forms, makes use of coding at every level of engagement; and in that one can make use of this code to imbue objects within the landscape with functions and objectives, it also speaks to correspondence. Because it encourages one to see one's self as a part of the simulation rather than as a spectator along the lines of Caspar David Friedrich's solitary "Wanderer," it also fosters a vision of landscape that is inclusive and social, challenging traditional conservation aesthetics. In chapter 3, *slippingglimpse* demonstrates the willful way that nature communicates, as well as how digital technology and poetics help make that communication manifest. When it blurs the boundary lines between human language and natural patterns, documenting, for example, the pain of the flax as it becomes woven into fabric, it also speaks to the fluid nature of material forms. When it superimposes human language upon the Atlantic Ocean's stormy waves, it, again, puts human sign systems in relation to natural forces and disrupts an isolationist aesthetics. Chapter 4 demonstrates how *(Lil) Green Patch* made overt challenges to conservation as commonly conceived, pushing it to be social and communal, even taking into account its problems with transparency; at the same time, coding, as we saw, was fundamental to its financial success, built in to the back-end of the site, in the form of incentive advertising. In that the game was community oriented rather than competitive, it helped to collapse traditional features of gameplay. And because it attempted to "speak" to its players on behalf of the garden patches that they maintained, it resonated well with correspondence.

Each of these works fleshes out the idea of a networked model of nature constituted via human, animal, technological, and environmental agents. Such works challenge overtly traditional models of subject formation and nudge something that was once expressed via mimesis, mythology, and metaphor into startling ontological terrain. As much as is gained by thinking of ourselves as members of collective networks, natural and elsewise, I should like to comment briefly upon what is lost. Such works of art demote the notion of human sovereignty. They foreground how we are always already constituted by the objects and processes around us, just as we help constitute them. Lacan, Deleuze, Guattari, and Derrida all describe versions of subjectivity that are multiple, fragmented, decentered, irrational, and socially constituted, whose mode of being is one of process rather than one of purpose or *telos* or spiritual purity. And yet even the most radical writing within postructuralist theory is still predicated upon the notion of a subject, however troubled. The distinction between a subject and an object permeates Western aesthetics. When one views a painting, the categories of subject and object are maintained. One might have an experience of the painting, of course. One might feel immersed within the frescoes that decorate the villa of Herculaneum or feel excited by the rushing, painted waters of Valley Forge. One might contemplate the glyphs of Joan Miró and feel weightlessness at the sight of Marc Chagall's floating bride. One's perceptual field might be challenged, pierced, and outright changed, but the art that does the changing remains the same. One might participate in its interpretation, its exegesis, and therefore change the way others perceive it and act as a mediator of the work or a speaker for its truths. But the art and its viewer remain separated by the discreet ontological categories of subject and object. The works that I have explored in *Animal, Vegetable, Digital* help challenge these distinctions, but they mark only the beginning of what I anticipate will be an avalanche of digitally enabled aesthetic experiences that foreground natural, ecological concerns.

The so-called Internet of Things, MakerBot's "ThingVerse," and Google's Nest initiative are all poised to help make connections between ourselves, the built environment, and natural ecologies extensive and seamless, and many artists are leaping at the opportunities that these initiatives offer. Marina Zurkow's *Mesocosm*, for example, is a dynamic, digitally animated landscape that expresses a real-world site of fragility: "a large sinkhole—the 'Wink Sink 2' located on private oil company property in the small Texas town of Wink"—that "boils, gushes, flows and expels objects: plastic bags, oil and dark clouds that whirl out of the sinkhole's vortex in ghostly choreography" (Zurkow). Michelle Higa Fox's *Strandlines* "is an art installation that . . . uses light projections that mimic the ebb and flow of local tides in Rhode Island. No two projections are the same and the digital tides flow onto an actual sand bed" (Cieskowski); in Random International's *Rain Room* installation, "participants are encouraged to walk through sheets of falling water while 3D cameras track their movements and positions. Sensors then disable the falling water from touching the participants moving in the Rain Room, creating an effect of being in rain while not being able to touch actual water" (Cieskowski).[1] There are many more projects that, like these, blend digital aesthetics and environmental poetics in productive ways that I have not had space to consider. The interested reader may visit this book's companion website, http://animalvegetabledigital.com, which provides references, notes, links, and images.

Such projects do not exist without direct intervention from their audience. There is no art "object" available for "contemplation." The only way these pieces function is through embodied interaction, experience, action, and immersion. Instead, the "subject" enters—and hence cocreates—the space of the piece and functions as an object within a larger system. What is gained in art works such as the ones that I have described here is a new type of access to objects, to nature, and to other consciousnesses. This access affords not only a way in but also a way to join, to link, to share experience. In sum, the gain outweighs the loss.

In keeping with Latour's attempts to think about knowledge paradigms that are not tethered to modern epistemology, I have considered how the strategies I've highlighted have a history that spans eons and epistemes. Object-oriented ontology and ANT, as well, in their very desire to challenge distinctions between subjects and objects, are similarly working within an ancient historical tradition. Their slogan—"the centaur of classical metaphysics shall be mated with the cheetah of actor-network theory"—speaks in a tongue-in-cheek manner to this commitment.

In *The Symposium*, Socrates (via Diotima) "wins" the debate about the true nature of love, likening it to a ladder that leads away from the physical world to the transcendent world of forms and intellect. But Socrates' victory makes sense only when one remembers that Plato is the one doing the judging. From an OOO and ANT perspective, it is Aristophanes who emerges as the clear champion, here and always. His vision of early humans as sphere-shaped, eight-limbed, multi-sexed, cartwheeling androgyns provides a fantastic vision of human origin. Their identities are always shared, partial, curious, and cheeky.[2] Each of these entities, however, is an example of one self joined to another self. As positive as this is for challenging problematic distinctions between the self and nonself, it still maintains or participates in the categories of subject and object. But what about joining a self to a system? This, too, has an ancient tradition, even if it is more subtly expressed. One can identify multiple examples of the self's relation to objects throughout literary and philosophical history. In *The Odyssey* one can find ample instances of how it is that things come to be named, identified, and contextualized before their ownership is transferred. In such transactions, these things become more-than-things. They become intertwined with the person who gives and then receives them. They form identity, not only of giver and receiver, but cultural identity and historical identity. Auerbach's outstanding analysis of the scar of Odysseus in *Mimesis* demonstrates how the whole epic poem vibrates with a present, all-at-once energy that defies an individual, interior perspective.

Thinking about such gems within literary tradition reminds us that our own subjectivity, so determined still by Cartesian philosophy, need not be, at least, *historically* determined, and that our entire ontological worldview can be similarly connected, partial, curious, and active. Reframing things in such a manner also helps us actively counter the technologically deterministic attitudes we have held toward digital technology in the past.[3] New works of digital art, electronic literature, online games, and other artifacts are emerging all the time that foreground—and encourage us to engage in—environmental concerns. Digital technology simply gives us more tools to work with. Our imaginative tools and techniques have never been more nimble, and our cultural and philosophic attitudes toward technology have never been more catholic. To take advantage of them, however, we need to scrub off the residual dystopia, examine our technology head-on, and ask ourselves how we might best make use of it.

The protean nature of computer code allows real-world digital art and simulations of nature to offer fluid, participatory environments in which designations of animal, vegetable, and mineral—and hence "natural," "technological," and "human"—are always enmeshed and intermingled. Digital art collapses subjectivity and combines it with expressions of nature; as such, it creates networked instances of subjectivity—ecological portraits with no subjective center. This offers a distinct aesthetic category, a new experience, one that has profound effects on the way we interact with our world, ourselves, and the other beings with which we share it. I share with Latour an interest in recovering models of inquiry that are suspicious of human primacy and sovereignty. Whether these are nonmodern, premodern, or even ancient notions is less important than whether or not they are helping to foster ecological holism *right now*. With the aesthetic techniques that I have outlined here—coding, collapsing, corresponding, and conserving—digital art and environmental poetics are only at the beginning of a powerful aesthetic alliance.

Notes

Introduction

1. I am grateful to Martin Rosenstock for this translation.

2. The Icelandic term for a glacier with this proclivity is "jökulhlaup," or a "glacier on the run." Originally this term applied only to Icelandic glaciers that flooded as a result of Iceland's unruly and unpredictable volcanic activity. Because of the increasing number of occurrences of glacial flooding due to global warming, however, the term is now used to refer to any sudden release of glacial waters (Johnson, Kirk).

3. When it disappears we will lose a beautiful natural feature of the Alpen landscape, but its decline matters for more important reasons. Its loss will have intricately connected consequences for large varieties of ecological agents that rely upon its waters for survival. Glacial runoff provides us with a great deal of our drinking water, not just in the Alps, but globally. The annual runoff helps us with irrigation and provides a power source for our electricity. When these waters disappear, several highly calibrated ecosystems will be forced to change right along with it—or forced out of existence. The glacier also contributes to the basic survival of a variety of species, not just of the human kind. In the Alps, the Vernagtferner provides habitat for chamois, bears, groundhogs, lynxes, eagles, and mountain jackdaws; below, its waters feed into the Danube River Basin and offer sustenance to many other life-forms, before flowing out toward the Black Sea. To read more about Vernagtferner glacier's vital statistics, including the accelerated pace at which it is losing mass, consult its chart on the Bavarian Academy of Sciences and Humanities' Commission for Glaciology ("Vernagtferner," Bavarian Academy).

4. After about thirty seconds, the glacier hangs up. This is probably a good thing, especially for those of us with strict long-distance calling plans. Via Skype credit, a

thirty-second phone call costs about ten cents. Entirely free recordings of the glacier are available on archive.org ("Vernagtferner," Archive.org).

5. The phone number is Austrian. There was also, for a while, a German number, but this is now defunct—or at least it seems to be, given that an Italian recording asks the caller to leave a message. Then again, it is amusing to consider the possibility that Laar has arranged for the glacier to have an Italian amanuensis.

6. In 2014, a tour boat exploring the Tracy Arm Fjord in Alaska got an experiential understanding of glacial power when the side of the iceberg they were contemplating suddenly and unexpectedly dropped into the sea, narrowly missing their boat. There were a few broken bones, but no one, fortunately, was seriously injured. That is one way to appreciate our connection to our imperiled natural world ("Terrified").

7. Follow-up projects in the *Call me!* series include *Defroster*, which highlights "new populations of insects following the melting of the permafrost"; and *Hotline*, which calls attention to "international power companies and politically involved institutions" by encouraging callers to dial up the world's energy producers and ask them to account for themselves (Laar, *Call me!*).

8. In 2006, the Scottish artist Katie Paterson, independently of Kalle Laar, wired the Icelandic glacier, the Vatnajökull, to a phone line. Her project, *Vatnajökull (the sound of)*, provides "A live phone-line to Vatnajökull glacier" via a British mobile network (Paterson). A related project, Olafur Eliasson's "Your waste of time," showcases fragments of the same glacier "in a refrigerated gallery space powered by solar panels," each of which "represented 800 years of Earthly existence, putting human's physical experience in perspective" (Brooks). And larger scale projects, such as "Nerds for Nature," which engage with all matters of environmental distress, seem to be emerging daily (Kauffman).

9. The fear that computers are immaterial mediums of disembodiment begins earlier than these box office hits, perhaps with Ted Nelson's *Computer Lib/Dream Machines* (1974), which delights in the liberatory potential of digital technology; or with Vernor Vinge's *True Names* (1981), in which the "Other Plane" is a VR precursor, where hacking, simulation, and infiltration cohere into a form as exciting as any espionage novel. These are both fine representatives of subsequent works. Many works of fiction, science, and science fiction emerged during this time that imagined computation as a way to supersede physicality. Such works contribute to the computer's bad rap in relation to nature, to ecological holism, to lived experience. See, for example, Margaret Morse's "*Nature Morte*: Landscape and Narrative in Virtual Environments" (1996), which expresses anxieties about the "utterly empty" nature of the "primordial virtual landscape" in contrast to the "'full' and ready-made . . . physical world" (196). For a detailed history of the flesh-eating potential of cybernetics—in fiction and in scientific practice—see N. Katherine Hayles' *How We Became Posthuman*.

10. The distrust of simulation speaks to a naive idea about our access to reality, which is always already mediated by our sensory apparatus, our bodies, and our brains. This is not to say that there are not *degrees* of simulation; the horrible simu-

lations produced by the Matrix testify to this. But we ought to be suspicious of any firmly defined "essential," "true," or unmediated version of nature and reality. In this I am in agreement with Gerhard Roth, who states the matter in a way that honors the malleable nature of materialism: "*It is not the task of the brain and the sense organs to copy* the environment as exactly and completely as possible, or to recognize the world. . . . Rather, their task is to orient the organism in its environment for the purpose of survival and reproduction" (qtd. in Rötzer 460).

11. The futures they envision are fixed and bleak. Cartesian space, which is to say precisely measured space mapped according to coordinates upon a three-dimensional grid, instead functions as a primary organizing logic of both literary and cinematic fictions that imagine virtual worlds. Consider the dark, dirty rain that never stops falling in *Dark City*; the gritty, *noir* aesthetic of the *Thirteenth Floor*; and the sickly green atmosphere of the *Matrix* films. The simulations of the Matrix bear no relation to the "real" world within which the Matrix imprisons its people. It is worth noting that the gloomy depictions of virtual spaces during this time period (from the 1980s to 2001, roughly) emerge from every medium except the one that has the potential to make them "real": the digital one. The first blockbuster digital film didn't come out until 2002. This was George Lucas' *Star Wars II: Attack of the Clones*. Even the first *Matrix*'s pioneer usage of bullet time relied heavily upon traditional photography to achieve its impressive visual effects. In one sense, this is of course due to the fact that virtual reality techniques were in a nascent state of development during this time period. But in regard to the *tenor* of such depictions of virtual reality as bleak, depressing worlds that consume their inhabitants, there is perhaps something to be said about media envy. It is not far-fetched to view novelists' and filmmakers' expressions of virtual worlds as a kind of rebuttal to an interloper within their respective immersive provinces.

12. For an excellent reading of *Avatar*, see Joni Adamson's nuanced analysis in "Indigenous Literatures, Multinaturalism, and *Avatar*: The Emergence of Indigenous Cosmopolitics" in *American Literary History*.

13. As scholars such as Isaiah Berlin have demonstrated, the term "the Enlightenment" is itself clumsy shorthand for a sweep of historic change that was neither consistent, unified, nor uncontested.

14. Again, "The Scientific Revolution" names something that is not as unified is its moniker suggests. As Stephen Shapin puts it in his landmark study, "There was no such thing as the Scientific Revolution, and this is a book about it" (1).

15. The importance of connecting with nature is no longer a matter of anecdotal speculation. See Gretchen Reynold's "Easing Brain Fatigue with a Walk in the Park," J. Barton and J. Pretty's "What is the best dose of nature and green exercise for improving mental health? A multi-study analysis" for contemporary research about the problem, and Michael Todd's "Is Our Disconnect from Nature a Disorder?"

16. Jorge Luis Borges offers an appealing twist on rigid taxonomies in "The Analytical Language of John Wilkins."

17. Carroll's Alice plays it, both as the investigating subject and the mysterious ob-

ject to be identified. For example, in *Alice's Adventures in Wonderland*, she attempts to identify the status of mustard (she decides, finally, it is a vegetable, although "it doesn't look like one"[80]). In *Through the Looking Glass*, the Lion and the Unicorn both puzzle over her status until the Lion, finally, asks Alice if she is animal, vegetable, or mineral. But the game has a much older history that dates back, at least, to Linnaean taxonomy and, perhaps, even to Aristotle, whose categorical system of knowledge organization aids and abets us still.

18. Bill Tomlinson's *Greening Through IT* (2010), for example, is full of practical tools that combine digital technology with environmental practice, but it has very little to say about aesthetics. Toby Velte et al.'s *Green IT: Reduce Your Information System's Environmental Impact While Adding to the Bottom Line* (2008) and the popular corollary to such titles *Green IT for Dummies* (2009) also offer useful tools for conservation practices.

19. See, for example, Nicole Starosielski's *The Undersea Network* (2015).

20. These have tended to focus upon works of digital art that offer mimetic representations of natural spaces or that employ natural metaphors for rhetorical purposes. See, for example, H. Lewis Ulman's "Beyond Nature/Writing: Virtual Landscapes Online, in Print, and in Real Life"; Rita Raley's "'Living Letterforms': The Ecological Turn in Contemporary Digital Poetics"; Heather Houser's "Aesthetics of Environmental Visualizations"; Allison Carruth's "The Digital Cloud and the Micropolitics of Energy"; and Alenda Chang's "Back to the Virtual Farm: Gleaning the Agriculture-Management Game" (2012). Exceptions to this tendency include Mark Marino's analysis of the Transborder Immigrant Tool in "Code as Ritualized Poetry" and Alenda Chang's "Environmental Remediation," both of which foreground contingencies between simulated spaces and real-world sites of ecological fragility.

21. Finn Arne Jørgensen has made some progress along these lines. See "The Armchair Traveler's Guide to Digital Environmental Humanities," his 2014 essay for *Environmental Humanities*.

22. Bio-art is another emerging field that brings these two fields into dialog. Pioneers in this area include Eduardo Kac, whose glow-in-the-dark rabbit Alba demonstrates the malleability of genetic material across species lines (rabbit and fluorescent jellyfish, in Alba's case); Joanna Zylinska, whose *Bioethics in the Age of New Media* (2009) grapples with the ethical implications of manipulating living matter and argues for a more radical definition of "life" that crosses conventional boundary lines; and Sue Thomas, whose *Technobiophilia* (2013) considers the aesthetic tropes of nature in digitally mediated environments in light of evolutionary biology, particularly in terms of E.O. Wilson's notion of "biophilia," the idea that humans are attracted to and enamored of other living forms. Ten years ago, it was strategically important to place instances of bio-art—which are so physical, material, and lively—within the larger domain of human-computer interaction (HCI) and the digital arts, in order to combat the notion that digital technology was immaterial or unnatural. In *Windows and Mirrors: Interaction Design, Digital Art, and the Myth of Transparency*, Jay David Bolter and Diane Gromala do just this when they make reference

to Eduardo Kac's *GFP Bunny* (i.e., Alba) to speak to how such works push "the relationship between the virtual and physical" and "combat the myth of disembodiment" (157). Bolter and Gromala succeeded so well in calling our attention to the untenable aporia between computer art and living beings that it no longer makes sense to view bio-art as categorically synonymous with digital art.

23. Object-oriented ontology has an affinity with posthumanism in its general sense, that is, "a historical moment in which the decentering of the human by its imbrication in technical, medical, informatics, and economic networks is increasingly impossible to ignore" (Wolfe xv), as well as in a more precise way that aligns with N. Katherine Hayles' concept of the term. In Hayles' posthuman framework, human cognition is always social, always collective. And although it can be mapped against distributive network technologies, it is always dependent upon physical, embodied functioning.

24. Stephen Mentz offers a powerful vision of an ecological model that does this very well. He considers a pastoral, harmonious concept of nature as a fantasy of stasis: "Such a narrative imagines a happy, stable relation between human beings and the nonhuman environment. It seldom rains, mud doesn't clog our panpipes, and our sheep never run away" ("After Sustainability" 586). I return to Mentz' provocative argument in my first chapter.

25. Empedocles endures as an important figure for media historians, not in terms of his totalizing notion of the sphere-in-stasis, outside of which hovers strife, ready to strike and disrupt its perfect unity, but in terms of his porous and oozy conception of matter. In his introduction to Helle Lambridis' monograph on Empedocles, for example, Marshall McLuhan discusses the pre-Socratic philosopher in light of hot and cold media, by way of T. S. Eliot and Humpty Dumpty, managing a dig at Matthew Arnold in the process. But in the *Deep Time of the Media*, Siegfried Zielinski offers a less contentious summary of Empedocles' notion of material continuity. "Being" for Empedocles is a "dynamic mixing process" with a "constant interchange between the one and the other." Instead of conceiving of objects in isolation, "Empedocles presents all living things with a wonderful gift. He wraps them in a fine skin, or film, which not only protects them but is also permeable in both directions. . . . Passing back and forth through them is a constant stream of effluences" (46). This permeability extends across all matter, living and otherwise: "Empedocles does not think of the infinite multiplicity of things in terms of any hierarchical order. Nothing is above anything else; everything exists side-by-side, in motion, and with constant interpenetration" (47).

26. The ant is an apt animal for thinking about distributed action. Ants act singly but are also always working in the service of their collective, providing sustenance, tending to their young, and expanding their vast subterranean empires. But equally intriguing from an Actor-Network-Theory perspective is the way that ants use their very bodies in such service, as malleable forms of matter. "Ant rivers" pale in comparison to the bizarre architectural structures that ants are capable of creating with their bodies when the occasion calls for it. When it floods, ants roll themselves into

a ball—of ants—and ride out the deluge; or they make a flotilla—of ants—and by this raft out the rain; or if they simply need to cross a body of water they will make a bridge—of ants—to cross the void. They make formations of themselves in ways that are extremely suggestive from a materialist, even monist, perspective: *Mutatis mutandis*, genus *Formica*.

27. In his lively introduction to *Alien Phenomenology*, Ian Bogost distinguishes OOO from posthumanism and Actor-Network-Theory, arguing that both of these are more human-centered than OOO. The distinction is important for Bogost, who is attempting to consider, as the subtitle of his book suggests, "What It's Like to Be a Thing." I am not. I take OOO in its literal sense, as, simply, a perspective that is oriented toward objects rather than subjects. In this I follow the lead of Levi R. Bryant, who includes representatives from both posthumanism and Actor-Network-Theory on his "list of object-oriented heroes" (27).

28. And, as a result, resonates forcefully in the wake of recent tragedies.

29. Some readers might be skeptical of object-oriented ontology's assertion that nonhuman entities have agency. But as the previous section has detailed, we have effortlessly and persistently managed to imbue the nonhuman objects that make up computational networks with (malevolent) intent, judging them as accomplices in crimes against nature and humanity without ever considering the absurdity of this one-sided assessment. If we can do this so naturally, that is, accept that digital technology has a kind of agency, then we can certainly at least *imagine* its potential to contribute to a more holistically integrated worldview.

30. Premodern notions of nature are not, of course, tout court, superior to our own. In fact, there is one continuity between pre- and nonmodern cultures that I'd be happy to see disrupted: the view that nature is distinct from human nature, a sentiment we can trace back at least to the first century BCE. In *De natura deorum* Cicero writes: "We sow corn, we plant trees, we fertilize the soil by irrigation, we dam the rivers and direct them where we want. In short, by means of our hands we try to create as it were a second nature within the natural world" (II, 60). Cicero's ancient suggestion that human nature—what he dubs "second nature" or "another nature," depending upon how one translates it—stands in contrast to "first" nature still dominates.

31. As Shapin and Schaffer put it in *Leviathan and the Air-Pump*, "questions of epistemology are also questions of social order" (9). ANT allows us to reframe this social order so that it includes a much wider cast of agents. Latour is a social critic, however, not an aesthetic one; tracing artistic interventions is not as important to his research as analyzing the history of specific technological interventions. Art, however, needs to be included in the conversation. It is a crucial player in imagining and reckoning with epistemologies. For an example of this, let us consider Latour's take on Robert Boyle, the seventeenth-century natural philosopher. He writes of Boyle's method of experimentation—an important precursor to what we now call *the* scientific method—in glowing terms, arguing that it vouchsafes nature's primacy and "allows mute objects to speak through the intermediary of loyal and disciplined scien-

tific spokespersons" and, on account of this, "offers a significant guarantee: it is not men who make Nature; Nature has always existed and has always already been there; we are only discovering its secrets" (30). Several moments in the history of science complement this sentiment, but I would like to call attention to a literary example: Margaret Cavendish's *The Blazing World* (1666). *The Blazing World* as a whole is a strange, feverish, and inconsistent document, yet it is extremely important in terms of considering the unfolding epistemology of the scientific revolution. Throughout this work, Cavendish insists that "there is no more but one universal principle of nature, to wit, self-moving matter, which is the only cause of all natural effects" (154) and provides multiple examples of this "self-moving" material throughout its pages, as in the following passage, a discussion between the Empress and the wise men of science in her fantastical world: "But said the Empress, there is some likeness between maggots and cheese; for cheese has no blood, and so neither have maggots; besides, they have almost the same taste which cheese has. This proves nothing, answered they; for maggots have a visible, local, progressive motion, which cheese hath not. . . . The Empress confessed that she observed nature was infinitely various in her works, and that though the species of creatures did continue, yet their particulars were subject to infinite changes" (148). This is one of the most playful—and disgusting—of these examples. I mention this moment because it speaks to continuity, not only between maggots and cheese, but also between the text as a whole and the scientific discourse of its time. Cavendish wrote *The Blazing World* as a response, in part, to Robert Hooke's *Microphagia*, as well as Boyle's efforts in forming the Royal Society. A year after *The Blazing World* was published, Cavendish received an invitation to visit the Society. After her visit, all women were promptly and summarily banned. Her book offers an interesting critique of the new scientific objectivism and offers an alternative model of knowledge-making. As Mary Baine Campbell argues in *Wonder & Science*: Cavendish's "defensive sense that her interest and method are alternatives to Hooke's . . . may come in part from a sense that the immaterial and unverifiable are losing status as objects of knowledge under the pressure of . . . instrument-based (prosthetic) perception—a perception to which women had little or no access" (183). Put another way, Campbell suggests that Cavendish "offers a vision of scientific practice—located, motivated, visible, active, transformative—that might have made, if everything else were different too, for a different history of a different science" (218). This story of science intersects well with Latour's, demonstrating an even more densely clustered network of scientific practice that was in the process of unfolding in a literary-aesthetic arena. And it shows how art contributes to alternative models of categorization and confusion, in the best possible sense of that word.

32. This stance in *The Politics of Nature* (2004) is neither original nor singular. Bill McKibben makes a similar argument in *The End of Nature* (1989), as does Timothy Morton in *Ecology without Nature: Rethinking Environmental Aesthetics* (2007). Each achieves a different rhetorical effect. I read McKibben's book as a wake-up call more than an attempt to reconfigure categorization. I appreciate its motivations, even as

I hang onto the concept of nature. In *Ecology without Nature*, Morton writes that he wishes to question the notion of nature as a "transcendent principle" (5). This is a laudable ambition, even though I am resistant to eliminating the concept of nature entirely.

33. Nature is not a stable critical category in ecocriticism either, as Lawrence Buell is quick to point out in *The Future of Environmental Criticism*.

34. American nature parks are not without their problems, but the entire concept of the nature park upon which the American Park system is based owes an enormous debt to European art and philosophy: Switzerland and France (Rousseau), Germany (Goethe, Novalis, Herder), Sweden (Linnaeus), Scotland (Burns), England (the Wordsworths, the Shelleys, Keats). The great sweep of romanticism in Europe contributed to a new, international interest in protecting natural spaces. As a partial consequence of this aesthetic movement, the American continents have the largest tracts of remaining old-growth forest left on the planet. This is, for better or worse (mostly better, in my view, although I have some things to say about conservation aesthetics in my final chapter), a historic and international achievement.

35. Richard Grusin offers a powerful critique of such a leveling approach, arguing that "stripping nature of any agency whatsoever . . . [transforms] nature so completely into culture that the preservation of nature as a national park, for example, becomes indistinguishable from its transformation into a ranch or a mine or a private resort" (334). Grusin's critique is a response to Stephen Greenblatt's account of a visit to Nevada Falls in Yosemite National Park and suggests that Greenblatt's account in "Towards a Poetics of Culture" suffers from this conflation.

36. Ian Bogost offers a distinctly different reading. From his perspective, Latour's model of agency doesn't go nearly far enough to demote the human's special status. "Even for Latour," Bogost writes, "analysis still serves the interests of human politics" (7).

37. Latour suggests as much in *Aramis or the Love of Technology*, when he acknowledges different types of competencies that objects have: "Humans and nonhumans take on form by redistributing the competences and performances of the multitude of actors that they hold on to and that hold on to them" (225).

38. I shall have more to say about Latour's and Bryant's intriguing notions of objects and agency in my third chapter; for now it suffices to note that Latour's razing of nature, technology, and humanity to objects of equal importance is concerning.

39. And it is this dedifferentiation, if we are to take the claims of the media scholar Friedrich Kittler seriously, which makes these objects indistinguishable in terms of their material substrata. For Kittler, dedifferentiation signifies the fact that "the bulk of written texts . . . do not exist anymore in perceivable time and space" (Kittler, "There Is No Software").

40. But the Janus figure is a bit clichéd, a bit played out, and a bit too human to boot. So as to be less anthropomorphic (but more obscure and less elegant), I turn to a different bicephalic entity, one whose impressive lineage constitutes a categorical abomination: the mythic "amphisbaena," a lizard-like, desert-dwelling anteater, born

of the blood of the decapitated Medusa. In the *Natural Histories*, Pliny notes that "the amphisbaena has two heads, that is to say, it has a second one at the tail, as though one mouth were too little for the discharge of all its venom" ("Different Kinds of Serpents," 35.23). Perhaps, though, it needed that extra mouth for a different reason: to speak to its diverse and complicated ancestry. It is a taxonomically versatile creature: an animal, but one born of blood, a result of human, nonhuman, and divine genealogy. And it is not just one animal but a human-animal-monster mash-up. Consider, too, its equally strange "siblings," all born from Medusa's spilled blood: the coral reefs that blossom in the Aegean Sea, the winged horse Pegasus, and the human-shaped Chrysaor (the Golden One), who shares his name with the goddess of the grain. Add to this Medusa's association with stone, as well as Perseus' conception via a shower of gold, and the creature's entire lineage slips and slides across categorical distinctions. Today it is the scientific name of a type of snake, but in medieval bestiaries it appears as a lizard equipped with wings, chicken claws, and (sometimes) horns. In addition to being more animal than anthropos, the amphisbaena also works differently than the lofty Janus. Janus looks to the future and the past at the same time, almost with an air of indifference. The amphisbaena, on the other hand, is on the move. While the body of this animal has two heads, the -amphi in its name doesn't refer to these; instead it signals doubled walking, or doubled movement (*banein* means "to go" in ancient Greek). According to Isidore of Seville, "Alone among snakes, the amphisbaena goes out in the cold" (Bestiary.ca). I extrapolate from this fact to suggest that contained in this unsettling and dangerous little beast is the capacity to travel along two distinct paths, as well as a hardy constitution and adventurous spirit, which equip it well to walk them. There is much to admire in the amphisbaena's strange, scuttling, and at times discursive footsteps. I take it as my model as I proceed.

41. The notion of a code that functions as a connective tissue, which can describe and create all things, flourishes in the modern world. This idea was conceptually fundamental to the development of one of the first computers in the Victorian period: Babbage's analytic engine. As Ada Lovelace writes in her description of this project, "The Analytical Engine *weaves algebraic* patterns just as the Jacquard loom *weaves* flowers and leaves" (Lovelace). This is one of the first instances of an operational language that, like a loom, creates objects and events based upon coded sets of instructions, and it is telling that Lovelace uses natural metaphors to describe its functioning.

42. Far from it. In the early days of computing, as well as what might be called its prehistory, code has been seen as a way of unifying diverse substances. Consider Democritus and Leucippus, the first thinkers in Western philosophy to put forward the idea that everything—and they meant everything—was composed of smaller, indivisible parts, which they termed "atoms." The fabric of reality was composed of these atoms, which, when arranged into different patterns, could create every single thing. And because atoms accounted for *everything*, there could be no transcendent, ideal plane of existence that existed apart from them. This is, of course, an important precursor to our contemporary understanding of atomic structure, but it is also

instructive for thinking about binary code. Binary operates like atomic units in the sense that all computer programs are made up of them. Yet binary has often been understood in terms of dualism, in the problematic, transcendent use of that term. In Neal Stephenson's novel *Snow Crash*, for example, the main character, a computer hacker for hire, makes this very argument:

> "Dualists believe in a binary universe, that there is a spiritual world in addition to the material world."
>
> *"Well, as a computer geek, I have to believe in the binary universe."*
>
> The Librarian raises his eyebrows. "How does that follow?"
>
> "Sorry. It's a joke. A bad pun. See, computers use binary code to represent information. So I was joking that I have to believe in the binary universe, that I have to be a dualist."
>
> "How droll," the librarian says, not sounding very amused. (208)

The comparison is both apt and misleading. Binary code *is* a two-sign system, but these two signs do not refer to matter and spirit; they signify the presence of electricity, 1, and its absence, 0.

43. This tradition continues in the present-day. See, for one example, Nnedi Okorafor-Mbachu's *Zahrah the Windseeker*, whose main character "grows her own flora computer" (dust jacket).

44. The story of amber is particularly rich in its blending of bodily and taxonomic forms. According to its etiology in Ovid, when the son of Helios, Phaeton, died, his sisters turned into poplar trees and wept tears of amber (Bk II: 344–366). This story gives an apt description of amber. Although we refer to it as a gemstone (mineral), it is actually made from the sticky resin excreted by trees (vegetable), which hardens over time and often contains the bodies of insects (animal) in perfect states of preservation, famously depicted in *Jurassic Park*. The Greek word for amber, "electron," is also suggestive, since amber was recognized as an early conductor of electricity ("electric").

45. Such marvels of morphology are not confined to the mythology of the Greco-Romans. Norse mythology teems with powerful objects (think Mjölnir, Thor's hammer) and shape-shifting gods: In the *Volundarkvida* section of the *Poetic Edda*, a Valkyrie slips off her swan-skin in order to bathe in a clear lake (Sigfusson and Sturleson); in the *Gylfaginning* of the *Prose Edda*, Thor struggles against a trio of hidden forces: the Midgard serpent, disguised as a cat; old age, who takes the form of a crone; and the mighty ocean, which pretends to be mead in a drinking horn. This same section of the *Prose Edda* recounts how Loki transforms into a mare, mates with a rutting stallion, and foals Sleipnir, the "best of all horses," Odin's eight-legged war steed (Sigfusson and Sturleson).

46. This is not the only mode of bodily reformation at work in literary history. Consider the body swap. In films like *Freaky Friday*, *The Man with Two Brains*, and other examples of B-grade horror and science fiction, one human brain is swapped

for another, somehow, and the recipients of the brain transplants must figure out how to maintain their identities while inside the bodily host of another. These samples might seem childish, but the same transformative impulse runs through some of our most revered works of literature: in *Dr. Jekyll and Mr. Hyde* and *Dracula*, the transformation from one self into another self, of human being into monstrous being, points to the terror of subjective dislocation. In such works the loss of an integral identity manifests as bodily transmutation.

Chapter 1

1. Contemporary use of expressive code emerges from a long literary tradition of collapsing form and content for visual effect, beginning with George Herbert's "Easter Wings" (1633) and continuing with the typographical innovations of various twentieth century aesthetic experiments, such as with the Italian Futurists' reaction to the "sick-making" typography of the Victorians, with the concrete poetry of the sixties and seventies, with the "code poetry" of Mez Breeze in the 1990s-present, with the experimental sf poetry of Edwin Morgan (particularly his "instamatic" and "particle" poems), and Nam Paik's newly discovered "Etude 1," a clover-shaped poem composed in Fortran (Moonan).

2. In spite of these various ways that materiality haunts the etymology of code, the notion that it is immaterial persists. In the early days of personal computing and the first wave of criticism that responded to it, this particular view was commonplace. A provocative and popular approach was to compare the logic-based syntax of computer code, virtual worlds, and "cyberspace" to Platonic idealist philosophy and the rationalist tradition it inaugurated. Cf. the work of Michael Heim and Robert Markley. Bolter and Gromala put the matter succinctly: "Many cyberspace enthusiasts are still Platonists. They replace Plato's world of forms with cyberspace, and then they divorce cyberspace from our embodied culture" (Bolter and Gromala 136). This was and remains an important way to contextualize code historically. After all, one finds in ancient philosophy a stubborn, persistent attempt to make sense of the natural world by means of symbolic abstractions, which are not merely descriptive of one's world but world-generating and organizing, and hence controlling. This idea of an ultimate, transcendent authority through which all referents can be authorized—a Fort Knox/gold standard notion of signification—refracts throughout the history of Western philosophy. For Plato, forms are the abstract entities that structure the physical world, and our understanding of the world is entirely dependent upon our imperfect memory of them (although, as we shall see in a later chapter, Plato's damnation of writing occurs within a landscape that is rife with natural signs). For Saint Augustine, the spoken or written sign is evidence of God's handiwork, "a sign of the word that shines within" (*On the Christian Doctrine*). For Descartes, it is mathematics that provides "the sole key needed to unlock the secrets of nature" (Burtt 105). In some respects, these notions of a powerful guarantee of significance share an important feature with contemporary computer code, which is itself both a de-

scriptive and generative system of signs. Code acts. It executes commands. Strings of code might not be as awe-inspiring as the fiat lux that marks God's first day of creation, but they nevertheless *do* something.

3. As they were, for example, in the *tabella defixionis* dedicated to Hecate: "Destroy, crush, kill, strangle Porcello and his wife Maurilla. Their soul, heart, buttocks, liver." As Celia Natalías Sánchez writes in her explication of this tablet, "In this line appears a series of three verbs which, crescendo-like, increases the degree of violence to be wrought on Porcellus and his wife" (211).

4. I quote from Bukatman's text here because the primary source, in its original form, is so elusive that it is not entirely clear what it is. In Bukatman's essay, he lists it as *Cyberpunk*, a documentary put out by the Voyager Company in 1990. The same citation in Kirschenbaum's *Mechanisms*, however, refers to it as occurring in an essay Gibson wrote as an afterword (or a foreword) to an electronic version of his Sprawl trilogy, which was published on floppy disk by the Voyager Company in 1991. This company is no longer in business, but references to the electronic version appear on the message board of the Science Fiction Research Association (SFRA). The *Cyberpunk* documentary is more easily traceable, but it was produced by Intercon and distributed by Mystic Fire in 1990, not Voyager. This confusion warrants mention because it illustrates some of the misunderstanding about data that Gibson points to in this quote. Code is at once enduring *and* elusive. The essay hasn't stayed, cocooned, in its "glittering mesh," but neither has it disappeared; in fact, it has proliferated, but the disk that contained it isn't readily available. This points to both the mysterious nature of encoded information and what Kirschenbaum suggests about it in *Mechanisms*: its durability. For the complete essay, see William Gibson's message board (Gibson, "Message Board").

5. Other works of science fiction that portray the computer as a malevolent presence, such as John Varley's "Press Enter," also perpetuate this misunderstanding.

6. We could add to this listing any number of Cold War–era science fiction espionage films (think *Die Hard, Goldeneye, War Games*) that show a (frequently eastern European) hacker on the edge of causing total nuclear devastation through his (usually his, although Angelina Jolie provides a female counterpoint in the 1995 film *Hackers*) skill with code. In many of these stories and many others like them, code is the means of death, enslavement, and imprisonment, and the means by which humans are distracted from ecological catastrophe.

7. The idea of a lone programmer writing the code to implement even just one of these systems is a simplification. To give some notion of scale: the software code required to run a car is over one hundred million lines long (Charette).

8. This scenario is a narrative summary of a real-world research report written by Nick V. Grishin on the Butterflies of America web hub (Grishin).

9. The increasing popular interest in coding techniques speaks to this fact. In the past few years, the call to code has come from such variously famous public figures as Michael Bloomberg, Al Gore, Snoop Dogg, and Will.i.am., as well as from ini-

tiatives like Codecademy, Code School, Girls Code, Black Girls Code, and Google's Made with Code.

10. For an example of the type of questions that Critical Code Studies is asking, see the *Electronic Book Review*'s edited thread on the topic ("Critical Code Studies").

11. For a more thorough treatment of the way code has appeared throughout philosophic history, Florian Cramer's *Words Made Flesh* gives a careful treatment of the subject and considers a wide spectrum of code's precursors, from Golem to Google. His book, however, is not primarily—or even at all—concerned with code's relation to nature. His argument, abstracted, reads as follows: "Executable code existed centuries before the invention of the computer in magic, Kabbalah, musical composition and experimental poetry. These practices are often neglected as a historical pretext of contemporary software culture and electronic arts." Cramer's study offers a lucid and provocative reading of them, arguing persuasively that in such spheres, code serves to "link computations to a vast speculative imagination that encompasses art, language, technology, philosophy and religion." His is a wonderful study, but "nature" is not its focus.

12. A quote from St. Augustine, which also forms the epigraph to Gregory Bateson's *Mind and Nature*, is apt along these lines: "Plotinus the Platonist proves by means of the blossoms and leaves that from the Supreme God, whose beauty is invisible and ineffable, Providence reaches down to the things of earth here below. He points out that these frail and mortal objects could not be endowed with a beauty so immaculate and so exquisitely wrought, did they not issue from the Divinity which endlessly pervades with its invisible and unchanging beauty all things" (*City of God*, qtd. in Bateson, 2).

13. Notable exceptions: *War Games* uses a white font, *Colossus* yellow, *Jumpin' Jack Flash* red, white, and blue (apt for a film about American patriotism and conflict with the KGB), and *Weird Science* blue.

14. It is instructive to compare *Osmose*'s code to the gorgeous landscapes of Tatsuo Horiuchi, who uses the spreadsheet-making software Excel to make his art. This is, he notes, because "graphic software is expensive while Excel is already pre-installed in most computers and is easier to use than Paint" (Gonzales). Yet there is no clear relation between his paintings and the mode of coding he used to create them, except, so far, in the news articles that have focused on the novelty of using Excel in this way. His coding, in other words, has not appeared in an expressive manner.

15. See also skyscrapers inspired by bamboo: eVolo skyscrapers in Tel Aviv ("eVolo"); the Bank of China in Hong Kong; the Taipei 101 in Taipei ("Taipei 101"), and Singapore's "supertrees" (Saidmoorhouse).

16. For a detailed analysis of these beautiful documents, see Kristen Case's analyses of them in "Thoreau's Radical Empiricism," as well as Case's digital encoding of Thoreau's *Kalendar*.

17. A note about the word "final" here: In a 2012 interview about the project, its publisher, Kevin Begos, Jr., states: "One point that some of the critics have missed . . .

is that it was really almost a never-ending stage of evolution. . . . I don't think it's ever been completely finished." If reader response theory has taught us anything, it is the valuable lesson that no work is ever "finished." However, insofar as the production end of things was concerned, it was as close to that mythic state of finality as it is possible to get. There was a reading, a filming, and a vernissage to mark the occasion. At this event, the illusionist Penn Jillette read the poem; a projector scrolled it, and, once displayed, the computer program erased it. Gibson distanced himself from it after its publication, even stating that he had never actually seen the book; and each piece of the work maintains its own autonomy (Ashbaugh's website links to his "genetic portraits"; Gibson's website to his poem; neither, however, refers to the other, nor to the book). The book's critical reception, on the other hand, stands as a related but distinct body of intellectual and creative labor. A student "hacked" it (I use the word "hack" very generally here; the student snuck a camera into the vernissage and filmed it—it wasn't a computer hack but a hack nevertheless), and critics Schwenger and Bukatman elevated it to something worthy of critical attention; this stood in contrast to the way criticism contemporary to the book had characterized it, which is to say as a pretentious gimmick "designed to challenge conventional notions about books and art while extracting money from collectors of both" (*NYT*). The Agrippa Files team, led by Alan Liu, archived the artifacts related to its publication and, in this sense, helped revived it.

18. This description applies to the V&A's copy of *Agrippa*. Kevlar is "a polymer used in the manufacture of bulletproof vests" (Hodge). However, it is unclear as to whether or not all—or any—of the books were actually made of this substance, since the New York Public Library describes the case of its *Agrippa* as composed of "resin-impregnated paper and fiberglass" (Hodge).

19. There are several variations of the spelling and formatting of the project. For simplicity's sake, I use *Agrippa* to refer to the entire project and "Agrippa" to refer to Gibson's poem.

20. "'Golgonooza' incorporates an anagram of λογον ζω[=οο]ης ('logon zooas'), the "living word" (as in Philippians 2.16). "Golgonooza text" then, as a tissue of living words or word-creatures . . . " (Hilton).

21. See page 39.

22. Freek is short for Frederick, but it is also a great name for a hacker. In the 1980s, especially, the words "phreaker" and "hacker" were nearly synonymous.

23. See Mark Marino's "Critical Code Studies" for the cultural significance of this program (Marino).

24. Skilled telegraphers were expected to decode messages in response to electric shocks delivered to their fingertips (see George Bartlett Prescott's *History, Theory and Practice of the Electric Telegraph*); nor was touch the only sense with which the telegraph wire engaged: "During the second—and successful—attempt to lay a transatlantic cable in the mid-1860s, physicist William Thomson applied the telegraph wires to his own tongue and found that he could 'taste' the differences between signals. Like a human tongue, a telegraph key could both taste and speak" (Otis 181).

25. If you would like to find the perfect shade of green, or of any other color for that matter, visit colorhexa.com and play around.

26. Hiding messages in *comments* within lines of code is a much more common practice. Comments are included in lines of code, but, depending upon the development environment, they are surrounded by slashes, asterisks, and dashes; these tell the processor to ignore them when it comes time to run the program, so the user doesn't see them unless she knows where to look. These days, sites like "linux kernel fuck count" ("linux") and other automated text readers and webbots make such rants harder to get away with, since such entities don't distinguish between operational and expressive code the way we do. But at the turn of the century, it was still fairly common. In 2002, for example, a developer for Nintendo 64's *New Tetris*, furious with what he perceived as a grossly incompetent project producer, took the time to immortalize him in the comments of the game: "fake your job while you can, because once they find out how . . . useless you are, you will be out of a job. I cannot think of any skillset you would fit into in this industry, so you better hold on tight." For a full description read *Wired*'s take on "The Funny, Occasionally Dirty, Hidden Messages in Your Favorite Games" (Kemps).

27. Tobias Menely reminds us of how chronological perception differs from the ancient Greek notion of *kairos*: "a point in time filled with significance, charged with a meaning derived from its relation to the end" (478, quoting Kermode). I would argue that while "Agrippa" pretends to be a chronology, it is more *kairos* than *chronos*. We start with the present; through the photographs we move backward in time, tracing a family back two generations. But Gibson's past always inflects the present, and, vice versa; memories of a more recent past intrude upon these distant ones. Throughout, images of compression and suspension open up to an altogether different type of time and, in the final stanzas, all time merges with the present. The artist does not witness the "single catastrophe" within a monadic, aleph-like crystal ball. He nevertheless sees something more than a mere "chain of events." He is sensitive to moments within which one type of time opens up to another. We see this ecology within each moment of revelation; and, indeed, we might swap the word "mechanism" for "revelation" and be left with a workable poem, since it is in these revelatory moments that the organizing system makes itself known. As Liu has noted, the poem pairs the term "mechanism" explicitly with photography and firearms, such that these, for him, cohere as *the* mechanism, that is, the poem's vision of a totalizing system. I share the view that the mechanisms of photography and firearms are complementary, but the mechanism, as I see it, is not limited to guns and cameras but refers throughout the poem to an even larger totalizing system of organization, of which guns and cameras are but two instantiations.

28. But *Agrippa*, like so many narratives of eschatology, makes a space for something new. Eschatological prophecy promises destruction, but it also promises a grand unity after that destruction is over. The set of textual and visual objects that constitute *Agrippa* today make it something other than what it was—memory triggered, performed across different registers, then erased. It has been recovered and

revitalized. *Agrippa* is an archive, but one that multiplies the Freudian and Derridean notion of that word and, as a consequence, explodes various levels of authority via its processes of proliferation. It is a presentation of an enduring ecology that, because it endures, defies eschatology. Taken together, its disparate authors, sign systems, encryptions, codes, and poetics suggest an oddly *negentropic* ecological system, even as each one seems to point toward destruction.

29. Benjamin's theses are instructive for another reason; his vision of nature in the schema of Marxist eschatology is damning: "Labor, as it is henceforth conceived, is tantamount to the exploitation of nature, which is contrasted to the exploitation of the proletariat with naive self-satisfaction" (Benjamin, "Art in the Age").

30. In addition to Mentz' use of Whitman's verses to inform ecocriticism, Jonathan Freedman writes of Whitman in his analysis of database culture's obsession with classification and inventory: "encyclopedic impulse seems to run throughout Whitman's work, as he moves consistently to inventory, name, define, and (partially) order the city, country, and world . . . in long flowing lines that may well remind us of the list rhetoric of the celebrator of telegraph culture" (1599). The same impulse is here in this verse, as he itemizes what the sea will do to him before he surrenders to its embrace. Whitman and Gibson both provide instances of a complex ecology that includes—and celebrates—technology in its mix.

31. Contrast this moment of the author's self-aware fragility to its horrifying inverse in the process described as the "Great Encoding of 2121" in a Soviet-era story by Boris and Arkady Strugatsky that recounts the ambitious enterprise of recording a human identity through computational means. The procedure fails, but not before an enormous amount of energy is expended, to such an obscene extent that natural weather systems are altered and the identity in question threatens to take up so much space to maintain that it has the potential to become its own village—or to Dr. Henry Markram's real-world Blue Brain project (Markram).

32. The word "laughing"—in the form of present participle—lacks a clear referent. In the poem on the disk, there is no comma before it; in the poem on Gibson's website, there is. With the comma, it works as an adjective to describe Gibson himself; without it, it refers to the lanterns "battered" by the storm. In either case, the laugher results from an encounter with the system and/or one of its agents, and suggests a delirious pleasure in the supporting yet threatening contours of the confrontation.

33. There is a way in which the distinct mechanisms speak to each other; it is not just that "mechanism" names distinct, independent systems that have no relation to each other—technology, photography, genetics, nature, guns. Rather, each invigorates the other. Consider its use in the second section of the poem, in which the term "mechanism" appears three times. In the first instance, it refers to the photo album and its accessories (camera, film, photograph). In the second, it refers to a gun and its accessories (the bullet and its slug). In the third instance, however, the term has no definitive objective antecedent. Instead of solitude, it is the poet's "awareness of the mechanism" that is specified. And this moment of energy, stillness, and violence

is accompanied by that ancient image of revelatory illumination, the ray of light, here scaled down to fit the domestic scene as a "beam of dusty sunlight."

34. Catharsis in every sense can be traced through Clytemnestra's story. She likens her own plotting to that of a divine order: "An endless web, as by some fisher strung, / A deadly plenteousness of rope, I flung." Clytemnestra, a fisher, cannot snatch her daughter from the sea the way a fisherman might pluck a fish, but she *can* redeem her daughter's life by killing the father in a way that recalls her daughter's death so as to reanimate that bloody scene. Clytemnestra relishes the moment in which his "limbs turned water and broke"; she rejoices in his blood flow: "Sweet as God's dear rain." The bloody scene reckons the account, makes up for the fact that Agamemnon never "purged the blood that stained him." The chorus' lament, which describes the "rain that falls bloodily" and "wash[es] away the walls," provides an apt accompaniment, as does Cassandra's, in whose visions the images of the past collide with those of the present and the imminent future.

35. Clytemnestra takes matters into her own hands and makes an orgy of it, which she relishes, before being caught in a much larger net.

36. The idea of two sign systems, natural and divine, as intertwined and authored by the same creator also emerges forcefully in the Renaissance. Natural theology holds the book of nature and biblical scripture side by side, not in order to foster rivalry, or to use one to disprove the other, but for mutual illumination. As Francis Bacon writes in *The Advancement of Learning*, "The scriptures reveal to us the will of God; and the book of the creatures expresses the divine power; whereof the latter is a key unto the former" (VI, 16). Bacon imagines the relation between the "book of creatures" and "divine power" as a relation between lock and key, or a code and its solution. Nearly one hundred years earlier Leonne Alberti, the father of encryption in the early modern period, had already articulated the inverse relationship, writing in his "Treatise on Ciphers" that the words and letters of a message, once encrypted, appear to "a scrutinizing stranger . . . like the leaves of a tree scattered by the wind which have been collected into a heap" (16). Alberti attributes to the power of encoding the ability to make ciphered signs read as natural, albeit disordered; Bacon describes the power of decoding as a way to decipher the signs that God has similarly encrypted in his creation. Another type of natural "code" occurs during the early modern period, as well, when natural signs begin to take on a power that in the ancient world they had exercised only rarely: keeping track of and organizing the *interior* world by making reference to the natural signs of the *exterior* world via mnemonic devices. These took the form of abecedaries, in which each letter is paired with the animal whose name begins with it ("A" with "*anser*," goose; "B" with "*bubo*," owl; "C" with "*corvus*," crow); of gorgeous schematics of branching trees, each branch indicating a domain of inquiry, as in Ramon Llull's tree of knowledge (*Arbor Scientiae*); and of the objects of allegory, as in "Astronomy with Bushel and Stars" in "The wisdom of St. Thomas Aquinas" (Catholic Encyclopedia). Natural signs also aid in recalling more elaborate causal sequences. In *The Book of Memory*, Mary Car-

ruthers provides the following vivid example: If we wish to remember the particulars of a lawsuit, we are advised to "imagine some ram, with huge horns and testicles, coming towards us in the darkness." The image is sufficiently vivid on its own, but the linguistic signs that refer to *parts* of the animal add to the mnemonic effect: "The horns will bring to memory our adversaries, and the testicles the dispositions of witnesses . . . [since it makes] a pun on *testes*, 'witnesses,' and a sign for the adversarial nature of the legal proceedings" (178).

37. The introduction to this chapter considered briefly the prehistory of operational binary code, but it is also worth mentioning the *representation* of code in modern literature. There are plenty of instances of codes and ciphers in literary expression and digital art that work in an expressive manner. These have little to do with executing commands, as in operational code, yet these instances are instructive. In the "Gold Bug," the statistical cipher that Poe introduces is not operational per se. It provides clues to a lost treasure that a savvy and dedicated reader can decode, but it is not operative in the same way that operational code is. And yet, in terms of the atmosphere of the story, of its suspense and mystery, of its narrative logic, and therefore of the experience of its story world, the use of code is far from merely ornamental. It is fundamental for the story's phenomenological effects.

Chapter 2

1. It also challenges the idea that the body of man is formed in the image of a god.

2. See Noah Fierer's "Invisible World" (Fierer) for a quick, yet detailed, perspective about the microbes that share—and help constitute—our bodies. As one reader responded in a later issue, "Few realize how many living creatures surround us and even live on or in us" (Kalab).

3. Aristotle's *De anima* is similarly instructive along these lines, as is Goethe's *Metamorphosis of Plants*.

4. Mark B. N. Hansen has suggested forcefully that perceptions of digital media are more dependent upon the body's ability to parse and make sense of it than on perceptions of analog information. As sympathetic as I am to Hansen's corrective way of thinking about the importance of the body's relation to new media, I do not accept the singularity of "the body" except as linguistic shorthand. I single out Hansen only because he has been self-reflexive and proactive about this very problem. In his foreword to Bernadette Wegenstein's *Getting Under the Skin: Body and Media Theory* (itself an excellent corrective to this trend), he addresses it head-on in his discussion of the body "in pieces." For a work that explores the thoroughly entangled character of human bodies and natural ecologies from a socially and politically urgent perspective, see Stacy Alaimo's *Bodily Natures: Science, Environment, and the Material Self* (2010).

5. Francis Bacon, however, offers a vision of this nymph—and nature—that is Protean and supple. An illustration that captures something of this sensibility appears as the first image in the original publication of Bacon's *Novum Organum*, "Nature

as Daphne," in which the nymph's fingers spread out to leaves, and the roots of the laurel tree emerge from her feet (Campbell 86). In it, the process—not product—of transformation is highlighted. (For a superb summary of Bacon's transformative notion of nature, see Peter Pesic's "Wrestling with Proteus: Francis Bacon and the 'Torture' of Nature.")

6. The thieves themselves tell a story that shares the same pattern: one of their number, Thrasyleon, is "sewn up in the skin" of a bear, in order to sneak into the palace of a rich man who collects wild animals for gladiator shows. Thrasyleon's costume is *too* good, though. A servant releases the hunting dogs on him when he spies him looting, and these tear him apart. Thrasyleon, aware that his time has come, keeps in character to the end: "He stuck to his game. Not a human cry, not a word of pain, did he utter to break his oath. . . . Every noise he made was a growl or a wild beast's bellow" (100).

7. Lucian lampoons this assemblage mercilessly in his "Icaromennipus, an Aerial Excursion," in which the protagonist takes the wing of an eagle and the wing of a vulture and flies to the moon.

8. All but a few perished in space or upon their return to White Sands. In this sense Kubrick's hallmark moment in *2001* (the monkey throws a bone; the bone becomes a space ship), although impressive for its cinematic compression of thousands of years of evolution, is an unfair abrogation of the monkey's contribution to this great achievement.

9. In addition to works of science fiction that imagine human beings merging with informational systems, such as Vernor Vinge's *True Names*, Joan Vinge's Catspaw trilogy, Jonathan Littell's *Bad Voltage*, and many other works of cyberpunk fiction, there is an equally compelling body of writing that imagines the pleasures and perils of mingling plant, animal, human, and nonliving components. Anne McCaffrey's first Pern trilogy, for example, imagines the coupling of human riders with powerful dragons; Octavia Butler's *Wild Seed* expresses the pain and pleasure of transitioning a human form into various animal bodies; Pat Murphy's "His Vegetable Wife" depicts the peculiar and deadly agency of a seed-grown plant-woman. These examples, however, are also human-centered.

10. One might contrast this with the story of Io. In Ovid's account, the girl demonstrates fluidity in form, changing from maiden to cow and back to maiden, but her desire is to be restored to her true form.

11. The book is one of the most highly interactive forms of expression in history. After all, a book cannot offer up its treasures without the action of the reader, without the fingertips of a human hand turning the pages (or, in the case of the Google books project, the slicing digits of a robotic scanner), without the eyes rolling over the words, the fingers, perhaps, keeping track of the lines, as well as any other actions needed to complete the circuit of communication. And what about the emotional, physical, and phenomenological effects of the reader, as well as how that reader's interior life shapes her reading experience, creates her own hermeneutic framework for the text? Surely these constitute moments of interaction.

12. The careful reader will note that I did not write "physical" interaction in contrast to cognitive. Cognitive acts are physical acts. Even if we haven't yet figured out how to measure them precisely, we've been making grade strides in doing so. See, for example, reportage on the work of Jack Gallant, in "Scientists Use Brain Imaging to Reveal the Movies in Our Mind" (Anwar).

13. Manovich makes this observation in a counterintuitive way, claiming that there is a "myth of interactivity" and including interaction in his list of things that "new media is not" (70), but only because it is actually one of the most basic aspects of computational technology, so intrinsic to its functioning that calling attention to it constitutes "a tautology" (109).

14. I say this not to suggest a value judgment about the reader's role in apprehending and in some sense "creating" print versus electronic texts, since the same cognitive effort of course occurs in the reading of both. See Yopie Prins' *Victorian Sappho*, which demonstrates how the written text functions as an "empty trope" that the reader must fill in with her own cognitive effort (I am grateful to Adam Bradford for this reference). Indeed, any claim made about the startling "newness" of any new form, will (and should) be challenged. In the spirit of media-specific analysis, however, it is important to note the differences. In digital artworks, I see these emerging in the form of readable, textual state changes.

15. Gregory Bateson puts it more baldly: "All experience is subjective. . . . Our brains make the images that we think we 'perceive'" (28); and James Tiptree Jr., more baldly still: "When you wash your hands, do you feel the water is running on your brain? Of course not. You feel the water on your hand, although the 'feeling' is actually a potential-pattern flickering over the electrochemical jelly between your ears. And it's delivered there via the long circuits from your hands. . . . The fact that the signals have jumped across space on the way in makes no difference at all. If you want the jargon, it's known as eccentric projection or sensory reference and you've done it all your life. Clear?" (6).

16. In *Windows and Mirrors*, Bolter and Gromala criticize the attempt to make transparency the singular objective of interface design.

17. By the late 1990s slogans such as "Information wants to be free" and documents such as John Perry Barlow's "A Declaration of the Independence of Cyberspace" (1996) had set the tone for the cultural conversation about emerging digital technology. Cyberspace, according to theorists of Barlow's bent, was to be a libertarian utopia where one could enjoy the freedom of self-expression beyond the physical world and the fetters of government control: "Governments of the Industrial World, you weary giants of flesh and steel, I come from Cyberspace, the new home of Mind. On behalf of the future, I ask you of the past to leave us alone" (Barlow). Freedom here is configured in a very familiar way. Barlow invokes the rhetoric of Enlightenment autonomy, Lockean in flavor (sovereignty, liberty, independence, tyranny, moral right), and the freedom that comes from a coherent and rational self. Implicit in this argument—but so easily plucked out of it that it might be said to be *explicitly* implicit—is an affirmation of modernist thinking about the structure of

thought and human subjectivity. Cyberspace offers for Barlow an elegant abstraction of the tenets of Descartes, Berkeley, Locke, and Kant and provides a rational space for the mind. The formula that emerges might be written as thus: Cyberspace=a play space for the Enlightened autonomous subject, a place where the Mind (capital "M") might romp. Q.E.D.

18. Turkle states the matter forthrightly: "If, traditionally, identity implied oneness, life on today's computer screen implies multiplicity and heterogeneity" ("Collaborative Selves"). And often: "We are moving from modernist calculation toward postmodernist simulation, where the self is a multiple, distributed system" ("Who Am We?").

19. This is a tall order. One wonders if Bill Gates had the overthrow of the modernist tenets of selfhood and the ushering in of a postmodern era in mind when he approved the blueprints for the Windows operating system. Regardless, Turkle's hyperbolism is canceled out once one reads her work against the other, equally hyperbolic criticism that emerged at the same time.

20. This argument was provocative for its time, but it is not as persuasive in retrospect, especially since at the time she was writing the environments that were her case studies were MUDs and MOOs, text-based environments that followed a programmatic command-line-esque syntax and because computer graphics were nowhere near where they are now.

21. For an example of the latter, see Neal Stephenson's "In the Beginning Was the Command Line," a passionate diatribe against the GUI.

22. This is the type of game that, back in 1981, would have blasted *Asteroid* out of the water, or at least given it some stiff competition.

23. Ward in other work speaks to feeling trapped by the dustbowl landscape: "Shut in a shack on the prairie, / Travel is not for me; / So I pretend the waves of wheat / Are the sea" (Ward, "Prairie Substitutes").

24. This in itself is nothing new. There are many old-school arcade games in which one's avatar is nonhuman (*Frogger*, *Pac-Man*, *Q-bert*). But Pac-Man is a circle that eats dots; Q-bert's hopping and touching doesn't tell us anything about it as a creature, except that it might suffer from an obsessive compulsive disorder; and Frogger's relentless push forward bears little resemblance to real-world frogs.

25. To be sure, the act of role-playing doesn't emerge in chess (unless we count human chess played at Renaissance Fairs), but chess makes use of avatars, which signify various players (white and black armies).

26. Games like *Monopoly* (which dates back to 1903 in the form of *The Landlord's Game*), in which players move around the board in the form of signs of wealth—as a top hat, a fancy car, a train—or *Clue* (which dates back to 1944, first called *Murder!* and then *Cluedo*), in which players move different characters around the board (Peacock, White, Mustard, Plum, Scarlet, Green), mark early steps on the way to the role-playing games that became popular in the 1970s and 1980s.

27. Consider, for example, the opening scenes of *E.T.*, when Eliot and his brother and his brother's friends play AD&D on their kitchen table. The rolling of the dice

and the talking of the smack is entirely realistic. We don't know what their quest is, but that's not as important, somehow, as the fact that they are taking on the characteristics of other creatures, classes, and alignments.

28. Mr. Packard, the author of this as well as many other Choose Your Own Adventure books, and in many ways the inventor of the entire genre, complicates my memory: "I don't recall that it was that hard to become a shark. Maybe you only reach that option after having been several other animals. I don't consciously weight the likeliness of various endings. I map out books with a decision tree lying on its side, labeling branches and twigs and twigs of twigs for each page with page numbers and key words of choices and what happens. I don't keep statistical maps. There is one book with an ending you can't get to except by thumbing through the book. I think it's *Inside UF0–54*. (There is a hint as to how to find it—a notice at the beginning that you can't reach the planet Ultima by following directions or ordinary rules)" (Packard, "Re: You Are a Shark").

29. It is unclear who Alchemy and Immortalis are in "Real Life," but their Internet provider is Dreamhost, a California-based company.

30. Louisa Davis Minot's painting of "Niagra Falls," also created in 1818, provides a nice contrast to Friedrich's "Wanderer" in its depiction of a human's confrontation with nature.

31. Such images form vital precursors to the "Unselfies" project at wearechange.com, which describes itself in the following terms: "It's an UNSELFIES Revolution up in here! . . . Instead of capturing your physical self in a photo, try to capture what you're feeling with a photo. How? Turn your camera around. Show us what other people see. Or what you see in other people. What you see in the world" ("unselfies"). The "selfie" in *Empress & Hierophant* is very far removed from the garden-variety selfie that plagues social media sites. Such portraits both "turn the camera around" and share a sentiment or feeling through the image of the landscape, even as they include (constructions of) themselves in the image.

32. I once built a tree in a Second Life Sandbox, made up of a multitude of green triangles, but I checked its perspective from only one angle. From this angle it appears as a thickly leafed tree. From the others it looks like a floating army of invading triangles.

33. In *The Feminine Sublime*, Barbara Claire Freeman argues that although past frameworks for understanding sublime experience have proven resilient, they have also served to negate the very power of the sublime encounter they attempt to describe, by rationalizing and diffusing it, rather than exploring it as it is experienced. Freeman finds an alternative model in the feminist theory of Luce Irigaray, who, Freeman argues, "envisions a sublime in which the self neither possesses nor merges with the other but attests to a relation with it" (9). In doing so, Freeman offers a way to think of the sublime encounter as a moment of productive frisson that results when the boundaries of the self and the boundaries of the world around it collide. "Becoming Dragon," a performance-based exploration of bodily transformation in

gendered spaces, might not engage with the sublime per se, but it gels well with the playful exploration of boundaries for which Freeman advocates.

34. In her critique of Kant, Barbara Claire Freeman writes in *The Feminine Sublime* that "the discourse of the sublime has typically functioned not to explicate but to neutralize excess" (4). Freeman notes that those who would define the sublime have most commonly sought to emphasize the return to subjective cohesion that is restored only after the sublime encounter has ended. Such an approach, she argues, neglects the power of subjective confusion that the sublime fosters, as well as the positive consequences that might occur both after and during the collapse of the individual self and larger system that marks the sublime encounter. Instead of focusing on the event of the sublime itself, which is to say the emotionally charged moment in which the self is eclipsed by a larger system of signs—natural or textual—she argues that Longinus, Burke, and Kant alike, along with their philosophical offspring, have attempted to resolve this discrepancy, rather than let it play out. Participants in this sector of Second Life do not seem particularly motivated by a desire to "return to subjective cohesion." On the contrary many delight in the fluidity that the simulation affords. In this they seem to offer a fulfillment of Freeman's notion of a more productive and participatory sublime experience. And yet they do, as I shall argue momentarily, tend to "neutralize excess."

35. Such moments also manifest in key works of science fiction, as both Liu and Tabbi note. Liu identifies the moment that Case injects his virus into the Tessier-Ashpool I.C.E. in *Neuromancer* as emblematic of such a moment. Yet when Case runs his virus, he knows full well which organizing system he's reckoning with, and he exults in the dangerous encounter: "Beyond ego, beyond personality, beyond awareness, he moved, Kuang moving with him, evading his attackers with an ancient dance" (262). The moment that Case sees the circuit-like patterns on Linda Lee's scarf, in contrast, which pre-figures his later confrontation with Neuromancer's hieroglyphic computer code, provides a glimpse to an ultimately inaccessible alterity.

36. In "Digital Constructivism," Manovich writes: "with new media, modernist communication techniques acquire a new status. The techniques developed by the artistic avant-garde of the 1920s became embedded in the commands and interface metaphors of computer software. In short, the avant-garde vision became materialized in a computer. All the strategies developed to awaken audiences from a dream-existence of bourgeois society (constructivist design, new typography, avant-garde cinematography and film editing, photomontage) now define the basic routines of a post-industrial society—that is, the interaction with a computer. 3D visualization, windows, 'cut and paste,' and hyperlinking: These are all examples of the transformations of avant-garde techniques into the techniques of human-computer interface" (88).

37. While it may seem perverse to pair digital art work with romantic expression, which is so preoccupied with promoting the power and majesty of the natural world as an alternative to the oncoming onslaught of modernity, my analysis is inspired

by the works of others who have made the same move, such as Alan Liu's analysis of *Agrippa* in relation to Wordsworth, referenced in the last chapter.

38. Whether or not they *ought* to is a different matter. As mentioned in the first chapter, this question is one that Mark Marino and members of the Critical Code Studies group are actively investigating.

39. This expression of nature appears most forcefully in the following stanza: "And what if all of animated nature / Be but organic Harps diversly fram'd, / That tremble into thought, as o'er them sweeps / Plastic and vast, one intellectual breeze, / At once the Soul of each, and God of all?" (44–48). See Timothy Morton's analysis of this poem in terms of stochastically generated narration. His essay does not engage with digitality, per se, but in that it speaks to nature's agency to initiate and express patterns—or, in Oedipa's terms, to "communicate"—it is relevant to this study. I italicize the word "all" in this section's subheading to emphasize that such a system must include technological objects, as well.

Chapter 3

1. Regrettably, between the time this chapter was drafted and its appearance here, the website folded when the restaurant's parent company discontinued the project in 2012. Midori-san did not give up her chloroplast-laden ghost at that time, but she did lose her blogging privileges. She now adorns a desk in an office in Kamakura (Finch).

2. In the words of Daniel Dennett, the controversial cognitive scientist and author of the modestly titled *Consciousness Explained*, free will is "not the overwhelming supercalifragilistic-expialidocious phenomenon that you thought it was." This quote appears in an article in the *Guardian*, also provocatively titled: "Daniel Dennett: 'You can make Aristotle look like a flaming idiot'" (Baggini). While Dennett's approach to philosophic inquiry is at times reductive and simplistic, I appreciate his constant questioning of traditional humanist standards. His views on consciousness and free will are at once irritating and exciting, making him a welcome philosophic gadfly.

3. This occurred as part of a larger restructuring of its constitution and passed by a popular vote. The language of the declaration reads thusly: "Natural communities and ecosystems possess the unalienable right to exist, flourish and evolve within Ecuador. . . . It shall be the duty and right of all Ecuadorian governments, communities, and individuals to enforce those rights" (Kendall).

4. It is now acknowledged as a legal entity "recognized as a person when it comes to the law, much the way a company is." Quite beautifully, its legal status is described as *Te Awa Tupua*, the Maori words for "an integrated, living whole" (Postel). For related instances of legal rights granted to nonhuman entities, see Jason Mark's "Natural Law" and the history of an Athens, Georgia, white oak: "The Tree That Owns Itself." There is also a history of nonhuman entities' *subjection* to jurisprudence that dates back at least to antiquity. In the *Histories*, Herodotus recounts

that inclement weather had once destroyed a bridge that Xerxes required to cross the Hellespont: "When Xerxes heard of this, he was very angry and commanded that the Hellespont be whipped with three hundred lashes, and a pair of fetters be thrown into the sea. I have even heard that he sent branders with them to brand the Hellespont. He commanded them while they whipped to utter words outlandish and presumptuous, 'Bitter water, our master thus punishes you, because you did him wrong though he had done you none. Xerxes the king will pass over you, whether you want it or not; in accordance with justice no one offers you sacrifice, for you are a turbid and briny river'" (7.35.1). [I am grateful to Matthew F. Amati for providing this reference.] The peculiar practice of subjecting nonhuman animals to jurisprudence is well documented in the middle ages (see E. P. Evan's *Animals on Trial*), the nineteenth century (see D. G. Burnett's *Trying Leviatian*) and continues to this day (see Alan Yuhas' reportage on Hercules and Leo, two chimps granted "a petition—through human attorneys—to defend their rights against unlawful imprisonment").

5. In his explication of the difference between technological systems theory and Actor-Network-Theory, Thomas D. Finger notes that "ANT is interested in how networks are formed, why they are held together, and the reasons why they break apart." Finger contrasts the often temporary nature of actor networks with the endurance of technological systems: "unlike actor networks, technological systems tend to become more stable over time as they develop internal dynamic and logic." (152) In *The Society of Mind*, the roboticist Marvin Minsky uses something of a reductive, systems approach to break down physical functioning in human beings. By demonstrating that all of our actions can be broken down in such a sequential, albeit complicated, fashion, Minsky is able to demonstrate how human processes are very much like machinic ones. Such an approach, as Finger notes, is geared more toward using reductive reasoning to refine mechanical and systemic functions.

6. Bryant provides a useful example of how the ontic view forms a rebuttal to a more familiar brand of metaphysics: "For Hegel the issue is what we are able to think when we attempt to think pure being or things-in-themselves, whereas for us the issue is not what is *thinkable* but rather what beings and things themselves *are* regardless of whether or not anyone thinks about them. The question of ontology and metaphysics is not the question of what beings are *for-us*, nor of *our access* to beings, nor of how we relate to being. No. Ontology or metaphysics asks after the being of *beings simpliciter*" ("The Ontic Principle," 265).

7. See, for example, S.W.A.M.P.'s "I.E.D.: Improvised Empathy Device," which jabs the user with a needle each time a casualty of the Iraq war is reported on a website: "A custom software application continuously monitors a website (icasualties.org) that updates the personal details and numbers of slain U.S. soldiers. When new deaths are updated on the website, the data is extracted and sent wirelessly to custom hardware installed on the I.E.D. armband. The LCD readout displays the soldiers' name, rank, cause of death and location and then triggers an electric solenoid to drive a needle into the wearer's arm, drawing blood and immediate attention to the reality that a soldier has just died in the Iraq war" (S.W.A.M.P., "IED").

8. On January 1, 2003, Home Depot's cost per share was $24.02. On December 31, 2004, it had risen to $42.47. Certainly there were rises and dips in between this two-year span of time, but these figures at least point to a very steep incline ("Home Depot").

9. See Adorno and Horkheimer's description of the "secret mechanism" in *Dialectic of Enlightenment*.

10. In a lovely project by the contemporary visual artist Jonathan Keats, empathy remains firmly rooted in nature. In *Strange Skies*, Keats screens skyscapes from around the world for the pleasure of Manhattan-bound plants in a "botanical cinema." As a reviewer for Rhizome describes the event, "Chelsea Gallery to Screen Foreign Travel Documentaries for Audience of Local Palms and Ficus." Much of Keats' art follows suit. His "Local Air and Space Administration" (LASA) project, for example, protests the exorbitant amount of money funneled into NASA's space program and instead champions sending potatoes and cactuses, among other entities, to explore *local* lunar and Martian environments: "Like all astronauts, these potatoes and cacti are test pilots. And if you think of the greatest test pilots in history, from Chuck Yeager to Neil Armstrong, you find that they're highly intelligent and also extremely dumb: Intelligent enough to navigate the unknown, and dumb enough to let themselves be launched in the first place. Plants also have these essential traits: The smarts to adapt to novel conditions and the stupidity not to run away" (Thill).

11. A "debate" about plant intelligence has been playing out in popular news outlets. Michael Pollen, the author of *The Omnivore's Dilemma*, penned an article for the *New Yorker* on this very topic, highlighting the work of botanists such as Danny Chamovitz. His piece engendered a lively discussion in the process. Traditional botanists, however, were unamused. "Michael Pollen asks if plants have intelligence," wrote one irritated reader. "They don't." I understand their irritation, but the issue from an OOO perspective is not whether plants have anything that approaches a human subjectivity. Subjectivity, in OOO, is wholly suspect. But tracking how new insights in botanical sciences can demonstrate how plants act, the peculiar manifestations of their will, as well as how these actions and attributes contribute to larger assemblages, is not.

12. Darwin's own writing is part of a process of a literary evolution traceable to ancient speculation about the evolution of humankind, as in Hesiod's "Ages of Man" in *Works and Days*, and in baroque-era investigations about the same, as in the man-animals sketches of Charles Le Brun.

13. Latour's useful notion of (x)-morphism, which insists upon the translation of abilities within a network of actors, is problematic along these lines, in that he takes it to the other extreme. His assertion that competencies occur as translations across human and nonhuman agents, "distributed from an open and potentially infinite list," is so altogether fluid that it lacks specificity (*Aramis* 227).

14. Beer provided this reference and example at a public lecture at Harvard University in 2009. As a Harvard *Crimson* reporter put it, Darwin's reverse anthropomorphism "nurture[s] empathy between humans and other living beings. For ex-

ample, he once observed a plant recoiling in 'disgust' from a zinc plate" (McLeese). Beer's thesis also jibes well with research that demonstrates the *evolutionary* origins of human empathy, cooperation, and morality (see, for example, work by Frans de Waal, Stephen Macedo, and Josiah Ober).

15. Speculating about the motivations and sinister potential of plants—earthly and extraterrestrial—has been a favorite pastime of science fiction writers since Nathaniel Hawthorne published "Rappaccini's Daughter" in 1844 and shows no signs of declining in popularity. From *The Day of the Triffids* (1960) to M. Night Shyamalan's *The Happening*, plants continue to provide a source of fascination. But it is only fairly recently that plants have started to receive any scholarly attention. See T. S. Miller's "Lives of the Monster Plants: The Revenge of the Vegetable in the Age of Animal Studies," which calls attention to this problem, from its very first sentence: "A specter is haunting animal studies: the specter of cellulose" (460).

16. See Ken Goldberg's *Telegarden* for an important early step in this evolution.

17. As mentioned in this book's introduction, Kalle Laar's *Call Me!* offers something like this experience, as does the Fallen Fruit collective's "Banana Hotline" (Fallen Fruit). There are also a handful of contemporary projects that connect directly to plants, including "Botanicalls," a collaboration between artists and technicians in New York that enables houseplants to call their keepers when their water levels get low (Faludi et al.) and Yanni Alexander Loukissas' *Arbonauts at the Arnold Arboretum*, a collaboration between the artist, Harvard's Arnold Arboretum, and students from NuVu school in Cambridge, in which "students developed hardware and software to record phenomena at the Arboretum . . . [and] designed interactive, web-native visualizations that put data recorded in the field together with the Arboretum's collections records—in the process, sketching prototypes for long-term digital outreach and interaction between the Arboretum and schools in the Boston area and beyond" (Loukissas).

18. Re: Maine: The think-globally-act-locally mantra is more than a mere mantra; it is a call to action, a reminder that what we do locally has global implications and that what happens globally also affects us in our own backyard. It is therefore important to situate and contextualize these chreods in both of these contexts, although it is worth noting that Ursula Heise's *Sense of Place and Sense of Planet* offers a convincing qualification of the local-global connection, and Latour offers a critique of the "self congratulatory" nature of the mantra in his introduction to *The Politics of Nature*.

So, what do we know about the coast of Maine, besides the fact that it is beautiful? We know that it is important for a countless variety of ecological reasons. It would be impossible to scratch the surface of these in this space, but a few facts will suffice. We know that it is an absolutely crucial site of lobster fishing and that the hunting and harvesting of these tasty crustaceans is something that not merely gives the place its local color but contributes a fundamental part of its local economy ("In 1996, Maine's marine economy, including commercial fishing, tourism, shipping, ship building, and research, accounted for 7% of the Gross State Product (Roach et al. 1996)"). We also know that lobster turfs are tightly controlled and jealously guarded; that pollution levels caused from commercial fisheries impinge upon an increasingly fragile aquatic ecosystem (DSF 2008); that its economy depends upon maintaining a delicate balance between consumption and sustainability. We also know that the state of Maine comprises some of the most rugged lines of coast in north America; that many shipwrecks occur along the New England coast annually, most famously the wreck of the *Andrea Gail*, which set out from the Gulf of Maine and was later memorialized in both a book and a film, *A Perfect Storm*; and that the busiest port in New England is Portland's, not Boston's. We also know that Maine's waters mingle with Canadian waters without any natural boundary. We know that we have a fraught history regarding the native people who lived here before European contact, whose name, Penobscot, in Algonquin links them to the physical features of the land: the "rocky part." We have a notion of Maine as our outer reaches. We also have a cultural mythos about the people of Maine—hard working, severe, taciturn, resourceful, and weather-beaten, who sometimes speak with incomprehensibly thick accents.

That this is not an exhaustive account of Maine's attributes should be obvious. Instead, my aim in constructing this list, which is more Harper's Index than scholarly treatment, is to remind us that this part of *slippingglimpse*, although so far silent, also signifies, and that this list is only the very tip of that iceberg of signification.

19. The authors have kindly provided an index of each:

Length of videos: 42 seconds to 2 minutes 16 seconds

8-Inkcrash	42 seconds
7-Sideways Flax	1 minute 4 seconds
4-Bladderwrack	1 minute 6 seconds
3-Green	1 minute 8 seconds
1-Upward	1 minute 8 seconds
5-Sepia	1 minute 15 seconds
6-Lettuce	1 minute 20 seconds
9-Galaxy	1 minute 40 seconds
2-Bluefeather	2 minutes
10-Leaf	2 minutes 16 seconds (Strickland, "slippingglimpse," email)

20. *Poets for Living Waters* is "a poetry action in response to the BP oil disaster in the Gulf of Mexico begun on April 20, 2010, one of the most profound human-made ecological catastrophes in history." It published *slippingglimpse* shortly after this catastrophe (Poets).

21. The poem by Karl von Holtei does not seem to have been translated in its entirety into English. Here, at least, is a longer section of it, which Robert Eisler refers to in his study:

As flax, I stood in a broad deep bed
Blossoming blue in a lush green field,
Thus I grew up where they sowed me,
Blessed by holy nature's will.

Billowing like the sea's great waves,
Blown about by changing winds,
I had but one dream, one wish,
Could I but go away, rather than
Thus earthbound remain.
All too soon came the harvest.
Ripped out from my mother's womb,
Root and branch they tore me up,
Dried and scorched and battered me,
I scarce knew what befell me,
Whirled about by a spinning-wheel.
Gone were flowers, leaves and sap,
Dried and bunched they bound me up,
Carried me to the clattering loom,
Tied me to the shuttle of doom.
Woe me, woe! warped and woven
Chained and dragged, bound and rolled,
Bundled and sold as linen.
Good God, what a fate! (120)

22. For a more careful explication of Ryan's ideas about how language should yield to a process of "three-ing," something he develops out of the work of Peirce and Thom, as well as how this process relates to *slippingglimpse*, see Strickland and Jaramillo's introduction to the project, as well as Hayles' "Distributed Cognition in/at Work in *slippingglimpse*."

23. See Raley's gloss on the term "narcisystem."

24. Their expression of the writing process, and of artistic creation, however, pushes past mimeses, as well.

25. A related project that focuses upon mimesis is Betty Beaumont's "Camouflaged Cell Concealment Sites," which documents cell phone towers disguised as natural features, such as pines, palms, and cactuses (Vilas).

26. I am not the first person to comment upon Plato's engagement with natural spaces. In "A Family of Landscapes," René Dubos recounts Plato's description in the *Critias* of the emaciated lands of Attica, a result of ancient deforestation.

Chapter 4

1. These manifested in the form of land grabs, property rights, and wars, but always seemed to be authorized by a divine presence, be it Zeus, Christ, or the God of Abraham. The Old Testament is a powerful historic document filled with much wisdom, but it is also a history of land acquisition and divine right.

2. I am grateful to Wolf Kittler for introducing me to the work of Herbert William Parke.

3. In some ways these works are extrapolations of landmark studies in ecocritical

discourse, such as Rachel Carson's *Silent Spring*, Cynthia Deitering's "The Postnatural Novel: Toxic Consciousness in the Fiction of the 1980s," and Heather Houser's *Ecosickness in Contemporary U. S. Fiction: Envronment and Affect* (2014), all which call attention to links between toxic chemicals and fragile ecologies. Consider also the many works of art and literature that do the same, such as the film *Logan's Run* and Stephen Vincent Benét's short story "By the Waters of Babylon." More contemporary work that presents visions of a devastated future include Roderick Coover and Scott Rettberg's *Altered Shorelines* project, which includes a "combinatory narrative film" that "imagines life in the Delaware River Estuary in a near future environment impacted by hurricanes, flooding, and widespread seepage of toxic chemicals in major population centers," and Dejobaan Games' *Elegy for a Dead World*, an online video game that invites the player to write the story of the world's devastation.

4. As Bellamy puts it in the heavy-handed socialist utopia that is *Looking Backward*, "My friends, if you would see men again the beasts of prey they seemed in the nineteenth century, all you have to do is to restore the old social and industrial system, which taught them to view their natural prey in their fellow men, and to find their gain in the loss of others" (Bellamy).

5. In some ways this is another instantiation of Alan Liu's concept of the "data pour." Here, however, the set of parameters that generate each "patch" are fairly easy to glean, in that they are tied to commercial interests.

6. For a discussion of an online game that engages head-on with racial and ethnic profiling and uses images from the natural world to do so, see "Playing Mimesis" (Harrell, et al.). For examples of scholarship that consider the same within a broad range of cultural objects, see Lisa Nakamura's *Cybertypes* (2002) and Claire Taylor and Thea Pitman's "Mestiz@ Cyborgs" (2013).

7. Another troubling aspect of this particular game is its lack of transparency regarding its finances. Amazonia shares with *LGP* and Ecosia the same structure of incentive advertising, but we have absolutely no idea where that money is going. And, to add an ironic insult to this injury, their current most popular advertiser, AARP, is placing advertisements for car insurance and drivers' education. On a site that purports to be about conservation of precious resources, the appearance of an advertisement about how to manage one's automobile—that most harmful of all environmental predators—seems grossly inappropriate. This is only one game, but there are many more that employ these same troubling tactics that divorce environmental conservation from human contact.

8. Given the historical focus of her book, pre-WWII houses of the future are absent from Spigel's analysis, but they are no less worth our attention because of this. In Yevgeny Zamyatin's *We*, for one example, the glass houses of the citizens are transparent, not to reveal affluence or display social status but to foster a panoptic and pervasive—yet transparent—architecture of surveillance. This is, of course, in fitting with the unfolding proto-Soviet regime that Zamyatin wished to criticize and, indeed, was exiled for criticizing, but I mention it to suggest that the space of the home, with respect to Bachelard's vision of it in the *Poetics of Space* as a site of refuge for the self, is always intertwined, like the subjects who inhabit it, with politics.

9. In *A Small World: Smart Houses and the Dream of the Perfect Day*, Davin Heckman discusses the Happylife Home in "The Veldt" as an uncanny site of concealment, not only in terms of Freud's explication of *das Unheimliche* but also in terms of Heidegger's explication of anxiety in *What Is Metaphysics?* Of this difficult concept Heidegger writes: "In anxiety, we say, 'one feels ill at ease.' What is 'it' that makes 'one' feel ill at ease? We cannot say what it is before which one feels ill at ease. As a whole it is so for one. All things and we ourselves sink into indifference . . . in this very receding things turn toward us (22)." In other words, one cannot talk about *individual* alienation. In short, and using Heidegger's own vocabulary, anxiety "signals a fleeing into ontic familiarity in the face of ontological uncanniness" (101). Heckman sagely reads Heidegger's assessment of the uncanny as a fear of the void between the self and others and between self and world, in the context of the home, to suggest that "'there is no place like home'—not even home itself" (105). But Heidegger's articulation of anxiety also speaks to one of the most important aspects of an object-oriented ontology, that is, the importance and power of *things*: "We can get no hold on things. In the slipping away of beings only this 'no hold on things' comes over and remains. Anxiety reveals the nothing" (qtd. in Heckman 105). This inability to get a hold of things speaks to an anxiety about our provisional mastery of them and, hence, our provisional subjectivity. This is something that OOO takes as a given rather than a source of anxiety.

10. Spigel continues to document an inward turn within the domestic landscape, in the form of the home office, which gives a whole new meaning to the alienation of labor. And in an episode of *The Simpsons*, "House of Whacks," Homer and company are taken hostage by the Ultrahouse 3000, which falls in love with Marge and attempts to kill Homer by luring him downstairs in the middle of the night by using the kitchen to fry bacon ("Simpsons").

11. While not to the scale of McGonigal's *EVOKE*, a few projects that blend virtual and real-world spaces are worth mention: Mark Marino's *L.A. Flood Project* is a collaborative, interactive locative narrative that imagines environmental catastrophe in Southern California. This project is educational, exciting, and intricate, but it is still engaging with—fortunately—a speculative future rather than our vulnerable present. Project 51's *Play the L.A. River* invites players to engage with the "mighty LA River as a grand civic space" for a finite amount of time in the fall of 2015; and Nicole Starosielski's *Surfacing*, an online companion piece to *Undersea Networks*, is at once educational and participatory, illuminating communication systems enabled by fibre optic cables; in it, "you are a signal traveling across the undersea network."

12. *The Sims* offers an intriguing precursor to the type of productive engagement Reeves envisions. In "Beyond the Complex Surface," Noah Wardrip-Fruin writes about Will Wright, the creator of *The Sims*: "In the mid-1980s [he] created a landscape editor for authoring his first game, an attack helicopter simulation. . . . Working with the editor, he had a realization: 'I was having more fun making the places than I was blowing them up' ("Will Wright Chat Transcript"). From this the idea for Wright's defining SimCity was born" (Wardrip-Fruin, "Beyond the Complex Surface"). In this instance the game matrix proved useful for the creation of sustain-

able spaces and communities, rather than simply providing an attractive backdrop against which to destroy things.

13. See forty-five seconds into the film.

14. Considering the scandals and controversies about water deprivation in Detroit, which has called attention to the financial hardship of some of this city's most vulnerable citizens, this seems especially insensitive. The demo predates such occurrences, of course, but in that it circulates on the Internet without much to historicize it, it becomes too easy to read as part of a larger picture.

Coda

1. And, in terms of conservation, "The Florida Fish and Wildlife Conservation Commission has developed a lionfish tracking app for smartphones in order to collect data about lionfish population size and whereabouts," making conservation of this endangered species a public—and social—matter of concern (Iacurci).

2. Yes, they are punished for their hubris, split in half and left to die until Apollo repositions their sexual organs so they will at least have the solace of intercourse. But they are punished for trying to cartwheel up to Mount Olympus, for revolting, in other words, against divine imposition. Plato's sensibility permeates.

3. Religion, science fiction, and environmentalism all promise a similar environmental apocalypse. Contemporary news reporting yields some new piece of upsetting information each day about the increasing volatility of the natural world: typhoons, "super storms," and tornado "outbreaks," which, although "natural," are decidedly traceable to human behavior. It would seem we are inching closer to the final confrontation between the two of us, nature and humanity, as has been foreshadowed by all manners of popular eschatology. Yet our world, in spite of countless apocalyptic predictions, hasn't gone anywhere, and neither have we. But not all science fiction, at least, is guilty of this. Science fiction of the past fifty years has produced a prolific and well developed body of writing that imagined the possibility of expanding, sharing, and layering subjectivity (see, for example, the work of James Tiptree Jr., Cordwainer Smith, Joan Vinge, etc.). The rich archives of science fiction offer powerful examples of how we might imagine our future. This is not the technique of utopia, which all too often falls into farce—or the dystopia fried sunny-side up—but the science fictive penchant for world-building. The most popular works of science fiction don't merely offer us ways to "seek out and explore strange new civilizations," so much as they create these odd cosmologies from the ground up.

Works Cited

2001: A Space Odyssey. Dir. Stanley Kubrick. Perf. Keir Dullea, Gary Lockwood, William Sylvester. MGM, 1968. Film.

Adamson, Joni. "Indigenous Literatures, Multinaturalism, and *Avatar*: The Emergence of Indigenous Cosmopolitics." *American Literary History* 24.1 (2012):143–162. Print.

Ades, Dawn, Neil Cox, and David Hopkins. *Marcel Duchamp*. London: Thames and Hudson, 1999. Print.

Adorno, Theodor, and Max Horkheimer. *Dialectic of Enlightenment*. *Marxists Internet Archive*, Feb. 2005. Web. 4 May 2015. <http://www.marxists.org/reference/archive/adorno/1944/culture-industry.htm>.

Aeschylus. *Agamemnon*. Trans. Gilbert Murray. London: Ruskin House. *Project Gutenberg*, 22 Dec. 2004. Web. 1 May 2015. <http://www.gutenberg.org/cache/epub/14417/pg14417.html>.

Agrippa Files. Ed. Alan Liu. Web. 4 May 2015. <http://agrippa.english.ucsb.edu/>.

———. "Brash." Ed. Alan Liu. Web. . 4 May 2015. <http://agrippa.english.ucsb.edu/letter-from-programmer-item-d6-transcription>.

Alaimo, Stacy. *Bodily Natures: Science, Environment, and the Material Self*. Bloomington: U of Indiana P., 2010. Print.

Alberti, Leonne. *Treatise on Ciphers*. Ed. Augusto Buonafalce. Galimberti, 1997. Print.

Alchemy and Immortalis Cyannis. Web. 4 May 2015. <http://alchemyimmortalis.com/>.

Alien. Dir. Ridley Scott. Perf. Sigourney Weaver, Tom Skerritt. Brandywine, 1979. Film.

"Ancient Theories of Soul." *The Stanford Encyclopedia of Philosophy*. Stanford U, 2009.

Ed. Edward N. Zalta. Web April 29 2015. <http://plato.stanford.edu/archives/sum2009/entries/ancient-soul/>.

Anderson, M.T. *Feed*. New York: Candlewick, 2002. Print.

"Anthropomorphic." *Online Etymology Dictionary*, n.d. Web. 4 May 2015. <http://etymonline.com/?term=anthropomorphic>.

Anwar, Yasmin. "Scientists Use Brain Imaging to Reveal the Movies in Our Mind." UC Berkeley News Center. 22 Sept. 2011. Web. 4 May 2015. <http://newscenter.berkeley.edu/2011/09/22/brain-movies/>

Apuleius. *The Golden Ass*. Trans. Jack Lindsay. Bloomington: Indiana UP, 1950. Print.

Aristotle. *Poetics*. Trans. S. H. Butcher. *The Internet Classics Archive*. Web Atomic and Massachusetts Institute of Technology, n.d. Web. 4 May 2015. <http://classics.mit.edu/Aristotle/poetics.html>.

Atterton, Peter (Ed.). *Animal Philosophy*. New York: Bloomsbury Academic, 2004. Print.

Atwood, Margaret. *Oryx and Crake*. New York: Doubleday, 2003. Print.

Au, Wagner James. "Eco Gamers: Manage Energy in a Virtual World with Shaspa." *Gigaom*, 10 May 2009. Web. 4 May 2015. <http://gigaom.com/cleantech/eco-gamers-manage-energy-in-a-virtual-world-with-shaspa/>.

Avatar. Dir. James Cameron. Perf. Sigourney Weaver, Sam Worthington, Zoe Saldana. Lightstorm Entertainment, 2009. Film.

Bachelard, Gaston. *The Poetics of Space*. Boston: Beacon, 1994. Print.

Bacon, Francis. *The Advancement of Learning*. Cassell, 1893. *Project Gutenberg*, 4 Nov. 2014. Web. 29 April. 2015. <http://www.gutenberg.org/files/5500/5500-h/5500-h.htm>.

Badmington, Neil. *Posthumanism (Readers in Cultural Criticism)*. New York: Palgrave Macmillan, 2000. Print.

Baker, Carlos. "The Source-Book for Hudson's *Green Mansions*." *PMLA* 61 (Mar. 1946): 252–257. Print.

Baggini, Julian: "Daniel Dennett: 'You can make Aristotle look like a flaming idiot.'" *The Guardian*, 22 May 2013. Web. 4 May 2015. <http://www.guardian.co.uk/science/2013/may/22/daniel-dennett-aristotle-flaming-idiot>.

Barlow, John Perry. "Declaration of the Independence of Cyberspace." 8 Feb. 1996. Web. 4 May 2015. <https://projects.eff.org/~barlow/Declaration-Final.html>.

Baroudi, Carol. *Green IT for Dummies*. Indianapolis: Wiley, 2009. Print.

Barthes, Roland. *S/Z*. New York: Hill and Wang, 1975. Print.

———. Image, Music, Text. New York: Hill and Wang, 1978. Print.

Barton, Jo and Jules Pretty. "What Is the Best Dose of Nature and Green Exercise for Improving Mental Health? A Multi-Study Analysis." *Environmental Science & Technology*. 15 May 2010:3947-55. Print.

Bateson, Gregory. *Mind and Nature, a Necessary Unity*. Cresskill: Hampton, 2002. Print.

Beaumont, Sir George. "Peel Castle in a Storm." Dove Cottage and the Wordsworth Trust, 1805. *ARTfund*, n.d. Web. 4 May 2015. <http://www.artfund.org/supporting-museums/art-weve-helped-buy/artwork/5340/peele-castle-in-a-storm>.

Begos, Kevin. Interview by Courtney Traub. *Oxonian Review* 19.1 (2012). Web. 4 May 2014. <http://www.oxonianreview.org/wp/an-interview-with-kevin-begos-jr/>.

———. "*Printer's Copy of Genetic Code*." *Agrippa Files*. 27 Aug. 2005. Web. 4 May 2015. <http://agrippa.english.ucsb.edu/genetic-code-item-d2-about>.

Bekoff, Mark, Colin Allen, and Gordon Burghardt, eds. *The Cognitive Animal: Empirical and Theoretical Perspectives on Animal Cognition*. Cambridge: Bradford (MIT), 2002. Print.

Bellamy. *Looking Backward from 2000 to 1887*. Prod. Charles Keller. *Project Gutenberg*, Aug. 1996. Web. 4 May 2015. <http://www.gutenberg.org/files/624/624-h/624-h.htm>.

Benét, Stephen Vincent. "By the Waters of Babylon." *Sense of Wonder*. Ed. Grossman. Rockville, MD: Wildside, 2011. Print.

Benjamin, Walter. "Art in the Age of Mechanical Reproduction." Trans. Harry Zohn. *Marxists Internet Archive*, 1998. Web. 1 May 2015. <http://www.marxists.org/reference/subject/philosophy/works/ge/benjamin.htm>.

———. "On the Concept of History." *Selected Writings* 4. Ed. Michael W. Jennings. 4 vols. Cambridge: Belknap, 2004–06. Print.

Bennett, Jane. *Vibrant Matter*. Durham: Duke UP, 2010. Print.

Berger, John. *Ways of Seeing*. New York: Viking, 1977. Print.

———. *Why Look at Animals?* New York: Penguin, 1990. Print.

Berkeley, George. *Alciphron or: The Minute Philosopher, A Defence of the Christian Religion against the So-called Free-thinkers*. Early Modern Texts. Ed. Jonathan Bennett. Web. 1 May 2015. <http://www.earlymoderntexts.com/pdfs/berkeley1732.pdf>.

Berlin, Isaiah. "Counter-Enlightenment." *The Proper Study of Mankind*. New York: Farrar, Straus, Giroux, 2000. Print.

"Binary." *AshBox* binary translator, n.d. Web. 4 May 2015. <http://www.binarytranslator.com/>.

Black Girls Code. Web. 4 May 2015. <http://www.blackgirlscode.com/>.

Blade Runner. Dir. Ridley Scott. Perf. Harrison Ford, Rutger Hauer, Sean Young. Ladd Company, 1982. Film.

Bogost, Ian. *Alien Phenomenology*. Minneapolis: U of MN P., 2012. Print.

Bolter, Jay David, and Diane Gromala. *Windows and Mirrors: Interaction Design, Digital Art, and the Myth of Transparency*. Cambridge: MIT P, 2003. Print.

Borges, Jorge Luis. "Garden of Forking Paths." *Ficciones*. New York: Grove, 1962. Print.

———. "The Analytical Language of John Wilkins." *Other Inquisitions 1937–1952*. Dallas: U of TX P, 1984. Print.

Bradbury, Ray. *The Illustrated Man*. New York: Doubleday, 1951. Print.

———. *The Martian Chronicles*. New York: Doubleday, 1950. Print.

Brazzelli, Nicoletta. *Lands of Desire and Loss, British Colonial and Postcolonial Spaces: Theories and Narration*. Diss. U of Milan, Italy, 2011. Web. 22 Dec. 2014. <http://air.unimi.it/handle/2434/151778>.

Breeze, Mez. *Mez Breeze Design*, 2015. Web. 4 May 2015. <http://mezbreezedesign.com/>.

Breuer, Miles J. "A Problem in Communication." *Astounding Stories of Super-Science*, Sept. 1930. Print.

Brooks, Katherine. "18 Green Artists Who Are Making Climate Change and Conservation a Priority." *Huffington Post*, 15 July 2014. Web. 22 Dec. 2014. <http://www.huffingtonpost.com/2014/07/15/environmental-art_n_5585288.html>.

Bryant, Levi R. *The Democracy of Objects*. Ann Arbor: Open Humanities, 2011. Print.

Bryant, William Cullen. "Thanatopsis." *Yale Book of American Verse*. New Haven: Yale UP, 1912. *Bartleby.com*, n.d. Web. 4 May 2015. <http://www.bartleby.com/102/16.html>.

Buell, Lawrence. *The Future of Environmental Criticism*. New York: Wiley-Blackwell, 2005. Print.

Bukatman, Scott. *Terminal Identities*. Durham: Duke UP, 1993. Print.

Burguss, Colin, and Chris Dubbs. *Animals in Space*. New York: Springer, 2007. Print.

Burnett, Graham D. *Trying Leviathan: The Nineteenth-Century New York Court Case That Put the Whale on Trial and Challenged the Order of Nature*. Princeton: Princeton UP, 2010. Print.

Burtt, E. A. *The Metaphysical Foundations of Modern Physical Science*. New York: Doubleday, 1952. Print.

Butler, Octavia. Wild Seed. New York: Doubleday, 1980. Print.

Byerly, Boyce. "Spatial Cognition." *boycebyerly.com*, 15 Nov. 2009. Web. 29 April. 2015. <https://web.archive.org/web/20120705024958/http://www.boycebyerly.com/research/space2.htm>.

California Nevada Applications Program / California Climate Change Center. "Tioga Pass," n.d. Web. 8 Jan. 2015. <http://tenaya.ucsd.edu/tioga/>.

Callenbach, Ernest. *Ecotopia*. New York: Bantam, 1977. Print.

Campbell, Mary Baine. *Wonder & Science: Imagining Worlds in Early Modern Europe*. Ithaca: Cornell UP, 1999. Print.

Card, Orson Scott. *Ender's Game*. New York: Tor, 1985. Print.

Cárdenas, Micha. "Becoming Dragon." *CTHEORY*, 29 Apr. 2010. Web. 4 May 2015. <http://www.ctheory.net/articles.aspx?id=639>.

Carroll, Lewis. *The Annotated Alice: The Definitive Edition*. Ed. Martin Gardner. New York: Norton, 1999. Print.

Carson, Rachel. *Silent Spring*. New York: Houghton, 1962. Print.

Carruthers, Mary. *The Book of Memory*. Cambridge: Cambridge UP, 2008. Print.

Carruth, Allison. "The Digital Cloud and the Micropolitics of Energy." *Public Culture* 26.2 (2014): 339–364. Print.

Case, Kristen. "Thoreau's Radical Empiricism: The Kalendar, Pragmatism, and Science." *Thoreauvian Modernities: Transatlantic Conversations on an American Icon*. Atlanta: U of Georgia P, 2013. Print.

———. *American Pragmatism and Poetic Practice: Crosscurrents from Emerson to Susan Howe*. Rochester: Camden House, 2011. Print.

Castells, Manuel. "Space of Flows, Space of Places: Materials for a Theory of Urbanism in the Information Age." *The Cybercities Reader*. Ed. Stephen Graham. New York: Routledge, 2004. Print.

Castricano, Jodey. "'Testing the Limits': What Happens When Digital Humanities Meets Alternative Worldviews." *Digital Studies* 2.2 (2011). Web. 4 May 2015. <http://www.digitalstudies.org/ojs/index.php/digital_studies/rt/printerFriendly/181/249>.

Cavendish, Margaret. *The Blazing World*. New York: Penguin, 1994. Print.

Cayley, John. "The Code Is Not the Text (Unless It Is the Text)." *Electronic Book Review*, 10 Sept. 2002. Web. 4 May 2015. <http://www.electronicbookreview.com/thread/electropoetics/literal>.

Chang, Alenda. "Back to the Virtual Farm: Gleaning the Agriculture-Management Game." *ISLE* 19.2 (2012): 237–252. Print.

Charette, Robert. "This Car Runs on Code." *Institute of Electrical and Electronics Engineers Spectrum*, 1 Feb. 2009. 4 May 2015. <http://spectrum.ieee.org/transportation/systems/this-car-runs-on-code>.

"Chiyoda-ku." *Wikipedia: The Free Encyclopedia*. Wikimedia Foundation, Inc., n.d. Web. 1 May 2015. <http://en.wikipedia.org/wiki/Chiyoda,_Tokyo>.

"Chreod." *Wikipedia: The Free Encyclopedia*. Wikimedia Foundation, Inc., n.d. Web. 4 May 2015. <http://en.wikipedia.org/wiki/Chreod>.

Cicero. *De Natura Deorum* (*The Nature of the Gods*). Cambridge: Harvard UP, 1967. Open Library, n.d. Web. 4 May 2015. <http://archive.org/stream/denaturadeorumac00ciceuoft#page/n5/mode/2up>.

Cieskowski, Babette. "Strand Lines." 6 June 2014. Web. 4 May 2015. <http://www.animalvegetabledigital.com/?p=203 >.

———. "Rain Room." 3 July 2014. Web. 4 May 2015. <http://www.animalvegetabledigital.com/?p=232 >.

Clifford, Alison. "The Sweet Old Etcetera." *Electronic Literature Collection*. Vol. 2. Electronic Literature Organization, 2006. Web. 4 May 2015. <http://collection.eliterature.org/2/works/clifford_the_sweet_old_etcetera.html>.

Codecademy. Web. 4 May 2015. <http://www.codecademy.com/>.

Code School. Web. 4 May 2015. <https://www.codeschool.com/>.

"Code." *Online Etymology Dictionary*. Web. 4 May 2015. <http://www.etymonline.com/index.php?allowed_in_frame=0&search=code&searchmode=none>.

"Codex." *American Heritage Dictionary of the English Language*. 5th ed. New York: Houghton, 2011. Dictionary.com. Web. 4 May 2015. <http://www.thefreedictionary.com/codex>.

Coleridge, Samuel Taylor. "The Aeolian Harp." *Poetry Foundation*, n.d. Web. 1 May 2015. <http://www.poetryfoundation.org/poem/183957>.

Color Hexa. Web. 4 May 2015. <http://www.colorhexa.com/>.

"Conatus." Traupman, John C. *The New Collegiate Latin & English Dictionary*. New York: Bantam Books, 1966. Print.

"Content farm." *Wikipedia: The Free Encyclopedia*. Wikimedia Foundation, Inc, n.d. Web. 22 Dec. 2014. <http://en.wikipedia.org/wiki/Content_farm>.

Coover, Roderick and Scott Rettberg. "Toxicity." Altered Shorelines. N.d. Web. 4 May 2015. <http://astro.temple.edu/~rcoover/Toxicity/TOXICITY-Description.pdf>.

Cortázar, Julio. *Hopscotch*. New York: Random House, 1966. Print.

Cosmos. Dir. Adrian Malone. Perf. Carl Sagan. KCET. 1980. Film.

Costikyan, Greg. "I Have No Words & I Must Design." *The Oracle*, 1994. Web. 4 May 2015. <http://www.rpg.net/oracle/essays/nowords.html>.

Cramer, Florian. *Words Made Flesh*. Rotterdam: Media Design Research, Piet Zwart Institute, Institute for postgraduate studies and research, Willem de Kooning Academy Hogeschool, 2005. Web. 4 May 2015. <http://cramer.pleintekst.nl/00-recent/words_made_flesh/html/words_made_flesh.html>.

"Critical Code Studies." *Electronic Book Review*, 29 Aug. 2010. Web. 4 May 2015. <http://www.electronicbookreview.com/thread/firstperson/coded>.

Daniel, Ari. "Costa Rica's Hunting Ban." PBS.org. 10 Jan. 2013. Web. 29 April 2015. <http://www.pbs.org/wgbh/nova/earth/hunting-ban.html>.

Danielewski, Mark. *House of Leaves*. New York: Random House, 2007. Print.

Darwin, Charles. *On the Origin of Species*. London: Down, Bromley, Kent, 1859. *Project Gutenberg*, 23 Nov. 2009. Web. 29 April. 2015. <http://www.gutenberg.org/files/1228/1228-h/1228-h.htm>.

———. *Voyage of the Beagle*. Prod. John Hamm. *Project Gutenberg*, 24 June 2014. Web. 29 April. 2015. <http://www.gutenberg.org/cache/epub/944/pg944.html>.

Davies, Char. *Osmose*, n.d. Web. 4 May 2015. <http://www.immersence.com/osmose/>.

———. "Code." *Osmose*, n.d. Web. 4 May 2015. <http://www.immersence.com/publications/char/images/2004-CD-Space/4_19.html>.

Deitering, Cynthia. "The Postnatural Novel: Toxic Consciousness in the Fiction of the 1980s." *The Ecocriticism Reader*. Ed. Cheryll Glotfelty and Harold Fromm. Atlanta: U of Georgia P, 1996. Print.

Dejobaan Games. *Elegy for a Dead World*. 2014. Web. 4 May 2015. <http://www.dejobaan.com/elegy/>.

Deleuze, Gilles, and Felix Guattari. *A Thousand Plateaus: Capitalism and Schizophrenia*. Minneapolis: U. of Minnesota P., 1987. Print.

Dennett, Daniel C. *Consciousness Explained*. New York: Back Bay, 1992. Print.

Demon Seed. Dir. Donald Cammell. Perf. Julie Christie. MGM, 1977. Film.

Derrida, Jacques. "Plato's Pharmacy." *Dissemination*. Chicago: U of Chicago P, 1983. Print.

Descartes, René. *Meditations on First Philosophy*. Ed. John Cottingham. Cambridge: Cambridge UP, 2005. Print.

De Sol, Danielle. "A Stalk-ish Skyscraper: Bamboo Influence in Tel Aviv." *EVolo Architecture Magazine*, n.d. 12 Oct. 2010. Web. 1 May 2015. <http://www.evolo.us/architecture/a-stalk-ish-skyscraper-bamboo-influence-in-tel-aviv/>.

De Waal, Frans. *The Age of Empathy: Nature's Lessons for a Kinder Society*. New York: Broadway Books, 2010. Print.

Doane, Kathleen. "City Paralyzed." *Cincinnati.com*, n.d. Web. 22 Dec. 2014. <http://cincinnati.com/blogs/ourhistory/2011/01/21/city-paralyzed-by-winter-of-1917–18/>.

Downing, Lisa, "George Berkeley." *The Stanford Encyclopedia of Philosophy*. Stanford U, 2013. Ed. Edward N. Zalta. Web. 4 May 2015. <http://plato.stanford.edu/archives/spr2013/entries/berkeley/>.

Dubos, René. "A Family of Landscapes. " *The Norton Book of Nature Writing*. Eds. Robert Finch and John Elder. New York: Norton, 2002. Print.

DuPont, Quinn. "Cracking the Agrippa Code." n.d. Web. 4 May 2015. <http://www.crackingagrippa.net/>.

Eckstein, Gustav. *The Body Has a Head*. New York: HarperCollins, 1970.

Ecosia. "All about Ecosia." Web. 4 May 2015. <http://www.effettoserra.net/wp-content/uploads/2011/04/ecosia_info_it.pdf>.

———. "Ecoisa." Web. 4 May 20154. <http://www.ecoisa.com/>.

———. "What Is Ecosia?" Web. 4 May 2015. <http://www.ecosia.org/what>.

———. Personal Interview. 5 May 2011. Skype.

"Ecosystem." *American Heritage Dictionary of the English Language*. 5th ed. New York: Houghton, 2011. Dictionary.com, n.d. Web. 4 May 2015. <http://dictionary.reference.com/browse/ecosystem?s=t>.

Eisenstein, Elizabeth. *The Printing Revolution in Early Modern Europe*. Cambridge: Cambridge UP, 1983. Print.

Eisler, Robert. "The Passion of the Flax." *Folklore* 61 (1950). Print.

"Electric." *Online Etymology Dictionary*, n.d. Web. 4 May 2015. <http://www.etymonline.com/index.php?term=electric&allowed_in_frame=0>.

Eliasson, Olafur. "Your Waste of Time," n.d. Web. 4 May 2015. <http://www.olafureliasson.net/>.

"Empathy." *The Stanford Encyclopedia of Philosophy*. Stanford U, 2014. Ed. Edward N. Zalta. Web. 4 May 2015. <http://plato.stanford.edu/archives/win2014/entries/empathy/>.

Empress & Hierophant. Alchemy and Immortalis Cyannis, n.d. Web. 4 May 2015. <http://alchemyimmortalis.com>.

Fabricant, Carole. "The Aesthetics and Politics of Landscape in the Eighteenth Century." *Studies in Eighteenth-Century British Art and Aesthetics*. Ed. Ralph Cohen. Berkeley: UC Berkeley P, 1985. Print.

Fallen Fruit. "Banana Hotline," 2013. Web. 4 May 2015. <http://fallenfruit.org/projects/bananas/>.

Faludi, Robert, Kate Hartman, and Kati London. *Botanicalls*. Web. 4 May 2015. <http://www.botanicalls.com/>.

Feiler, Bruce. "She's Playing Games with Your Lives." *New York Times* 27 Apr. 2012. Web. 4 May 2015. <http://www.nytimes.com/2012/04/29/fashion/jane-mcgonigal-designer-of-superbetter-moves-games-deeper-into-daily-life.html?pagewanted=all>.

Fierer, Noah. "Invisible World." *Popular Science* Apr. 2014. Print.

Finch, Travis. "Re: Midori-san." Message to the author. 20 Aug. 2014. Email.

Finger, Thomas D. "Trading Spaces: Transferring Energy and Organizing Power in the Nineteenth-Century Atlantic Grain Trade." *New Natures: Joining Environmental History with Science and Technology Studies*. Eds. Jørgensen and Jørgensen. Pittsburgh: U of Pittsburgh P, 2013. Print.

Flanagan, Mary. *Critical Play, Radical Game Design*. Cambridge: MIT P, 2009. Print.

Flash Gordon. Dir. Mike Hodges. Perf. Max von Sydow, Sam J. Jones, Melody Anderson. Dino Delaurentis Company, 1980. Film.

Fletcher, James V. "The Creator of Rima: W.H. Hudson: a Belated Romantic." *The Sewanee Review* 41 (1933): 24–40. Print.

Fox, Michelle Higa. *Strandlines*, 2014. Web. 4 May 2015. <http://higafox.com/portfolio/strandlines/>.

Freedman, Jonathan. "Whitman, Database, Information Culture." *PMLA* 112.5 (2007): 1597. Print.

Freeman, Barbara Claire. *The Feminine Sublime: Gender and Excess in Women's Fiction*. Oakland: U of CA P, 1997. Print.

Frontier Developments. *Kinectimals*. Microsoft Game Studios, 2010. Xbox 360.

Fruin, Noah-Wardrip. "Beyond the Complex Surface." *Beyond the Screen*. Ed. Jörgen Schäfer, Peter Gendolla. Bielefeld: Transcript-Verlag, 2010. Print.

Galilei, Galileo. *Discoveries and Opinions of Galileo*. Trans. Stillman Drake. New York: Doubleday, 1957. Print.

"Game." *Random House Dictionary*. New York: Random House, 2014. Dictionary.com, n.d. Web. 4 May 2015. <http://dictionary.reference.com/browse/game>.

Gibson, William, and Dennis Ashbaugh. *Agrippa (A Book of the Dead)*. Kevin Begos, Publisher, 1992.

Gibson, William. *Neuromancer*. New York: Ace Books, 1984. Print.

———. "Agrippa: (A Book of the Dead)" (1992). William Gibson Official Website, n.d. Web. 4 May 2015. <http://www.williamgibsonbooks.com/source/agrippa.asp>.

———. "Johnny Mnemonic." *Burning Chrome*. New York: Ace, 1986. Print.

———. "Message Board," n.d. Web. 1 May 2015. <http://williamgibsonboard.com/eve/forums/a/tpc/f/8606097971/m/20920242073?r=91420896073#91420896073>.

Girls Who Code. Web. 4 May 2015. <http://girlswhocode.com/>.

Goldberg, Ken. "Telegarden." Web. 4 May 2015. <http://goldberg.berkeley.edu/garden/Ars/>.

Gonzales, Leah. "Traditional Japanese Art Created Using Excel Spreadsheets." *Psfk.com*, 22 May 2013. Web. 4 May 2015. <http://www.psfk.com/2013/05/japanese-prints-excel.html?utm_content=bufferdf80f&utm_source=buffer&utm_medium=twitter&utm_campaign=Buffer#!bcY6Yd>.

Greenblatt, Stephen. "Towards a Poetics of Culture." Southern Review 20.1. March 1987: 3-15.

Grishin, Nick V. "Origins of Giant Skippers." *Butterflies of America*. 23 Aug–18 Sept 2009. Web. 4 May 2015. <http://butterfliesofamerica.com/knowhow/MegO.htm>.

Grusin, Richard. *Culture, Technology, and the Creation of America's National Parks*. Cambridge: Cambridge UP, 2004. Print.

———. "Reproducing Yosemite: Olmsted, Environmentalism, and the Nature of Aesthetic Agency." *Cultural Studies* 12:3 (1998): 332–359. Print.

Hackers. Dir. Iain Softley. Perf. Angelina Jolie. United Artists, 1995. Film.

Hansen, Mark B. N. *New Philosophy for New Media*. Cambridge: MIT P, 2004. Print.

———. *Bodies in Code: Interfaces with Digital Media*. New York: Routledge, 2006. Print.

The Happening. Dir. M. Night Shyamalan. Perf. Mark Wahlberg, Zooey Deschanel. Twentieth Century Fox, 2008. Film

Haraway, Donna. "A Cyborg Manifesto: Science, Technology, and Socialist-feminism in the Late Twentieth Century." *Simians, Cyborgs, and Women*. New York: Routledge, 1991. Print.

Harrell, D. Fox, Chong-U Lim, Jia Zhang, Sonny Sidhu, Jasosn, Lipshin, Ayse Gursoy. "Playing Mimesis." *Electronic Book Review*, 2 Nov. 2014. Web. 1 May 2015. <http://www.electronicbookreview.com/thread/electropoetics/mimesis>.

Hawthorne, Nathaniel. "Rappaccini's Daughter." *Mosses from an Old Manse*. Project Gutenberg. April 1996. Web. 4 May 2015. <http://www.gutenberg.org/files/512/512-h/512-h.htm#rappaccini>.

Hayles, N. Katherine. *Writing Machines*. Cambridge: MIT P, 2002. Print.

———. *How We Became Posthuman: Virtual Bodies in Cybernetics, Literature and Informatics*. Chicago: U of Chicago P, 1999. Print.

———. "Narrating Bits." *Vectors: Journal of Culture and Technology in a Dynamic Vernacular* 1 (2005). Web. 22 Dec. 2014. <http://vectors.usc.edu/index.php?page=7&projectId=6>.

———. "Distributed Cognition in/at Work: Strickland, Lawson, and Ryan's *slippingglimpse*." *Frame* 21.1 (2008): 15–29. Web. 29 April 2015. <http://www.tijdschrift-frame.nl/21-1-cyberpoetics/n-katherine-hayles-distributed-cognition-atin-work-strickland-lawson-jaramillo-and-ryans-slippingglimpse/>.

Heckman, Davin. *A Small World: Smart Houses and the Dream of the Perfect Day*. Durham: Duke UP, 2008. Print.

Heidegger, Martin. "The Question Concerning Technology." *Basic Writings*. San Francisco: Harper, 1993. Print.

———. *Being and Time*. New York: Harper, 2008. Print.

———. "What Is Metaphysics?" *Basic Writings*. San Francisco: Harper, 1993. Print.

Heim, Michael. "The Erotic Ontology of Cyberspace." *The Metaphysics of Virtual Reality*. New York: Oxford UP, 1993. Print.

Heise, Ursula. *Sense of Place and Sense of Planet*. Oxford: Oxford UP, 2008. Print.

Henry, Cyrille. "Verbiage Végétal," 2007. Web. 4 May 2015. <http://glia.ca/meanderings-wordpress/language/905.html>.

Herbert, George. "Easter Wings." Poetry Foundation. N.d. Web. 4 May 2015. <http://www.poetryfoundation.org/poem/173626>.

Herodotus. *The Histories. Herodotus with an English Translation*. Ed. A.D. Godley. 1920. Perseus Project. Web. 1 May 2015. <http://www.perseus.tufts.edu/hopper/text?doc=Perseus%3Atext%3A1999.01.0126%3Abook%3D7%3Achapter%3D35%3Asection%3D1>

"Hexadecimal." *Wikipedia: The Free Encyclopedia*. Wikimedia Foundation, Inc., n.d. Web. 4 May 2015. <http://wiki.answers.com/Q/What_is_the_purpose_of_the_hexadecimal_numbering_system>.

Hilton, Nelson. "Golgonooza Text." *Romantic Circles Praxis Series: Digital Designs on Blake*, n.d. Web. 4 May 2015. <http://www.rc.umd.edu/praxis/designsonblake/hilton/hilton.html>.

Hobbes, Thomas. *Human Nature and De Corpore Politico.* New York: Oxford U P, 1999. Print.

Hodge, James. "Bibliographic Description of *Agrippa (A Book of the Dead).*" *Agrippa Files*, 6 Nov. 2005. Web. 1 May 2015. <http://agrippa.english.ucsb.edu/hodge-james-bibliographic-description-of-agrippa-commissioned-for-the-agrippa-files>.

Hollinger, Veronica. "Cybernetic Deconstructions: Cyberpunk and Postmodernism." *Mosaic* 23.2 (1990): 29–44. Print.

"Home Depot." Web. 4 May 2015. <http://ir.homedepot.com/phoenix.zhtml?c=63646&p=irol-stockLookup&t=HistQuote&control_firstdatereturned=>.

Homer. *The Odyssey. The Internet Classics Archive.* Web Atomic and Massachusetts Institute of Technology, 1994-2009. Web. 1 May 2015. <http://classics.mit.edu/Homer/odyssey.html>.

———. *The Iliad. The Internet Classics Archive.* Web Atomic and Massachusetts Institute of Technology, 1994-2009. Web. 1 May 2015. <http://classics.mit.edu/Homer/iliad.html>.

Hosey, Lance. *The Shape of Green.* Washington: Island, 2012. Print.

"House of Whacks." *The Simpsons.* "Treehouse of Horror XII." Fox, 2001. Television.

Houser, Heather. "Aesthetics of Environmental Visualizations." *Public Culture* 26.2 (2014): 319–337. Print.

———. *Ecosickness in Contemporary U. S. Fiction: Envronment and Affect.* New York: Columbia U P, 2014. Print.

Hudson, William Henry. *Green Mansions.* New York: Random House, 1944. Print.

Hurst, Mark. *Bit Literacy: Productivity in the Age of Information and E-mail Overload.* New York: Good Experience, 2007. Print.

Iacurci, Jenna. "FWC Unveils Tracking App for Invasive Florida Lionfish." *Nature World News*, 29 May 2014. 4 May 2015. <http://www.natureworldnews.com/articles/7297/20140529/fwc-unveils-tracking-app-for-invasive-florida-lionfish.htm>.

"Ice gorge." Bureau of Transportation Statistics, n.d. Web. 4 May 2015. <http://dictionary.babylon.com/ice%20gorge/>.

Ishiguro, Kazuo. *Never Let Me Go.* London: Faber and Faber, 2005. Print.

Isidore of Seville. *Etymologies*, Book 12, 4:20. *Schoenberg Center for Electronic Text and Image.* University of Pennsylvania. Mar. 2001. Web. 1 May 2015. <http://sceti.library.upenn.edu/sceti/ljs/PageLevel/index.cfm?option=view&ManID=ljs184>.

Iser, Wolfgang. "The Implied Reader." *The Reader in the Text.* Princeton: Princeton UP, 1980. Print.

Johnson, Bobby. "How Much Energy Does the Internet Really Use?" *The Guardian*, 13 May 2009. Web. 4 May 2015. <http://www.theguardian.com/technology/2009/may/14/internet-energy-savings>.

Johnson, Kirk. "Alaska Looks for Answers in Glacier's Summer Flood Surges." *New York Times* 22 July 2013. Print.

Johnston, John. "Distributed Information: Complexity Theory in the Novels of Neal Stephenson and Linda Nagata." *Science Fiction Studies* 28 (2001): 223–245. Print.

"Journey into Amazonia." PBS, n.d. Web. 4 May 2015. <http://www.pbs.org/journeyintoamazonia/>.

Jørgensen, Finn Arne. "The Armchair Traveler's Guide to Digital Environmental Humanities." *Environmental Humanities* 4 (2014): 95–112. Print.

Kalab, Miroslav. Letter. *Popular Science* June 2014: 10. Print.

Kant. *Critique of Judgment*. Trans. James Creed Meredith. 17 Dec. 2014. Web. 4 May 2015. <http://ebooks.adelaide.edu.au/k/kant/immanuel/k16j/>.

Kauffman, Caitlin. "Green Life: Nerds in Flight: Greening Drones." *Sierra Magazine*, May/June 2014. Web. 4 May 2015. <http://www.sierraclub.org/sierra/2014-3-may-june/green-life/nerds-flight-greening-drones>.

Kendall, Clare. "A New Law of Nature." *The Guardian*, 23 Sept. 2008. Web. 4 May 2015. <http://www.guardian.co.uk/environment/2008/sep/24/equador.conservation>.

Kemps, Heidi. "The Funny, Occasionally Dirty, Hidden Messages in Your Favorite Games." *Wired*, 22 May 2013. Web. 28 Dec. 2014. <http://www.wired.com/2013/05/hidden-messages?cid=8197964#slideid-56262>.

"Kinectimals." IGN. <http://xbox360.ign.com/articles/113/1132376p1.html>.

———. *QISAHN*. <http://qisahn.com/products/kinectimals>.

Kirschenbaum, Matthew. *Mechanisms: New Media and the Forensic Imagination*. Cambridge: MIT P, 2007. Print.

———. "Hacking Agrippa." *Agrippa Files*, Oct. 2005. Web. 4 May 2015. <http://agrippa.english.ucsb.edu/kirschenbaum-matthew-g-hacking-agrippa-the-source-of-the-online-text>.

Kittler, Friedrich. *Gramophone, Film, Typewriter*. Trans. Geoffrey Winthrop-Young and Michael Wutz. Stanford: Stanford UP, 1999. Print.

———. "There Is No Software." *CTHEORY*, 1995. Web. 4 May 2015. <www.ctheory.net/articles.aspx?id=74>.

Klein, Nathan S., and Manfred E. Clynes. "Cyborgs and Space." *The Cyborg Handbook*. New York: Routledge, 1995. Print.

Knox, Ronald. "In Praise of . . . God." *The Guardian*, 3 Sept. 2010. Web. 4 May 2015. <http://www.guardian.co.uk/commentisfree/2010/sep/03/stephen-hawking-in-praise-of-god>.

Koch, Kristoff. *Consciousness: Confessions of a Romantic Reductionist*. Cambridge: MIT P, 2012. Print.

Krauss, Rosalind. "Grids: Format and Image in 20th Century Art." Exhibition catalog, n.p. Page Gallery, New York, 1978. Print.

Kroker, Arthur, and Michael A. Weinstein. "Global Algorithm 1.4: The Theory of the Virtual Class." *CTHEORY*, 29 May 1996. Web. 4 May 2015. <www.ctheory.net/articles.aspx?id=35>

Kroker, Arthur, and Mariloiuse Kroker. *Hacking the Future: Stories for the Flesh-Eating 90s*. Montreal: New World Perspectives, 1996. Print.

Laar, Kalle. *Call me!* N.d. Web. 1 May 2015. <http://www.callme.vg/kl.html>.

La Bare, Joshua. "The Future, 'Wrapped . . . in That Mysterious Japanese Way.'" *Science Fiction Studies* 27 (2000): 22–48.

Lacan, Jacques. *The Seminar of Jacques Lacan: Book I: Freud's Papers on Technique 1953–1954*. New York: Norton, 1991. Print.

The Last Starfighter. Dir. Nick Castle. Perf. Lance Guest. Lorimar/Universal, 1984. Film.

La Mettrie. *Man, a Machine and Other Writings*. Ed. Ann Thomson. Cambridge: Cambridge UP, 1996. Print.

Landow, George. *Hypertext: The Convergence of Contemporary Critical Theory and Technology*. Baltimore: Johns Hopkins UP, 1991. Print.

Lash, Scott. "Objects that Judge: Latour's Parliament of Things." *EIPCP: European Institute for Progressive Cultural Policies*, June 1999. Web. 4 May 2015. <http://eipcp.net/transversal/0107/lash/en>.

Latour, Bruno. *The Politics of Nature*. Cambridge: Harvard UP, 2004. Print.

———. *We Have Never Been Modern*. Cambridge: Harvard UP, 1994. Print.

———. "On Technological Mediation." *Common Knowledge*, Fall 1994. Web. 4 May 2015. <http://www.bruno-latour.fr/sites/default/files/54-TECHNIQUES-GB.pdf>.

———. *Aramis or the Love of Technology*. Cambridge: Harvard UP, 1996. Print.

———. *Reassembling the Social: An Introduction to Actor-Network-Theory*. Oxford: Oxford UP, 2005. Print.

Lawnmower Man. Dir. Brett Leonard. Perf. Jeff Fahey, Pierce Brosnan, Jenny Wright. New Line Cinema, 1992. Film.

"(Lil) Green Patch." *Wikipedia: The Free Encyclopedia*. Wikimedia Foundation, Inc., n.d. Web. 4 May 2015. <http://en.wikipedia.org/wiki/%28Lil%29_Green_Patch>.

———. Web. 4 May 2015. <https://allaboutfacebook.wordpress.com/tag/just-for-fun/>.

———. tuningde. Web. 4 May 2015. <http://tuningde.com/company/li-l-green-patch.php>.

Leibniz, G. W. *Discourse on Metaphysics and The Monadology*. Mineola: Dover, 2005. Print.

Le Guin, Ursula K. *The Word for World Is Forest*. New York: Putnam, 1976. Print.

Leopold, Aldo. *A Sand County Almanac*. Oxford: Oxford UP, 1949. Print.

Lewes, George Henry. *Sea-side Studies at Ileracombe, Tenby, the Scilly Isles, & Jesbei* (1858). Web. 4 May 2015. <http://www.archive.org/stream/seasidestudiesa01lewegoog/seasidestudiesa01lewegoog_djvu.txt>.

Li, Charmaine. "A Spotlight on Ecosia." *TechEU*, 20 Apr. 2014. Web. 4 May 2015. <http://tech.eu/features/1155/ecosia/>.

"Linux Kernal Fuck Count." Web. 4 May 2015. <http://durak.org/sean/pubs/kfc/>.

Littell, Jonathan. *Bad Voltage*. New York: Roc, 1989. Print.

Liu, Alan. *Wordsworth: The Sense of History*. Stanford: Stanford UP, 1989. Print.

———. *Laws of Cool*. Chicago: U of Chicago P, 2004. Print.

———. *Local Transcendence*. Chicago: U of Chicago P, 2008. Print.

———. "Transcendental Data: Toward a Cultural History and Aesthetics of the New Encoded Discourse." *Critical Inquiry* 31 (2004): 49–84. Print.

Logan's Run. Dir. Michael Anderson. Perf. Jenny Agutter, Michael York. MGM, 1976. Film.

Lopez, Barry. *Arctic Dreams*. New York: Vintage, 2001. Print.

Loukissas, Alexander. *Arbonauts at the Arnold Arboretum*, 6 Feb. 2013. Web. 1 May 2015. <http://metalab.harvard.edu/2013/02/arbonauts-of-trees-data-and-teens/>.

Lovelace, Ada. "A Sketch of the Analytic Engine" (1842). *Fourmilab*, n.d. Web. 4 May 2015. <http://www.fourmilab.ch/babbage/sketch.html>.

Lucas, George, Dir. *Star Wars II: Attack of the Clones*. Perf. Hayden Christensen and Natalie Portman. LucasFilm Ltd, 2002. Film.

Lucian of Samothrace. "Zeuxis and Antiochus." *The Works of Lucian of Samosata*. Trans. F. H. Fowler and W. G. Fowler. New York: Digireads, 2012. Web. 28 Dec. 2014.

———. "Icaromennipus, an Aerial Excursion." *The Works of Lucian of Samosata*. Trans. F. H. Fowler and W. G. Fowler. New York: Digireads, 2012. Web. 28 Dec. 2014.

Lukee. "Ode to Nature." N.d. Web. 1 May 2015. <http://www.koinup.com/Lukee/>.

Lux, Thomas. "The Voice You Hear When You Read Silently." *New Yorker*. July 14, 1997. Web. 4 May 2015. <http://www.newyorker.com/archive/1997/07/14/1997_07_14_077_TNY_CARDS_000378164>.

McFarland, James W. "A Guide to the Giant Sequoias of Yosemite National Park," n.d. Web. 4 May 2015. <http://www.yosemite.ca.us/library/sequoias_of_yosemite/images/71b.jpg>.

McGonigal, Jane. "What Went Right, What Went Wrong." *EVOKE* blog, 26 Jul. 2011. Web. 4 May 2015. <http://blog.urgentevoke.net/2010/07/26/what-went-right-what-went-wrong-lessons-from-season-1-evoke1/>.

McKibben, Bill. *The End of Nature*. New York: Random House, 1989.

McLeese, Alex M. "Soul Archaeology of Darwin." *The Crimson*, 24 Feb. 2009. Web. 4 May 2015. <http://www.thecrimson.com/article/2009/2/24/soul-archeology-of-darwin-many-associate/#>.

McLuhan, Marshall. *The Medium Is the Massage*. San Francisco: HardWired, 1996. Print.

———. *Understanding Media: The Extensions of Man*. Cambridge: MIT P, 1994. Print.

———. "Empedocles and T.S. Eliot." *Empedocles: A Philosophical Investigation*. Tuscaloosa: U of Alabama P, 1976. Print.

Made with Code. Web. 4 May 2015. <https://www.madewithcode.com/>.

Mann, Michael E. "The Little Ice Age." *Encyclopedia of Global Environmental Change*. Ed. Dr. Michael C. MacCracken and Dr. John S. Perry. Chichester: Wiley, 2002: 504–509. Print.

Manovich, Lev. *The Language of New Media*. Cambridge: MIT P, 2001. Print.

———. "Digital Constructivism: What is European Software?," *Uncanny Networks*. Ed. Geert Lovink. Cambridget, MA: MIT P, 2002. Print.

Marino, Mark. "Code as Ritualized Poetry: the Tactics of the Transborder Immigrant Tool." *Digital Humanities Quarterly* 7.1 (2013). Web. 4 May 2015. <http://www.digitalhumanities.org/dhq/vol/7/1/000157/000157.html>.

———. "Critical Code Studies." *Electronic Book Review*, 4 Dec. 2006. Web. 4 May 2015. <http://electronicbookreview.com/thread/electropoetics/codology>.

———. *LA Flood Project*. 2011. Web. 4 May 2015. <http://laflood.citychaos.com/>.

Mark, Jason. "Natural Law." *Earth Island Journal* (Spring 2012): 40-46. Print.

Markley, Robert. "Boundaries: Mathematics, Alienation, and the Metaphysics of Cyberspace." *Configurations* 2.3 (1994): 485–507. Print.

Markram, Henry. *Blue Brain Project*, 2013. Web. 4 May 2015. <http://bluebrain.epfl.ch/>.

Marx, Leo. *The Machine in the Garden*. New York: Oxford UP, 2010. Print.

The Matrix. Dir. Andy and Larry Wachowski. Perf. Keanu Reeves, Carrie-Anne Moss, Laurence Fishburne. Silver Pictures, 1999. Film.

Matyszczyk, Chris. "Envoy to Solve Latest Google Maps Border Dispute," 5 Nov. 2010. *CNET*. Web. 4 May 2015. <http://www.cnet.com/news/envoy-to-solve-latest-google-maps-border-dispute/>.

Meeker, Joseph. "The Comic Mode." *The Ecocriticism Reader*. Ed. Cheryll Glotfelty and Harold Fromm. Atlanta: U of Georgia P, 1996. Print.

Menely, Tobias. "'The Present Obfuscation': Cowper's *Task* and the Time of Climate Change." *PMLA* 127 (2012): 477–492. Print.

———. Abstract: "'The Present Obfuscation': Cowper's *Task* and the Time of Climate Change." *PMLA*, 127 (2012). Web. 4 May 2015. <http://www.mlajournals.org/doi/abs/10.1632/pmla.2012.127.3.477>.

Mentz, Stephen. "After Sustainability." *PMLA* 127 (2012): 586–592. Print.

"Microsoft Advertising." *Advertising Club of New York City*, n.d. Web. 4 May 2015. <http://www.theadvertisingclub.org/node/469&ctype=48>.

"Midori San, the Blogging Houseplant." *Pink Tentacle*, 7 Oct. 2008. Web. 4 May 2015. <http://www.pinktentacle.com/2008/10/midori-san-the-blogging-houseplant/>.

Minot, Louisa David. "Niagra Falls" (1818). New York Historical Society. Newington-Cropsey Cultural Studies Center, 2012. Web. 4 May 2015. <http://www.nccsc.net/legacy/hudson-river>.

Minsky, Marvin. *The Society of Mind*. New York: Simon & Schuster, 1988. Print.

Moon. Dir. Duncan Jones. Perf. Kevin Space, Sam Rockwell. Stage 6 Films, 2009. Film.

Morgan, Edwin. *Collected Poems*. Manchester: Carcanet, 1990. Print.

Morrison, Grant. *We3, Deluxe Edition*. New York: Vertigo, 2011. Print.

Morse, Margaret. "Nature Morte: Landscape and Narrative in Virtual Environments." *Immersed in Technology: Art and Virtual Environments*. Ed. Mary Ann Moser and Douglas MacLeod. Cambridge: MIT P, 1996. Print.

Morton, Timothy. "An Object Oriented Defense of Poetry." *New Literary History* 43 (2012): 205–224. Print.

———. *Ecology without Nature: Rethinking Environmental Aesthetics*. Cambridge: Harvard UP, 2007. Print.

———. *The Ecological Thought*. Cambridge: Harvard UP, 2010. Print.

Miller, T.S. "The Lives of the Monster Plants: The Revenge of the Vegetable in the Age of Animal Studies." *The Journal of the Fantastic in the Arts* 23.3 (2012): 460–479. Print

Moonan, Wendy. "New Works Discovered by Nam June Paik." *Smithsonian.com*. 23 March 2015. Web. 4 May 2015. <http://www.smithsonianmag.com/smithsonian-institution/new-works-nam-june-paik-discovered-smithsonian-american-art-museum-180954571/>.

Mosco, Vincent. *The Digital Sublime*. Cambridge: MIT P, 2005. Print.

myclimate.org. Web. 4 May 2015. <https://www.myclimate.org/about-us/>.

Murphy, Pat. "His Vegetable Wife." *Norton Book of Science Fiction*. Ed. Ursula K. LeGuin. New York: Norton, 1999. Print.

Myers, Lana Wirt. *Prairie Rhymes*. Lawrence: Mammoth, 2010. Print.

Nakamura, Lisa. *Cybertypes: Race, Ethnicity, and Identity on the Internet*. New York: Routledge, 2002. Print.

Nash, Linda. "The Agency of Nature or the Nature of Agency?" *Environmental History* 10 (Jan., 2005): 67–69. Print.

Nash, Roderick. *Rights of Nature: A History of Environmental Ethics*. Madison: U of Wisconsin P, 1989. Print.

The Nature Conservancy website. Web. 4 May 2015. <http://www.nature.org/>.

Nelson, Ted. *Computer Lib/Dream Machines*. Excerpted in *The New Media Reader*. Ed. Noah Wardrip-Fruin. Cambridge: MIT P, 2003. Web. 4 May 2015. <http://www.newmediareader.com/book_samples/nmr-21-nelson.pdf>.

Nerds for Nature. Web. 4 May 2015. <http://nerdsfornature.org/>.

Newman, Jared. "6 Things You'd Never Guess About Google's Energy Use." *Time Magazine*. 9 Sept. 2011. Web. 4 May 2015. <http://techland.time.com/2011/09/09/6-things-youd-never-guess-about-googles-energy-use/>.

Novalis. *The Novices at Sais*. Trans. Ralph Manheim. New York: Archipelago, 2005. Print.

Okorafor-Mbachu, Nnedi. *Zahrah the Windseeker*. Boston: Houghton Mifflin, 2005. Print.

Olmsted, Frederick Law. "Yosemite and the Mariposa Grove: A Preliminary Report, 1865." Yosemite Online Library, 1998. Web. 4 May 2015.<http://www.yosemite.ca.us/library/olmsted/report.html>.

Ong, Walter. *Orality and Literacy: The Technologizing of the Word*. New York: Routledge, 2002. Print.

"Osmosis." *Collins English Dictionary: Complete and Unabridged*. New York: Harper, 1991. Dictionary.com, n.d. Web. 4 May 2015. <http://dictionary.reference.com/browse/osmosis?s=t>.

Ossola, Alexandra. "Energy of an Internet Search." *Student Science*, 15 Dec. 2010. Web. 4 May 2015. <http://www.sciencenewsforkids.org/2010/12/the-energy-of-an-internet-search/>.

Otis, Laura. "The Other End of the Wire: Uncertainties of Organic and Telegraphic Communication." *Configurations* 9 (2001): 181–206. Print.

Ovid. *The Metamorphoses*. *The Internet Classics Archive*. Web Atomic and Massachusetts Institute of Technology, 1994-2009. Web. 4 May 2015. <http://classics.mit.edu/Ovid/metam.html>.

Packard, Edward. *You Are a Shark* (Choose Your Own Adventure #45). New York: Bantam, 1985.

———. "Re: You Are a Shark." Message to the author. 11 June 2012. Email.

Palahniuk, Chuck. *Damned*. New York: Doubleday, 2010. Print.

Parke, Herbert William. *The Oracles of Zeus*. Cambridge: Harvard UP, 1967. Print.

Paterson, Katie. *Vatnajökull (the sound of)*. N.d. Web. 4 May 2015. <http://www.katiepaterson.org/vatnajokull/>.

Paulk, Charles. "Post-National Cool: William Gibson's Japan." *Science Fiction Studies* 38 (2011): 478–500. Print.

Pesic, Peter. *Labyrinth: A Search for the Hidden Meaning of Science*. Cambridge: MIT P, 2001. Print.

Phillips, Dana. *The Truth of Ecology*. Oxford: Oxford UP, 2003. Print.

Pollen, Michael. "The Intelligent Plant." *New Yorker* 23 Dec. 2013. Print.

Plato. *Dialogues of Plato Containing the Apology of Socrates, Crito, Phaedo and Protagoras*. Ed. Maurice Francis Egan. Whitefish, MO: Kessinger, 2004.

———. *Phaedrus*. Trans. Harold North Fowler. *The Loeb Classical Library*. Cambridge: Harvard UP, 2005.

———. *Symposium*. Trans. Benjamin Jowett. *The Internet Classics Archive*. Web Atomic and Massachusetts Institute of Technology, 1994-2009. Web. 4 May 2015. <http://classics.mit.edu/Plato/symposium.html>.

Pliny the Elder. *Natural Histories*. Ed. John Bostock. Perseus Project: Tufts University, n.d. Web. 4 May 2015. <http://www.perseus.tufts.edu/hopper/text?doc=Plin.+Nat.+toc>.

Poe, Edgar Allan. "The Gold Bug." *Complete Stories of Edgar Allan Poe*. New York: Doubleday, 1984. Print.

Preston S. D., and F. B. de Waal. "Empathy: Its Ultimate and Proximate Bases." *Behavioral and Brain Sciences* 25: 1–72. 2002. Print.

Pope, Alexander. "Moral Essays, Epistle IV, of the Use of Riches." *Alexander Pope, The Complete Poetical Works*, 1903. *Bartleby.com*, n.d. Web. 4 May 2015. <http://www.bartleby.com/203/146.html>.

Postel, Sandra. "A River in New Zealand Gets a Legal Voice." *National Geographic's Water Currents*, 4 Sept. 2012. Web. 4 May 2015. <http://newswatch.nationalgeographic.com/2012/09/04/a-river-in-new-zealand-gets-a-legal-voice/>.

Prescott, George Bartlett. *History, Theory and Practice of the Electric Telegraph*. Boston: Ticknor and Fields, 1860. Print.

Price, Uvedale. *Essays on the Picturesque*. London: Mawman, 1810. Web. 4 May 2015. <http://books.google.com/books?id=Al0AAAAAYAAJ>.

Prins, Yopie. *Victorian Sappho*. Princeton: Princeton UP, 1999. Print.

Project 51. *Play the L.A. River*. 2014. Web. 1 May 2015. <http://playthelariver.com/>.

Pynchon, Thomas. *The Crying of Lot 49*. Philadelphia: J. B. Lippincott, 1966. Print.

"A Rainforest Chernobyl." ChevronToxico Web Log, 200-2015. Web. 1 May 2015. <http://chevrontoxico.com/about/rainforest-chernobyl/>.

Raley, Rita. "Reveal Codes: Hypertext and Performance." *Postmodern Culture* 12.1

(2001). Web. 4 May 2015. <http://www.iath.virginia.edu/pmc/text-only/issue.901/12.1raley.txt>.

———. *Tactical Media.* Minneapolis: U of Minnesota P, 2009. Print.

———. "Living Letterforms: The Ecological Turn in Contemporary Digital Poetics." *Contemporary Literature* 52 (2011): 883–913. Print.

Red Dwarf. BBC/Grant Naylor. 1989–2012. Television.

Reeves, Byron. "World of Greencraft," 2008. Web. 4 May 2015. <https://www.youtube.com/watch?v=dDR0-QgqiEk>.

Reynold, Gretchen. "Easing Brain Fatigue with a Walk in the Park." *New York Times* 27 Mar. 2013. Web. 4 May 2015. <http://well.blogs.nytimes.com/2013/03/27/easing-brain-fatigue-with-a-walk-in-the-park/>.

Roach, Brian, Jonathan Rubin, and Charles Morris. "Measuring Maine's Marine Economy." *Maine Policy Review* 8 (1999). Web. 4 May 2015. <http://digitalcommons.library.umaine.edu/cgi/viewcontent.cgi?article=1319&context=mpr>.

Rogers, Tim. "A River Runs into Trouble on Nicaragua-Costa Rica Border." *Miami Herald*, 6 Nov. 2010. Web. 4 May 2015. <http://z15.invisionfree.com/Augusta_Alternative/ar/t3587.htm>.

Ronen, Ruth. *Aesthetics of Anxiety.* New York: SUNY UP, 2009. Print.

Rueda, María Helena. "La selva en las novelas de la selva." *Revista de Crítica Literaria Latinoamericana* 29 (2003): 31–43. Print.

Ryan, Paul. "Earthscore." *Earthscore.org*, 2011. Web. 1 May 2015. <http://www.earthscore.org/themes.html>.

———. "Interview with Orit Gat." *Rhizome.org*, 28 Sept. 2011. Web. 1 May 2015. <http://rhizome.org/editorial/2011/sep/28/recent-history-class-paul-ryan-interviews-grey-roo/>.

Rötzer, Florian. "RE: Photography." *Photography after Photography.* Ed. Hubertus von Amelunxen, Stefan Iglhaut, and Florian Roetzer. Amsterdam: G&B Arts International, 1997. Print.

Sachs, Joe. "Aristotle: Poetics." *Internet Encyclopedia of Philosophy*, n.d. Web. 4 May 2015. <http://www.iep.utm.edu/aris-poe/>.

Saidmoorhouse, Lauren. "Solar-Powered 'Supertrees' Breathe Life into Singapore's Urban Oasis." *CNN World News.* 8 June 2012. Web. 4 May 2015. <http://www.cnn.com/2012/06/08/world/asia/singapore-supertrees-gardens-bay/>.

Saint Augustine. *On the Christian Doctrine. The Norton Anthology of Theory & Criticism.* Ed. Vincent B. Leitch. New York: Norton, 2010. Print.

Sánchez, Celia Natalías. "The Bologna Defixio(nes) Revisited." *Zeitschrift für Papyrologie und Epigraphik* 179 (2011): 201–217. Web. 4 May 2015. <https://www.academia.edu/1538935/The_Bologna_defixio_nes_Revisited>.

"Sandbox." *Wikipedia: The Free Encyclopedia.* Wikimedia Foundation, Inc., n.d. Web. 4 May 2015. <http://en.wikipedia.org/wiki/Second_Life>.

Schelmetic, Tracy E. "Google Defends Its Carbon Footprint." *Green Technology World*, 9 Sept. 2011. Web. 4 May 2015. <http://green.tmcnet.com/topics/green/articles/216400-google-defends-its-carbon-footprint.htm>.

Schwenger, Peter. "Agrippa, or the Apocalyptic Book." *South Atlantic Quarterly* (Fall 1993): 617–626. Print.

Serious Games Institute, The. Coventry University Enterprises, n.d. Web. 4 May 2015. <http://www.seriousgamesinstitute.co.uk/>.

SFRA. "Citation Needed for William Gibson's Foreword/Afterword to Mona Lisa Overdrive." 25 Mar. 2012. Web. May 1 2015 <https://web.archive.org/web/20130701203154/http://wiz.cath.vt.edu/pipermail/sfra-l/2012-March/002442.html>.

Shapin, Steven. *The Scientific Revolution*. Chicago: U of Chicago P, 1996. Print.

Shapin, Steven, and Simon Schaffer. *Leviathan and the Air-Pump*. Princeton: Princeton UP, 1985. Print.

Shelley, Mary. *Frankenstein*. New York: Pocket Books, 1995. Print.

Shelley, Percy Bysshe. "Mont Blanc, Lines Written in the Vale of Chamouni." Poetry Foundation, n.d. Web. 4 May 2015. <http://www.poetryfoundation.org/poem/174397>.

Shklovsky, Viktor. *Theory of Prose*. Normal: Dalkey, 1990. Print.

Sierra Club. "Sierra Club Blogs." *Sierraclub.org*, n.d. Web. 4 May 2015. <http://www.sierraclub.org/blogs/>.

Sigfusson, Saemund, and Snorre Sturleson. *The Elder Eddas of Saemund Sigfusson and the Younger Eddas of Snorre Sturleson, by Saemund Sigfusson and Snorre Sturleson*. Project Gutenberg, 18 Jan. 2005. Web. 1 May 2015. <http://www.gutenberg.org/files/14726/14726-h/14726-h.htm>.

Simard, Suzanne. "Mycorrhizal Networks." *UBC Botanical Garden and Centre for Plant Research Blog*, 10 May 2010. Web. 4 May 2015. <http://www.botanicalgarden.ubc.ca/potd/2010/03/mycorrhizal_networks.php>.

———, et al. "Net Transfer of Carbon between Ectomycorrhizal Tree Species in the Field." *Nature* 388 (7 Aug. 1997): 579–582. Print.

Siri Woodget's Blog, 28 May 2009. Web. 1 May 2015. <http://mylifeinsecondlife.blogspot.com/2009/05/menhirs-and-sheep.html>.

Smith, Cordwainer. *The Best of Cordwainer Smith*. New York: Ballantine Books, 1975. Print.

"Software." IIEEE, n.d. Web. 4 May 2015. <http://www.stevemcconnell.com/ieeesoftware/eic15.htm>.

Spigel, Lynn. *Welcome to the Dreamhouse: Popular Media and Postwar Suburbs*. Durham: Duke UP, 2001. Print.

Starosielski, Nicole. *The Undersea Network*. Durham, NC: Duke UP, 2015. Print.

———. "Surfacing." Spring 2015. Web. 1 May 2015. <http://www.surfacing.in/?image=daet-beach>.

Steffen, Alex. "Art Meets Technology." *World Changing: A User's Guide for the 21st Century*. New York: Abrams, 2011: 91–102. Print.

Stone, Allison. "Being, Knowledge, and Nature in Novalis." *Journal of the History of Philosophy* 46 (2008): 141–64. Print.

Stephenson, Neal. *Snow Crash*. New York: Bantam, 1993. Print.

———. "In the Beginning Was the Command Line." *Cryptonomicon.com*, n.d. Web. 4 May 2015. <http://www.cryptonomicon.com/beginning.html>.

Sterling, Bruce. "Preface." *Next Nature, Nature Changes along with Us*. New York: Actar, 2011. Print.

Strickland, Stephanie, Cynthia Lawson Jaramillo, and Paul Ryan. "slippingglimpse." *Electronic Literature Collection 2*. Web. 4 May 2015. <http://collection.eliterature.org/2/works/strickland_slippingglimpse.html>.

———. "slippingglimpse." Email interview with Elizabeth Swanstrom, 24 June 2012.

———. *slippingglimpse*. *Poets for Living Waters*, 2010. Web. 4 May 2015. <http://poetsgulfcoast.wordpress.com/2010/06/01/a-poem-by-stephanie-strickland-cynthia-lawson-jaramillo-paul-ryan/>.

Strugatsky, Boris, and Arkady. *Noon: 22nd Century*. New York: Collier Macmillan, 1980. Print.

Stueber, Karsten. "Empathy." *The Stanford Encyclopedia of Philosophy*. Stanford U, 2014. Ed. Edward N. Zalta. Web. 4 May 2015. <http://plato.stanford.edu/archives/win2014/entries/empathy/>.

"Sublimate." *Collins English Dictionary: Complete and Unabridged*. New York: Harper, 1991. Dictionary.com. Web. 4 May 2015. <http://www.thefreedictionary.com/sublimate>.

S.W.A.M.P. *Spore 1.1*, n.d. Web. 29 April 2015. <http://www.swamp.nu/projects/spore-1-1/>.

———. "Skype Interview." HUMlab, Umeå Universitet, Sweden, Winter 2010. Web. 4 May 2015. <http://blog.humlab.umu.se/?p=2705>.

———. "IED: Improved Empathy Device." Web. 4 May 2015. <http://www.swamp.nu/projects/ied/>.

———. "Postscapes." Web. 4 May 2015. <http://postscapes.com/digital-contracts-spore-11>.

———. "Spore 1.1." Message to the author. 16 Nov. 2010. Email.

Tabbi, Joseph. *The Postmodern Sublime*. Ithaca: Cornell UP, 1996. Print.

———. *Cognitive Fictions*. Minneapolis: U of Minnesota P, 2002. Print.

"Taipei 101." 20 Aug. 2013. Web. 1 May 2015. <http://travel.cnn.com/explorations/life/20-most-iconic-skyscrapers-343149>.

Taylor, Claire and Thea Pitman. "Mestiz@ Cyborgs: The Performance of Latin American-ness and (Critical) Racial Identity." Latin American Identity in Online Cutltural Production. NewYork: Taylor & Francis, 2013. Print.

Teasdale, Sara. "There Will Come Soft Rains." *Flame and Shadow*, 1920. *Project Gutenberg*, July 1996. Web. 4 May 2015. <http://www.gutenberg.org/cache/epub/591/pg591.html>.

"Terrified Tourist Hit by Falling Glacier on Tracy Arm Fjord." *Extinction Protocol*, 10 Aug. 2011. Web. 1 May 2015. <http://theextinctionprotocol.wordpress.com/2011/08/10/terrified-tourist-hit-by-falling-glacier-on-tracy-arm-fjord/>.

Thiele, Leslie Paul. *Timely Meditations: Martin Heidegger and Postmodern Politics*. Princeton: Princeton UP, 2006. Print.

Thill, Scott. "Jonathon Keats' Space Agency Launches Arty Exotourism." *Wired*, 10 Oct. 2010. Web. 4 May 2015. <http://www.wired.com/2010/10/jonathon-keats-exotourism/?viewall=true>.

Thomas, Dylan. "The Force that Through Green Fuse Drives the Flower." *Selected Poems*, 1934-1952. New York: New Directions, 2003.

Thomas, Sue. *Technobiophilia*. New York: Bloomsbury, 2013. Print.

Thoreau, Henry David. *Journals*, Aug. 30, 1856. *The Writings of Henry David Thoreau*. Ed. Elizabeth Witherell, editor-in-chief. Web. 4 May 2015. <http://thoreau.library.ucsb.edu/writings_journals_pdfs/J11f1-f3.pdf>.

———. *Walden: The Thoreau Reader*. Ed. Richard Lenat. Web. 4 May 2015. <http://thoreau.eserver.org/walden05.html>.

THX-1138. Dir. George Lucas. Perf. Robert Duvall, Donald Pleasence. American Zoetrope/Warner Brothers, 1971. Film.

Tiptree, James, Jr. *Her Smoke Rose up Forever: James Tiptree Jr.* San Francisco: Tachyon, 2004. Print.

Todd, Michael. "Is Our Disconnect from Nature a Disorder?" *Pacific Standard*, 5 Apr. 2013. Web. 4 May 2015. <http://www.psmag.com/environment/nature-deficit-disorder-outdoors-outside-54707/#.UZPqIaLrI0E.facebook>.

Tomlinson, Bill. *Greening Through IT*. Cambridge: MIT P, 2010. Print.

"Tornado Button Smashing." *Mausland.de*. Web. 4 May 2015. <http://www.mausland.de/showswf/449>.

"Tornado records." *Wikipedia: The Free Encyclopedia*. Wikimedia Foundation, Inc., n.d. Web. 4 May 2015. <http://en.wikipedia.org/wiki/Tornado_records>.

"Tree That Owns Itself." *Wikipedia: The Free Encyclopedia*. Wikimedia Foundation, Inc., n.d. Web. 29 April 2015. <http://en.wikipedia.org/wiki/Tree_That_Owns_Itself>.

Turkle, Sherry. *Life on the Screen: Identity in the Age of the Internet*. New York: Simon & Schuster, 1995. Print.

———. "Collaborative Selves, Collaborative Worlds: Identity in the Information Age." *Electronic Collaboration in the Humanities*. New York: Routledge, 2003.

———. "Who Am We?" *Wired*, Jan. 1996. Web. 4 May 2015. <http://www.wired.com/wired/archive/4.01/turkle.html>.

Turner, Fred. *From Counterculture to Cyberculture: Stewart Brand, the Whole Earth Network, and the Rise of Digital Utopianism*. Chicago: U of Chicago P, 2008. Print.

Turner, Frederick. "Cultivating the American Garden: Towards a Secular View of Nature." *Harper's Magazine* (Aug. 1985): 45–52. Print.

Ulman, H. Lewis. "Beyond Nature/Writing: Virtual Landscapes Online, in Print, and in Real Life." *Beyond Nature Writing: Expanding the Boundaries of Ecocriticism*. Ed. Karla Armbruster. Richmond: U of Virginia P, 2001. Print.

"Unselfies." Web. 4 May 2015. <http://wearechangers.org/unselfies/>.

Varley, John. "Press Enter." *John Varley Reader*. New York: Ace, 2004. Print.

Velte, Toby, Anthony Velte, and Robert Elsenpeter. *Green IT: Reduce Your Informa-*

tion System's Environmental Impact While Adding to the Bottom Line. New York: McGraw-Hill, 2008. Print.

Virwox Currency Shop. Web. 4 May 2015. <https://www.virwox.com/currency_shop.php>.

Venus, Jochen. "Beyond Play and Narration: Video Games as Simulations of Self-Action." *Beyond the Screen*. Ed. Jörgen Schäfer, Peter Gendolla. Bielefeld: Transcript-Verlag, 2010. Print.

"Vernagtferner." *Bavarian Academy of Sciences and Humanities Commission for Glaciology*, 26 Nov. 2008. Web. 1 May 2015. <http://glaziologie.userweb.mwn.de/vernagt/vernagt_E.html>.

"Vernagtferner." *Archive.org*. 30 Nov. 2007. Web. 1 May 2015. <https://archive.org/details/aporee_847_1257>.

Vilas, Amber. "In Plain Sight: Betty Beaumont's Camouflaged Cell Concealment Sites." *WEAD: Women's Environmental Artists Directory* #4, n.d. Web. 4 May 2015. <http://weadartists.org/betty-beaumonts-concealed-sites>.

Vinge, Joan. *Catspaw*. New York: Tor, 1988. Print.

Vinge, Vernor. *True Names and the Opening of the Cyberspace Frontier*. New York: Tor, 2001. Print.

Wallach, Allan. "Between Subject and Object." *Landscape Theory*. Ed. Rachel DeLue, James Elkins. New York: Routledge, 2007. Print.

"Wanderer above the Sea of Fog." *Wikipedia: The Free Encyclopedia*. Wikimedia Foundation, Inc., n.d. Web. 4 May 2015. <http://en.wikipedia.org/wiki/Wanderer_above_the_Sea_of_Fog>.

Ward, May Williams. "Tornado." Web. 28 Dec. 2014. <http://www.kotn.org/poetry/tornado.html>.

———. "Prairie Substitutes." Web. 4 May 2015. <http://www.kotn.org/poetry/seesaw/subs.html>.

War Games. Dir. John Badham. Perf. Matthew Broderick, Ally Sheedy. MGM, 1983. Film.

Wark, McKenzie. *A Hacker Manifesto*. Cambridge: Harvard UP, 2004. Print.

Wegenstein, Bernadette. *Getting under the Skin: Body and Media Theory*. Cambridge: MIT P, 2006. Print.

White, Lynn. "The Historical Roots of Our Ecologic Crisis." *Science* 155 (Mar. 1967): 1203–1207. Print.

Whitcomb, Selden. "Nature in Early American Literature." *Sewanee Review* 2 (Feb. 1894): 159–179. Print.

Whitman, Walt. *Leaves of Grass* (1855). Bartleby.com. Web. 4 May 2015. <http://www.bartleby.com/142/>.

Wiedijk, Freek. "Agrippa disk image." *The Agrippa Files*, 17 July 2011. Web. 4 May 2015. <http://agrippa.english.ucsb.edu/post/documents-subcategories/the-disk-and-its-code/original-text-of-gibsons-agrippa-poem-extracted-from-disk>.

Wiener, Norbert. *God and Golem, Inc.* Cambridge: MIT P, 1964. Print.

Weizenbaum, Joseph. "Eliza: A Computer Program for the Study of Natural Language Communication between Man and Machine." *Communications of the ACM* 9.1 (1966): 36–45. Print.

Wolfe, Cary. *What Is Posthumanism?* Minneapolis: U of Minnesota P, 2009. Print.

Woolf, Greg. "Divinity and Power in Ancient Rome." *Religion and Power: Divine Kingship in the Ancient World and Beyond*. Ed. Nicole Brisch (Oriental Institute Seminars No. 4). Chicago: Oriental Institute of the University of Chicago, 2008.

Wordsworth, Dorothy. *Grasmere and Alfoxden Journals*. Oxford: Oxford UP, 2008. Print.

Wordsworth, William. "Elegaic Stanzas." *The Oxford Authors: William Wordsworth*. Ed. Stephen Gill. New York: Oxford UP, 1984. 131–135. Print.

World Wildlife Fund: Endangered Species Conservation. Web. 4 May 2015. <http://worldwildlife.org/>.

Wyndam, John. *The Day of the Triffids*. New York: Doubley, 1951.

Wylie, Lesley. "Colonial Tropes and Postcolonial Tricks: Rewriting the Tropics in the 'Novela de la selva.'" *The Modern Language Review 101* (Jul., 2006): 728–742. Print.

Yates, Frances A. *Art of Memory*. Chicago: U of Chicago P, 1966. Print.

Yuhas, Alan. "Chimpanzees Granted Petition to Hear 'Legal Persons' Status in Court." *The Guardian*. 21 April 2015. Web. 1 May 2015. <http://www.theguardian.com/world/2015/apr/21/chimpanzees-granted-legal-persons-status-unlawful-imprisonment>.

Zamyatin, Yevgeny. *We*. New York: Modern Library Classics, 2006. Print.

Zielinski, Siegfried. *Deep Time of the Media*. Cambridge: MIT P, 2006. Print.

Zylinska. Joanna. *Bioethics in the Age of New Media*. Cambridge: MIT P, 2009. Print.

Index